MUDHONEY

THE SOUND AND THE FURY FROM SEATTLE

MUDHONEY

THE SOUND AND THE FURY FROM SEATTLE

Keith Cameron

This 2014 edition published under arrangement between Omnibus Press and Voyageur Press, a member of Quayside Publishing Group, 400 First Avenue North, Suite 400, Minneapolis, MN 55401 USA

Voyageur Press titles are also available at discounts in bulk quantity for industrial or sales-promotional use. For details write to Special Sales Manager at MBI Publishing Company, 400 First Avenue North, Suite 400, Minneapolis, MN 55401 USA.

To find out more about our books, visit us online at www.voyageurpress.com.

ISBN: 978-0-7603-4661-7

Library of Congress Cataloging-in-Publication Data
Library of Congress Cataloging-in-Publication Data

Cameron, Keith (Music journalist), author.
Mudhoney : the sound and the fury from Seattle / by Keith Cameron.
pages cm
Reprint. Previously published: London : Omnibus Press, 2013.
Includes bibliographical references and index.
ISBN 978-0-7603-4661-7 (softcover)
1. Mudhoney (Musical group) 2. Rock groups--United States--Biography. 3. Grunge groups--United States--Biography. I. Title.
ML421.M8C36 2014
782.42166092'2--dc23
[B]

2013044546

Cover design: Fresh Lemon
Photo research: Jacqui Black

Printed in China
10 9 8 7 6 5 4 3 2 1

Contents

Introduction

A Riot of Our Own

London was unusually dry during May 1989—only two days out of the whole month saw any significant rainfall. Most of its total 12mm would arrive in a thunderstorm on the hot and humid 24th, but Friday May 12 was much cooler, with sporadic showers breaking out in the UK's capital. Perhaps the weather was doing its best to make two rock bands from the notoriously damp U.S. city of Seattle feel at home.

Inside the toilets at the University of London's School of Oriental and African Studies (SOAS), there was precipitation of a different sort. Beer seemed to be everywhere: lying in pools underfoot and around the urinals, where customers also had to beware of random piles of vomit. Beyond the toilets, and past some more dubious splashes on the floor, a corridor connected the student union bar to a hall where the air itself felt intoxicating: heavy with sweat, cigarette smoke, and an odor strongly suggestive of brewery effluent.

Onstage was one of the two Seattle bands, comprising four men on bass, drums, and two guitars. It was standard issue stuff, but the scene was a little odd. Firstly, there were some other people onstage too, members of the audience standing or dancing in amongst the band.

Odder still, some audience members sat atop the stacks of PA speakers on each side of the stage. Then there was the lighting—or rather the lack of it, with no sign of the spotlight rigs that add visual drama to rock gigs. Instead, some of the hall's house lights provided a strangely informal ambience to the music.

The band itself seemed completely unflustered, as if they'd played far stranger situations that this. Wearing a white T-shirt with the legend "Red Light District, Amsterdam," one of the guitarists seemed to shiver in time to the music's tense grind as he sang:

"I got a belly full of ouzo
A head full of hurt
I'll be digging your treasure, baby
See what I unearth.
Take you down to the dirt
Drag you through the mud
Drag you through the mud . . . "

Bodies were tumbling through the air, one after another; squirming limbs and smiling faces. Just outside the entrance to the hall a pair of police officers stared, bemused, perhaps wondering why they were there.

Such was the scene approximately 50 minutes into the biggest headlining performance in the UK thus far by Mudhoney. The crowd—maybe around 800 people, certainly more than felt safe—was pressed uncomfortably against the stage, which seemed too small for the size of the room and had been unsteadily augmented by trestle tables.

But still, the band was playing and the people were rocking.

Forty minutes earlier, however, it didn't seem as if there was going to be a show at all. Police were summoned to SOAS as the event organizers found themselves overwhelmed by the mayhem unfolding from the very beginning of Mudhoney's set.

With the audience so hemmed in, singer and guitarist Mark Arm decided to try to emulate the feat of his idol, Iggy Pop, who famously walked Christ-like upon the hands of his delighted fans at the 1970 Cincinnati Pop Festival. After all, the stunt had worked for Arm on a smaller scale six weeks ago in Newcastle.

Although only the opening act for New York art-rock legends Sonic Youth, their gig at Newcastle's Riverside Club was Mudhoney's UK debut and the audience was as excited by them as by the headliners. They were greeted by Arm stepping straight from the stage onto their heads.

Now, at SOAS, with twice as many people facing him, Mark Arm leapt backwards into the morass midway through the first song and was carried around before being deposited safely whence he came—minus his guitar. Back onstage, Arm watched, perhaps a little anxiously, as his pale blue Hagstrom made a circuit of the hall before it, too, was returned. He stepped up to the microphone, seemingly to appeal for calm.

"I'd like to take this opportunity to personally invite everybody to join us onstage!"

There was a near-instant collective response. Within seconds, dozens of people surged forward, up and over the makeshift barrier. The rush continued until there was no more room.

Mudhoney's drummer, Dan Peters, was trapped behind his kit, while Arm, bassist Matt Lukin, and guitarist Steve Turner laughed helplessly as their equipment was fondled by excited fans.

Minutes passed. Eventually, after some (but by no means all) of the invaders had been persuaded to return whence they came, the band struggled through a song. At which point, Mark Arm declared: "We're not going to play another note unless each and every one one of you gets on top of the speaker stacks!"

This was too much for one of the security staff, who made a lunge for Arm and had to be restrained by audience members. Even Arm himself was taken aback at the crowd's unthinking response to his latest requests: "I don't wanna be your fucking parent, but you should know better," he smiled. "Folks are less gullible where we come from."

Mudhoney continued their performance, but soon came to a halt again as the front of the stage collapsed. As well as holding back the crowd, the trestle tables were also makeshift platforms for the band's onstage sound monitors. With monitors disappearing and the lighting rigs wobbling dangerously against human bodies, the monitor engineer switched off his mixing desk and began packing up. The lighting engineer did likewise.

The handful of stage security guards seemed to have simply disappeared. Amidst the confusion, the band retreated to their dressing room where Peters started getting changed, on the reasonable assumption that the show was finished. Matt Cameron, his counterpart in opening band, Soundgarden, asked, "Does this happen every night with you guys?"

Back in the hall, with pieces of broken furniture being passed over people's heads, a tall, broad-shouldered Yorkshireman named Anton Brookes began grabbing anyone he recognized at the front of the melee and demanding they help him keep the crowd offstage. He explained that the show's promoters had panicked and called the police: "If we don't do something, they'll stop the gig, and we can't let that happen."

Brookes was Mudhoney's UK publicist, and people he knew in the building happened to be journalists from various weekly music magazines. Thus I was dragooned into acting as an ad hoc bouncer, attempting to protect the now-returning band and what was left of their equipment from trampling by the hordes.

Backstage, a compromise had been reached. The main PA would stay and the band would play without monitors or light.

Anton, meanwhile, was marshaling his citizens' security team. He might have been built for such capers, but most of the journalists in his orbit were God-help-us-if-there's-a-war material. Behind me, Mudhoney did their bit to defuse the situation by cranking "Chain That Door," a notably frantic selection from their repertoire and only the third song played in half an hour.

Thereafter, proceedings settled down into a benign chaos. The band delivered as best they could, given the missing equipment and the constantly stage-diving audience members we were unable to prevent clambering past us—not least because Anton himself kept getting carried away and joining in.

But the atmosphere was joyous. Sitting on top of the speaker stack to the left of the stage, where she had been deposited by the momentum of the stage invasion, Leila Kassir grinned broadly. She was in her final year at school in South Harrow, northwest London—her A-level exams were the following week—and the Mudhoney gig was a Friday night treat to celebrate the 18th birthday of her friend, Anna Cass, who sat next to her on the stack, looking equally delighted. Leila and Anna regularly took the long tube journey from the suburbs to inner London to see bands—the previous week they had been to the nearby University of London Union (ULU) for Dinosaur Jr—but Mudhoney were their favorites. Leila looked especially happy from her perch above the thrashing mass, because, as Mark Arm made one of his dives into the crowd, she reached down and touched his knee. Although she actually fancied Steve more, if any member of Mudhoney had a knee worth touching then it was definitely Arm.

Surveying the smiles and the mayhem, the band seemed amused, even satisfied by the outcome. Their set finished on an ecstatic high with "In'n'out of Grace"—fittingly, given that it was pretty much the ultimate Mudhoney song: a guitar-squalling, drum-flailing, throat-shredding rock'n'roll epiphany of precision and slop. Transcendence duly reached, the band took their leave. Everyone else stumbled out onto the damp streets of central London, stunned at what had just happened. This felt like the start of something.

Something different. Something special.

"How was the Mudhoney and Soundgarden gig?" a colleague in the *Sounds* office asked me the following Monday. "Oh, amazing," I replied. "Mudhoney caused a riot. A *friendly* riot . . . "

* * *

What took place at the School of Oriental and African Studies on May 12, 1989, was both the culmination of a process and the start of a revolution. It had deep roots and would have far-reaching ramifications.

In the UK, the "friendly riot" was a small but undeniable symptom of a depressed populace beginning to loosen up. Examining pictures of the time now, almost 25 years later, it's startling to note how gray Britain looked in 1989. City centers were scarred by closed-down shops and derelict spaces, while London had a permanent population of homeless people living on the streets, all by-products of the aggressive free-market economic policies of Margaret Thatcher, who had been in power for exactly 10 years. The cultural landscape felt equally barren and defeated. Pop music was in a state of denial, as the media acquiesced in the aggressively aspirational ethos and obsession with promoting style over content. The quintessential magazine of the eighties was entitled, aptly, *The Face*.

Dissenting voices were marginalized or co-opted by the hope of commercial crossover, a legacy of the post-punk era when artists were convinced they could somehow upset the established order from within a corporate system. Thus the independent record label Rough Trade, the crucible of British alternative pop culture, had begun the eighties as a workers co-operative but ended the decade as a quasi-major record label and distribution group, worrying about budgets and turnover and how to survive the departure of its most successful band, The Smiths, who, shortly before breaking up in 1987, had signed with EMI. In 1991, with its activities fatally overextended, Rough Trade collapsed—a trauma with lengthy repercussions for the UK record industry.

In artistic terms, for all their manifest qualities, The Smiths had effected a stifling hegemony over the British post-punk landscape. Their melding of Sixties beat pop and Seventies glam was sophisticated, even subversive, yet those who came in their wake failed to comprehend the subtleties.

So began an endless litany of cute nonentities, nostalgically cranking out tributes to an era they were too young to remember. Those repelled by the wan Smiths-lite of bands like The Railway Children, or for whom the amiable parochiality of The Wedding Present et. al felt too prim, increasingly sought to taste forbidden fruit.

The best chances of finding it lay in America, where an underground culture flourished free from the illusory prospect of commercial success and heavy rock wasn't stigmatized as it had been in Britain. As U.S. punk mutated into the brutalist velocity of hardcore—exemplified by Southern California's Black Flag and Washington D.C.'s Minor Threat—which then gave vent to an array of hybrid twists on traditional rock dynamics, from the mid-eighties onwards a genuinely new rock blueprint began emerging in the U.S., coalescing around the output of three record labels—SST, Homestead, and Touch & Go—and a vanguard trio of bands: Big Black from Chicago, The Butthole Surfers from Texas, and Sonic Youth from New York City.

In 1987, the UK independent label Blast First had released the latest albums by all three acts: Big Black's apoplectic, valedictory *Songs About Fucking*; The Butthole Surfers' queasy, LSD-saturated metal opus *Locust Abortion Technician* (both of the former licensed from Touch & Go); and Sonic Youth's *Sister*, licensed from SST (run by Black Flag's Greg Ginn), where the Lower East Side avant-rock inquisitors finally consummated their fascination with conventional song structures in music both savage and vulnerable.

Laced with transgressive themes and imagery, each record inhabited a far more visceral rock landscape than most British bands seemed capable of realizing. Throughout 1987 and 1988, discerning rock heads' attention was fixed on the New World by a string of key records: *You're Living All Over Me* by Dinosaur Jr the apogee of J Mascis' gonzoid Stooges-do–Neil Young guitar assault; *Surfer Rosa* by Pixies, surrealist nerd rock produced by Big Black's Steve Albini; the debut EP by Fugazi, a band comprising former members of Minor Threat and fellow D.C. hardcore progenitors Rites of Spring; and, in October 1988, both Sonic Youth's breathtaking double album, *Daydream Nation*, and Mudhoney's debut mini-LP, *Superfuzz Bigmuff*.

Collectively, alongside a few UK-spawned texts (most notably Spacemen 3's *Playing with Fire*), these records heralded a countercultural response to straitened times, running parallel to the euphoric oblivion of the nascent rave scene. Indeed, the two shared some common characteristics: the psychedelic predilections of The Butthole Surfers were not exactly veiled, while the spacey dissonance of Sonic Youth suggested its own form of altered consciousness. Perhaps most intriguing was Mudhoney's grounding in Seattle, where MDA, a chemical cousin of Ecstasy, had been prevalent during the mid-eighties. When added to the city's ingrained beer culture and the less rigid demarcations between traditionally adversarial punk and metal tribes, Seattle's unselfconscious new rock variant was primed to drop on London like a mind-bomb.

Further afield, in terms of the Seattle scene's bragging rights, the SOAS show in May 1989 was highly significant. It was the first time

Mudhoney had headlined over Soundgarden, as they would do again the next evening in Portsmouth. This detail might not have mattered to British audiences, for whom Mudhoney were clearly rising stars, but it certainly raised eyebrows among members of Soundgarden.

Formed in 1985, Soundgarden, with its intense amalgam of heavy rock and new wave, had established their reputation among observers of the Seattle underground, a small network of fans, bands, retailers, journalists, and college radio DJs, many of whose roles intersected. Later that year, Soundgarden offered their first recordings to the public as part of *Deep Six*, a compilation of the fledgling scene released by a new local independent label, C/Z Records. Among the other contributors were Green River, whose original lineup featured vocalist Mark Arm and guitarist Steve Turner, and The Melvins, whose bassist was Matt Lukin. In 1987, Green River and Soundgarden were the first bands to release records on Sub Pop, another new Seattle independent. Founded by Bruce Pavitt and Jonathan Poneman, two would-be music entrepreneurs who met via mutual friendship with Soundgarden guitarist Kim Thayil, the label's evangelical belief in the Seattle underground rock scene would propel first Soundgarden, then Mudhoney and, eventually, Nirvana to wider prominence.

As the world now knows, Nirvana changed rock music forever. Yet without the profound musical influence of Mudhoney or the marketing hustle of Sub Pop providing them with a platform, they might never have been heard beyond the Pacific Northwest, then an unfashionable and obscure corner of the U.S. Sub Pop not only released Nirvana's first records—the band's debut album, *Bleach*, came out the month after Mudhoney and Soundgarden's SOAS gig—it nurtured the Seattle underground scene to the point where international recognition for its music was possible.

Soundgarden, however, chose a different path. Of all the bands featured on *Deep Six*, they possessed obvious mainstream crossover potential—located chiefly in the glistening musculature of singer Chris Cornell, who combined the brooding lust appeal of Jim Morrison with the lung-busting holler of Robert Plant. Major record labels began courting Soundgarden soon after their 1987 Sub Pop debut, the *Screaming Life* EP; indeed, A&M funded some demo recordings in 1988.

However, the band members were wary of embroiling themselves in a corporate structure so early in their career. While negotiating with A&M, Soundgarden decided to release an album on an independent label. Much to the dismay of Pavitt and Poneman, they chose Greg Ginn's established SST over the fledgling Sub Pop, which had only recently taken up the lease on its first office and was already flirting with bankruptcy.

Soundgarden duly released an album for SST, the patchy *Ultramega OK*, then signed with A&M. They completed the recording sessions for *Louder Than Love*, their major label debut, in January 1989. With the record already in the can, Soundgarden made their UK live debut as the support band for Mudhoney, a group in existence for little more than 12 months and whose records were released by the very same Seattle independent they snubbed the previous year. To compound the insult, it was only six months since Mudhoney supported Soundgarden in Seattle and the riotous scenes at SOAS seemed to suggest they were dealing in hype and hysteria, rather than serious musicianship.

"We played what we thought was one of our best shows," says Thayil. "Mudhoney came out, made a few statements, lost their microphone, the crowd went crazy. Next day, that's all anybody could speak about, the near riot. It was amazing! They've played a song! Maybe two songs! We're tired, we're drunk, we thought, 'Damn, we kicked ass.' But then we realized there's another cultural phenomenon apart from music that's being traded in at that point."

Though Soundgarden played well and were enthusiastically received, everything about the experience was routine. Thereafter, for all the subversive overtones of their sensual take on heavy rock they projected to a mass audience, sometimes bridling at the compromises this entailed—such as opening for Guns N' Roses in arenas and stadia during 1991–92—they eventually reaped the ultimate reward in 1994, when their album *Superunknown* entered the *Billboard* album chart at number one. Just three years later, however, the band broke up, weary of each other and the business imperatives to which they'd consented but never wholeheartedly embraced.

Mudhoney, by contrast, proceeded to ride a wave of mania from an audience pumped by the media's fascination with Sub Pop, often without any clue as to where they were going or why. Their subsequent journey saw many highs and lows, but they never quit; indeed, they continue to this day. The principal reason why Mudhoney still exists—where so many of its peers faltered—is because the band never allowed commercial considerations to impact upon their music.

The other constant theme of the band's 25-year existence has been the reservoir of affection and respect among its audience, which feeds on the obvious camaraderie felt within Mudhoney towards each other, rather than the more traditional rock melodramas. Of the raggedy tribes who gathered at SOAS on May 12, 1989, the common currency was a smile. Late that night, after she'd got home on the last Metropolitan Line train, Leila Kassir wrote in her notebook: "The concert was held in a room no bigger than a school hall, which soon became filled with the scruffiest people I've ever seen at a gig. Apart from some students, the audience seemed to be made up of members of other bands. I somehow realised from the moment I arrived it was going to be a monumental and strange and unforgettable night."

Leila knew it—and the band knew it too.

"Early on, during soundcheck I didn't think there was anything in the air, but I remember coming back from dinner and walking through the crowd, and people were in the venue—and it definitely had this weird electricity," says Mark Arm today. "I don't know how to describe it, there was just a really weird sense to it. It was totally strange, actually. A lot of pheromones and testosterone, I suppose."

* * *

In 2012, the Reading Festival headliners were Foo Fighters, led by Dave Grohl, the man who holds the distinction of filling Dan Peters' shoes in Nirvana (now there's a story—which we'll get to later). As he prepared to lead his band into their encore, Grohl told the audience of the first time he met the other members of Nirvana, at a barbecue the day after the band played their gig at the Motorsports International Garage. The show had been the band's biggest thus far, to an audience of approximately 1,500; Grohl said he asked Peters what was the biggest audience Mudhoney had ever played to. Peters replied: "35,000 people." Grohl was amazed. "Where the fuck did Mudhoney ever play to 35,000 people?" he demanded. Whereupon Peters told him about the Reading Festival.

As Grohl explained to his 2012 crowd, Nirvana went on to play the Reading Festival in 1991, on Friday at mid-afternoon (not Saturday, as he mistakenly claimed), then again in 1992, when they closed the festival as headliners. It would be Nirvana's last ever UK show. Had it not been for Mudhoney's trailblazing impact, they would never have played Reading festival once, let alone headlined.

Mudhoney were the vanguard of the new rock sound that coalesced in Seattle at the end of the 1980s. Known as "grunge," it transformed rock music as well as impacted upon cinema, art, design, fashion . . . even (briefly) the soft drinks industry.

Nirvana eclipsed everything around them. When Kurt Cobain was found dead on April 8, 1994, Mudhoney was touring the U.S.'s East Coast as special guest of Pearl Jam—the band formed by Arm and Turner's former Green River colleagues, Jeff Ament and Stone Gossard, which, in the wake of Nirvana's success, had effected a similarly monumental commercial crossover.

There was talk of canceling that evening's show, at the Patriot Center in Fairfax, Virginia, but both bands decided to keep on going. It was what Mudhoney always did in the face of adversity—sometimes in defiance of common sense. They'd kept going in 1991, when Steve Turner decided to go back to college, and then as their relationship with Sub Pop frayed amid the label's latest near-fatal dalliance with bankruptcy. They kept going in 1992, as their debut album for a major label emerged half-baked and Mark Arm's heroin addiction reached a near-fatal low. They kept going as the early nineties grunge boom turned into a mid-nineties bust. They kept going despite being dropped by Warner Bros. and seeing their audiences dwindle. They kept going despite being the subject of a ruinous tax claim by the U.S. Internal Revenue Service in 1996, a dispute that dragged on until early 2001. They kept going even after Matt Lukin, for so many the ebullient totem of everlasting good times, quit the band, having become disenchanted with playing music, and returned to his previous job as a carpenter.

The recruitment of Lukin's successor, Guy Maddison, heralded a new phase of Mudhoney. Back in partnership with a revitalized Sub Pop, they released a new album, the vibrant *Since We've Become Translucent*, and began touring again—albeit now fitting their itinerary around grown-up responsibilities: Peters has three children, Turner has two; Maddison balances parenthood and music with his career as a critical care nurse at Seattle's Harborview Hospital; Arm is the warehouse manager at Sub Pop.

Perhaps the main reason Mudhoney have survived is thanks to a shrewd assessment of how important rock'n'roll really is. The conventional career strategy would have been to quit sometime in the mid-nineties under a cloud of acrimony and then, later, to reform for a lucrative reunion tour after a series of half-baked solo projects, amid much conciliatory hand-wringing. It's worked for more than one of their contemporaries. But Mudhoney have endured precisely because they never for one moment regarded making music as a career. Asked in 2013 for the secret of how to survive 25 years as a band, Mark Arm replied: "Not giving a shit."*

Since being forced to get regular jobs in order to continue, they've realized the true value of their band lies in their friendship—including that of Matt Lukin, still a Mudhoney member *in absentia*: "It makes me happier knowing that I didn't slow them down, or that I wasn't the cause of a breakup," he says. "I love it. I'll go and see them now and then. There was one show where they just did a really short set; they were playing none of the songs I recognized from me being in the band, and they all fucking rocked!" It's a perspective increasingly shared by others. In 2012, a Mudhoney documentary film, *I'm Now*, premiered at cinemas, while 2013 marked the band's 25th anniversary and saw the release of *Vanishing Point*, their ninth full album, on Sub Pop, the maverick Seattle label whose history is inextricably linked with their own.

* "Mudhoney: Touch Me I'm Old as Fuck" by David Lake, *The Seattle Weekly*, March 26, 2013.

According to Sub Pop's cofounder, Jonathan Poneman, Mudhoney are comparable to the Tower of London's ravens. "When Mudhoney left, the label went into decline," he says. "And when they came back, things reenergized. This sort of conjecture is foolish, but I really wonder: If there still was a Nirvana, would they be making records anywhere near as passionate and as timely as the records Mudhoney are currently making? I don't think so."

Speculating upon his band's ultimate legacy, Mark Arm once said with typical candor: "Steve always likes to say that we're a footnote. And probably in the greater scheme of things, that's at best what we'll be remembered as."* Maybe. But as this book will demonstrate, sometimes the most profound truths sit in the margins of history.

* *Our Band Could Be Your Life* by Michael Azerrad (Little, Brown, 2001), 453.

1

No Place Like Home

High Woodlands doesn't look like a hotbed of grunge. Its myriad streets curve into cul-de-sacs, each comprising mostly one-story houses with built-in garages and gray or beige exteriors. Overlooked by trees, the lawns are neat, going on immaculate. If crime is a concern in this neighborhood then most residents still don't seem to think fences are necessary—though an occasional sign helpfully states: "Private Property."

Driving past Our Redeemer Lutheran Church and the nearby Robert Frost Elementary School that he attended as a child, Mark Arm takes a right turn into the cul-de-sac on 118th Avenue NE and parks his Volkswagen Passat outside the bungalow where he grew up. This is, he acknowledges, definitive suburbia.

"When we first moved here, behind the house it was all woods. They were just starting to build what they call 'Kingsgate 3 & 4.' There are maybe 10 different types of house, replicated over and over again. All there was of the church was the parsonage. The church was so small they would just meet in the living room. They eventually built it up, my dad and the other men of the church. I remember helping with that as a kid."

Mark points at the road leading out of the cul-de-sac and sloping gently down towards the school and Our Redeemer. "This was considered a hill. Once I got into skateboarding, I spent so much time going down this hill. Or I'd be riding round into the cul-de-sac, imagining. . . . I'd read *Skateboarder* magazine and I'd seen them riding in pools. So I'd be pretending I was in a pool. Being an only kid."

Geographically, High Woodlands sits at the center of Kingsgate, a housing development subdivided into numerical sectors and belonging to the city of Kirkland, just off Interstate 405, the traffic-laden freeway that links Kirkland with Bellevue and Renton. Collectively, these and other nearby urban centers—such as Redmond and Bothell—are known as the Eastside suburbs, commuter satellites of the metropolis situated across Lake Washington: Seattle.

Tucked into the northwest corner of the state of Washington, itself a part of the most northwesterly region of the USA before it meets Canada, downtown Seattle is about 20 miles from Kirkland. In favorable traffic it's a half-hour drive, not far away at all. But in the mind of an only child in High Woodlands, whose horizons were defined by the short trips to church and school—or to the Kingsgate Library, or perhaps to the Safeway store near the Kingsgate Skate King—Seattle seemed a remote prospect.

As the opening lines of "Where Is the Future," the opening song on Mudhoney's 2006 album, *Under a Billion Suns*, truthfully state, Mark Arm was "born on an air force base in 1962"—on February 21 at Vandenberg Air Force Base in California, to be exact. He wasn't called Arm then, but Mark Thomas McLaughlin, the son of Calvin McLaughlin and Anita Schwab, who met in the aftermath of World War II and married in 1957. Calvin served in the U.S. Air Force based in Wiesbaden, near Frankfurt where Anita lived, and where she had been a promising opera singer before the war. "They were engaged for 10 years before they got married, while he was reassigned to the Pacific," says Mark. "I don't think my mom had many options, what with all the German males of her age being wiped out."

Mark's earliest memories are not of Vandenberg but Germany, where his parents lived for the last few years of his father's tenure in the air force before moving back to the U.S. After a brief stay in California, the McLaughlins finally settled in the Pacific Northwest, moving into the newly built High Woodlands in 1966.

"My mom wanted to come to some place with what she called 'culture,'" says Mark. "Which meant a thriving symphony [orchestra] and opera. So initially we went to San Francisco. I can remember going to the aquarium in Golden Gate Park, right off the Haight. At that point there was definitely the bubbling up of what was soon to be hippy culture, probably not yet super-visible so I don't know if my parents would have even noticed. But it's funny to think my dad's about the same age as Allen Ginsberg!" Mark's smile suggests that, besides both being born in the early twenties, Ginsberg and McLaughlin senior would have found little in common. "To call it the 'Beat Generation' I think is a misnomer. Because most people in that generation were not beats."

The young Mark McLaughlin was denied the opportunity of growing up amid the flower children when his father, having retired from the air force with a pension after 20 years' service, got a job at Boeing. Founded in Seattle in 1916, by the mid-Sixties the aviation giant was the largest single employer in the region, as the advent of the jet airliner fueled a population boom. When the McLaughlins arrived in their suburban idyll, as many as 80 percent of their neighbours also worked for Boeing.

While he had that much in common with his fellow High Woodlanders, in most aspects Mark felt a certain otherness. For one thing, he was an only child—though far more unusual was his having quite obviously middle-aged parents. Everyone else's mom and dad seemed to be 20 years younger than his; schoolfriends would assume his mother was his grandma, and not just because of her age. Anita's clothes were from a different continent and a different era. Fascinated as an adolescent by *The Mod Squad* and other attempts by American television to depict hippy-era countercultural themes, Mark had a recurring dream about his parents taking off their "old people masks" and throwing a wild party. "There was obviously something going on there psychologically!" he laughs.

At least he was permitted to watch television. Pop music was another matter entirely. His mother had very specific notions of what qualified as appropriate conduct. "There was a right way to fold your underwear, and everything else was wrong. That went right down the line. Music had to be classical, and *classical* classical—anything past the eighteenth century was shit in her eyes."

As was common—and indeed, from 1936, compulsory—for German girls in the thirties, Anita had been in the *Bund Deutscher Mädel*, the female division of the Hitler Youth, and Mark wonders if this shaped an inflexible perspective on life. As mainstream American culture began to dilute and absorb the impact of Woodstock and the Aquarian age, Anita McLaughlin's attitudes remained rooted in Old World propriety.

Much to his chagrin, she insisted on Mark taking piano lessons from an early age. "Even before I was born, my mom bought a baby grand and in her mind had this idea that I would be the next Van Cliburn. I think she started going through menopause as I was a kid—and she was high strung and nervy to begin with. I would be practicing and if I hit a wrong note, I would hear a shriek coming out of the kitchen: '*B flat*!!!' It was incredible. It got to the point where I actually hated the instrument, and when I got old enough to put my foot down and say I don't want to do this anymore, I completely turned my back on it. I wish that I had actually retained that stuff. I could play all right, and I did fine in recitals, but I wasn't a virtuoso."

So there was music in the McLaughlin household, but it had to be the right kind. Although he had a small record player, if Mark wanted to play anything other than a couple of approved children's 45s, he had to do so when his parents weren't at home. In order to obtain records, he had to secretly buy them with pocket money on family shopping trips to Seattle's Naval Air Station at Sand Point, where his father could claim ex-military discounts.

Seven-inch singles were small enough for Mark to hide under a coat until he got home, where he would hasten to his room and bury his contraband in a drawer. The first covert purchase was "Yo Yo," a big hit in 1971 for those wholesome Mormon singing sensations The Osmonds. Future acquisitions would include Terry Jacks' 1974 hit "Seasons in the Sun," a lachrymose *adieu* from a dying man to his family and friends—"a very emotional song to a 10-year-old"—adapted by Rod McKuen from a Jacques Brel original in which *le moribond* tells his wife that he knows of her unfaithfulness (Jacks' version would later be covered by Nirvana).

As Mark grew older, an illicit source of inspiration presented itself in the garage: the family Volkswagen Beetle didn't need the ignition switched on for the radio to work, so Mark would sneak in and listen to Top 40 hits, his ears perking up when anything vaguely edgy came on—for example The Rolling Stones, or even such cheesy period hits as "Green Eyed Lady" by Sugarloaf. "My parents tried to keep me away from rock'n'roll. That only made the attraction greater."

The lure of forbidden fruit began landing the pre-teen Mark McLaughlin in conflict with authority. For years, his transgressions extended no further than cycling to nearby Totem Lake, a large marshy pond where he and his friends indulged in standard-issue stupidity, like attempting to build a raft from pieces of wood and then to sail in it. Lives may have been put at risk, but no laws were broken.

That was to change with the arrival on the McLaughlins' cul-de-sac of a Californian family, featuring six lairy boys who rode BMX bicycles and spoke an exotic new language. "They said things like 'radical' and they were very appealing," says Mark. "An older boy actually rode motocross motorcycles. It seemed like every other kid had a BMX bike and I wanted one so bad. I had a 10-speed, but my mom for some reason was like, 'You can't have a BMX, it's dangerous, it's stupid.'"

Around the same time as the Cali crew breezed color into High Woodlands, Totem Lake Mall opened its doors. Today, like the nearby namesake water feature, it's dying, its business drained away by bigger, brighter malls in Bellevue. Back in 1974, however, Totem Lake Mall was as happening as things got in these parts, with such rarefied retail experiences as Lamont's Anchor department store, Schuck's Auto Supply, and Sportswest. It soon became a magnet for Mark and his disreputable new friends.

"I shoplifted a pair of I Ski sunglasses, which were all the rage. Kinda like cop glasses. I thought, 'I'll look so cool in these when I ski.' At the time they were $12, which if you were a kid was an exorbitant amount of money. I hid them in my drawer and my mom found them. My mom was *really* good at cleaning my room."

By now Mark was in the seventh grade, attending the local Kamiakin Junior High where his fledgling delinquency took tentative steps forward. Without the benefit of an elder sibling to keep him streetwise, he was initially confused as to where all his neighborhood peers went during break time, until someone took him to a nearby wooded area where everyone was smoking cigarettes—or even getting stoned. In an effort to get with the program, Mark fashioned a pipe for himself at the school's workshop; that he had no idea how to actually obtain anything to smoke seemed beside the point. Yet despite hiding it behind books on a shelf protected by glass doors, the intrepidly dusting Anita found that too.

One day, the Californian boys decided it was their mission to get Mark a BMX bike. Wandering over to Kingsgate Library, they spotted one parked outside and seized it. They ran for the woods, intending to leave it there until the fuss caused by the theft had subsided. In no time at all, however, they were back in the woods, drooling over their ill-gotten gain. The plan was to strip the bike for parts and then reassemble it in a different guise, though no one seemed very sure where the other parts were coming from. That dilemma was soon solved; they were busy dismantling the bike when its owner and his friends showed up.

"There's other woods further away that we should have gone to, but we were pretty dumb criminals," says Mark. "So they found us and we ran."

Scattering in all directions, the miscreants converged on the Californian boys' house. Needing to keep a low profile, it was decided that both the library and the Kingsgate Safeway, the nearby local hang-out, were out of bounds. Yet within a few hours they were back at Safeway. Inevitably, a police car pulled up. The boys were separated and interrogated, whereupon their prepared defense—that they had just stumbled across the bike in the woods—quickly unraveled. It was Mark who cracked first.

"They were saying things like, 'It's going to be much easier for you if you tell the truth.' When my dad got home that day, I've never seen him so angry. His face was beet red. He was always a very reserved, quiet guy, but I'd never seen him react that way. I remember him chasing me around the dining room table. It would probably have been funny had I not been so scared."

The farcical case of the stolen BMX was to have a fundamental impact on Mark McLaughlin's life. His parents decided drastic measures were needed to save their son from ruin. That summer, his father took him to Kansas, to the tiny community where Calvin had been born in 1923 and grew up as the youngest of 10—the son of a dirt farmer during the Dust Bowl era of the thirties.

Mark was startled to find that Centralia, the nearby "town" where Calvin and his farm friends would get into fights with the "townies," was nothing more than a road with a couple of shops on either side, barely more than a dot on the map in the very middle of nowhere. It was a stark insight to his father's upbringing. Then, for his eighth grade, he was enrolled at a new school: Bellevue Christian.

A private interdenominational institution situated in Clyde Hill, near the super-rich enclave of Medina where Microsoft magnate Bill Gates lives, according to its mission statement Bellevue Christian School seeks to "prepare young people to live fully for God in a rapidly changing world with the ability to understand, evaluate, and transform the world from the foundation of God's unchanging vision."

As far as the McLaughlins were concerned, its primary purpose was extricating 13-year-old Mark from the dubious influence of the boys next door. Ostensibly, the plan worked. Getting to school now required a 10-mile bus journey down I-405, as opposed to a five-minute hop along the road to Kamiakin Junior High. Mark no longer socialized with his neighborhood peers, except in controlled environments like church.

However, the move did nothing to quell his gnawing sense of isolation. At least his arrival at this alien environment coincided with Bellevue Christian ending its policy of compulsory school uniform. "I had been mortified by the prospect of having to stand there, at the bus stop, in my neighborhood, in a fucking uniform," he says. "I was a scrawny little kid, and easily bullied sometimes, and I felt odd with my weird older parents. I was just trying to fit in."

Yet on an intellectual level, going to Bellevue Christian was arguably the making of him—because it was there that he realized he was not alone in feeling out of step with the herd. The school roll drew from two separate demographics. First, there were the offspring of fundamentalist Christian parents seeking to minimize their children's interaction with the secular world, who began attending from infant level. But Bellevue Christian was also a popular option with parents like the McLaughlins, not necessarily devout believers but hoping that the school's religious strictures would quell "problem" behavior in children typically on the cusp of those troublesome teen years.

Consequently, its intake was far more cosmopolitan than the local high school's, and Mark now found himself interacting with kids from areas beyond his immediate vicinity: from Bellevue, the affluent Seattle suburb of Mercer Island, or the big city itself.

"Sometimes I wonder: What if I hadn't gone to Bellevue Christian and ended up going to Juanita High School, in my neighborhood, would I have continued to hang out with stoner dumb shits like I was hanging out with before, or would I have broken out of that and gotten into punk rock and started thinking differently? I think I ended up hanging out with much smarter and weirder and more devious kids. I don't think Bellevue Christian ruined my life at all—it probably made it better. It gave me something to question. And also, it's where I met up with Smitty."

"Smitty" was Jeffrey Smith, from south Bellevue, with whom Mark had much in common. Another only child, Smitty believes the motivation for sending him to Bellevue Christian was punitive: "To break my will." His father also had a military background—"He probably didn't make any effort to understand that things might have changed a little bit since 1947!"—and like Mark, Smitty felt stigmatized by his peers for having middle-aged parents.

"We were definitely both loners," he says. "I had a few friends. Sometimes I felt like Mark didn't have hardly any friends until we all became friends and started doing stuff a little bit later, after the end of high school, when we started playing music together."

The pair first met as teammates in intramural basketball: "Basketball for people that aren't good enough to play on the real team," according to Smitty. As fellow nosebleed sufferers, they also found themselves frequenting the school nurse. But although they were amicable with each other, Mark and Jeff belonged to distinct cliques and didn't become firm friends until their final year at high school, when music became a common bond.

With her son safely dispatched along the path of righteousness at Bellevue Christian, Mark's mother had relented somewhat on her zero tolerance attitude towards music. He was now allowed to buy his own records. In a conciliatory gesture, she even bought him Elton John's *Greatest Hits*. "By this point I wasn't really into Elton John anymore," says Mark. "But I had bought 'Fox on the Run' by The Sweet; I really, really dug that. Then 'Ballroom Blitz' came on the radio, and I went, 'Fuck—I'm buying that album!'"

The album was *Desolation Boulevard*, The Sweet's breakthrough U.S. release: a compilation of the erstwhile glam-pop hit machine's two previous UK LPs that revealed them chafing against the teen-bait material written by producers Nicky Chinn and Mike Chapman, offering up their own grittier compositions—some of which featured scenes of a sexual nature. The epic, Deep Purple-ish "Sweet FA," for instance, had the opening couplet: "Well it's Friday night and I need a fight/And if she don't spread I'm gonna bust her head." "A.C.D.C.," Chinn/Chapman's ode to the potential side benefits of a bisexual lover ("She's got some other women as well as me"), was demure by comparison.

What, though, would Anita McLaughlin make of her son's first legitimately purchased record? "She read the lyric sheet, and then said to me: 'I just hope you don't understand what they're talking about.' Which was pretty big of her. She could have just taken the record and smashed it, then said, 'I'm not letting you buy another record.' But I think at this point she realised there was no stopping it."

Although gripped by a typical 14-year-old boy's wonderment about sex, it would be several years before Mark discovered exactly how fascinating girls could be. One member of his Bellevue Christian social circle proved quicker on the uptake. Hanging out at the Kingsgate Skate King one evening in late 1976, Mark McLaughlin, Mark Davie, and Paul Zech turned round and were astonished to see their friend Kurt Walls talking to a girl.

"Then they started making out! We were like, 'Woah! This is weird,'" says Mark. "The next night, I was at home watching the Paul Lynde Halloween Special with KISS, and there's a knock at the door. It was Kurt, who's from Redmond—which is miles away. He says: 'I just got laid!' He met up with that girl again and they went to the bushes. Totally weird. I said: 'What was it like . . . ?!' I don't think he ever saw her again."

Sex education was most certainly not on the curriculum at Bellevue Christian—at least not for boys. Mark remembers his biology teacher dissecting a frog by way of attempting to explain the mechanics of procreation, freezing in horror as he uttered the word "penis." "He was proud of the fact that he and his wife had never kissed until after they were married, they just held hands. I didn't learn anything about reproduction from any adult."

Such repressed attitudes were consistent with Mark's life experience thus far. Be it at home or in school, the prevailing political and moral climates were deeply conservative. During his fifth grade at Robert Frost Elementary, in the runup to the 1972 presidential election the entire school had been gathered in the cafeteria and pupils were asked to raise their hands for either the Republican incumbent, Richard Nixon, or his liberal Democrat opponent, George McGovern. "Basically to find out what the parents are thinking, because at that age kids just parrot their parents," says Mark. "So of course, my hand shot up for Nixon. In fact, only two kids raised their hands for McGovern, and they were a brother and a sister. That's an indication of the mindset of this neighborhood. If I remember correctly, those kids' mom eventually came out of the closet."

As well as attending church every week, Mark was a member of that redoubtable bastion of good citizenship the Boy Scouts of America, for which his father was an adult volunteer. Perhaps accordingly, Mark McLaughlin's reaction to punk rock's revolutionary portent was not one of wholesale acceptance. He saw a report on Tom Snyder's late-night talk show about the insurgent youth cult then sweeping the UK. The film's stance was typical of the era's equivalent British media coverage: much tut-tutting about moral turpitude amid scenes of youths with safety pins in their faces.

"I watched this, going, 'Oh my God, I hope this stuff doesn't come here, this is crazy! What are these people thinking?!' And then for a little while they show this band, who I later realized was The Damned. I was thinking: 'Wow, that's like KISS, but faster and better!' I thought that, but I didn't let myself admit it. So I didn't get into punk in 1977."

Thanks to the repetitive diet of AM radio and the limited scope of his nearest record shop, DJ Sound City in Totem Lake Mall, Mark's penultimate (or junior) year at Bellevue Christian was soundtracked by a bovine rotation of KISS, Ted Nugent, REO Speedwagon, Foreigner, Styx . . . the stodgy staples of Middle American seventies rock. In such company, the genuinely edgy and lascivious Aerosmith stood out like Roman gods.

"I was a huge Aerosmith fan," says Mark. "My one great lapse at that time was listening to Rush. I think the appeal was they didn't sing about cars and girls, which most of that sterile shit did. . . . There was this overwhelming feeling that you'd missed something. Like the really good shit had happened in the sixties, with The Who and Hendrix, and what you had left was *this stuff*. Also, I thought that to be in a band you had to be a musician: you had to be technically proficient, know what you're doing."

Salvation was at hand, but only after a further run-in with the law. Towards the end of his junior year, Mark and two of his associates—collectively they dubbed themselves the "Zucchini Brothers"—were caught smoking behind the school water tower. Kurt Walls and Paul Zech were expelled from Bellevue Christian. Mark begged for clemency and was allowed to stay: "I must have made some insane concessions. I was on such thin ice with my parents, I couldn't afford them to be so pissed off with me. That's when I started hanging out more with Smitty."

His parents must have breathed sighs of relief as well as pride when, at 16, Mark became an Eagle Scout—the BSA's ultimate accolade, attained only by a small elite who had earned all 24 merit badges while also demonstrating service and leadership credentials. But his Scout spirit would steadily abate as he became enthralled with Smitty, whose wry skepticism inculcated a more subversive attitude towards authority than the standard delinquent teen clichés.

Collectively, Jeff Smith, Peter Wick, Tom Wolf, and a younger boy, Darren Morey, were a pretend band, whose name popped into Smitty's head one day while idling over a music magazine during one of Mr. Epp's mathematics lessons. "Mr. Epp was a really good teacher," says Smitty, "but he was very stoic and barely spoke. He was also the soccer coach. I think he had been drafted into the American soccer league back in the sixties. It paid so badly that being a teacher was better than being a pro soccer player in America. Kind of a strange guy. I was really bored in class one day and I started reading the *New York Rocker*—'Mr. Epp & The Calculations' is such a silly new wave-sounding name, but it sounded pretty cool in 1978 and I thought it would be a good name for a band."

Always friendly with the Zucchinis, as their senior (i.e. final) year at high school began, the ranks of Mr. Epp embraced Mark McLaughlin as a fully fledged recruit. Pretty soon the band began to blur the boundaries between imagination and physical reality. They would design T-shirts for tours that never happened or sleeves for nonexistent records—like Epp's 1979 debut *Hit the Creek*, its followup *Even More Live,* and 1980's *The Girl with the Diet Dr. Pepper Eyes*.

The boys found an alternative place of education at Rubato Records in downtown Bellevue. The only second-hand record shop on the Eastside, it was run by John Rubato, who played drums for local art-punks Student Nurse and actively encouraged his teenage clientele's musical quests. He didn't laugh at Mark when he bought a Dixie Dregs album, but instead suggested he might also want to check out New York Dolls, Brian Eno, or Captain Beefheart. Rubato was also responsible for convincing Smitty that making music (*outré* music in particular) was a realistic ambition.

"I walked in there once and this music was just so nuts and so loud and the guitars were so distorted. I said, 'What is this?' And it was Jimi Hendrix's 'Star Spangled Banner' . . . I'd heard a little bit of Jimi Hendrix, but just classic rock stuff. I was like, 'My God, this is unbelievable.' That and The Velvet Underground, especially *White Light/White Heat*, y'know, 'Sister Ray' and 'I Heard Her Call My Name,' the guitars are so feeding back, so thick and menacing. We were like, 'We wanna do stuff that sounds like that.'"

In June 1980, Mr. Epp had their first practice session in the unfinished basement of the Morey family home, situated on a finger of land projecting from the bottom of Clyde Hill into Lake Washington. Paul Morey ran a successful hair salon in downtown Seattle and was happy to let his son, Darren, and his friends mess around—"so long as we didn't burn anything down," says Smitty. Inspired by The Velvet Underground, it was an exercise in pure noise mischief, involving vacuum cleaners and various people taking turns at the drum kit Darren had inherited from his older brother.

The summer of 1980 was a key transitional period in the life of 18-year-old, punk-curious Eagle Scout Mark McLaughlin. Perhaps most significantly, given his later musical endeavors, he discovered The Stooges, having seen the name cited in music magazines as a vital punk forebear. Though their first two albums, 1969's *The Stooges* and its 1970 followup *Fun House,* were out of print and almost impossible to find at the time, 1973's *Raw Power* had been reissued as part of Columbia's Nice Price budget range. Mark found a remaindered copy in Rubato.

"I remember thinking, 'This doesn't sound like anything I'm familiar with at all,'" he says. "I mean, it was rock'n'roll, but the production on it was so weird and off-putting! I couldn't quite get a handle on it, at that time. This is a world of Styx and Foreigner and Journey—and then *this*! This makes no sense! But there was something about it that kept me coming back to it and made me want to find the other two records. It wasn't just like [I said], 'Oh, I've heard The Stooges,' and let it go."

Having graduated from Bellevue Christian, Mark was also about to start higher education at Linfield College in McMinnville, a town in northwest Oregon's Willamette Valley, 35 miles from Portland and a four-hour drive from Seattle. The far from obvious choice of college suggested conflicting impulses on his part, as well as parental influence. Linfield was a small private institution, founded in 1858 by the Oregon Baptist Educational Society. The religious grounding reassured Mark's parents, as did the fact that a neighbor's daughter attended the college.

His personal inclination had been for Evergreen State College in Olympia, the Washington state capital 60 miles south of Seattle. Opened in 1971 amid a countercultural backlash to the Ohio National

Guard's murder of four Kent State University students protesting against the Vietnam War, to this day Evergreen could almost be a parody of progressive liberal education: under its Latin motto *Omnia Lateres*—"Let it all hang out"—students are offered "Narrative Evaluations" instead of grades. Mark knew there was no chance he would be allowed to go; he was already confounding his parents' expectations by insisting on a liberal arts degree, although they had hoped he would follow his father into the air force.

So conservative Linfield was a compromise, but not purely to appease Anita and Calvin. He rationalized the choice to himself by the fact that, as a keen skier, he could take advantage of McMinnville's proximity to any number of Oregon's resorts. Fundamentally, however, after attending such a small high school, Mark had felt intimidated by the possibility of enrolling at the huge University of Washington, which, although handily situated in Seattle, had over 35,000 students and dominated an entire neighborhood of the city northeast of Lake Union, the so-called U-District. With a mere 1,500 undergraduates, there was no chance of him being overwhelmed at Linfield. There was, however, every chance that Mark McLaughlin would stick out—especially as, by the time he began his studies, he was no longer merely curious about punk.

★ ★ ★

Located at 1426 First Avenue, near Pike Place Market in downtown Seattle, The Showbox originally opened as an entertainment venue in 1939. For three decades its famous sprung dancefloor kept crowds moving to the popular sounds of the day: Al Jolson, Duke Ellington, Muddy Waters, Peggy Lee, and Frank Sinatra all performed there, as well as Pacific Northwest rock'n'roll pioneers The Kingsmen and The Wailers. By the end of the Seventies, however, it was a rarely used Jewish bingo hall known as The Talmud-Torah—its dilapidation indicative of Seattle's struggle after Boeing halved its workforce during the early part of the decade.

Enter Modern Productions, a group of young local music promoters with the vision to embrace the revolutionary energies unleashed by punk. The venue reopened on September 8, 1979, with a gig by Manchester art-rock existentialists Magazine—the audience included Jonathan Poneman, a 19-year-old from Ohio who had moved to Seattle just four days earlier. During the next 12 months, The Showbox became a vital source of nourishment for Seattle's underground music scene, an incentive for nonmainstream touring acts (both from the U.S. and overseas) to make the trip up the coast from California or across the Rockies from the Midwest. With a capacity of 1,000, it was larger than a dive bar but more intimate than a sports arena. Perhaps most significantly, it was an all-ages venue and was not restricted to over-21s. Thus a hitherto disparate audience of curious teenage nonconformists could congregate to potentially have their minds blown.

So it was for Mark McLaughlin on August 12, 1980, when he went to The Showbox to see Devo. The absurdist, post-punk freakshow from Akron, Ohio, then stood on the verge of an unlikely commercial breakthrough with the synth-heavy future-pop of "Whip It." Though enamored of the band's hysterically pent-up subversion of rock'n'roll, it was as much the tactile experience of the event that affected Mark.

"Seeing Devo spun my head around," he says. "I'd seen a couple of large-scale arena concerts, like Rush and The Kinks and Sammy Hagar. You'd tell yourself, 'Wow, this is great,' but just sitting in a far seat at a coliseum looking at these guys on a stage way down there, *somewhere*, it wasn't really all that captivating. And then I went to see Devo at The Showbox, which was this small club; it had a sprung dancefloor, and people were, I guess, pogoing. The whole place was going nuts, jumping up and down in unison and by two thirds into the show there's one person between me and the stage. It was incredible. One of the guitar players, one of the Bobs, was doing a guitar solo and he bent over the crowd and the neck of the guitar went over our heads so I reached up and touched it—and he hit me over the head with his guitar neck. I went, 'Yeeaah!' And I've never looked back since."

Life at college proved a stark contrast to this epiphany. Although it did have a record shop, Discus, where he bought Canadian import copies of the first two Stooges albums, McMinnville was "a cultural vacuum" and Mark returned home as often as possible, where he spent his time bingeing on the one precious resource Linfield could not offer: a community of kindred spirits.

"I was one of two punk rockers there," says Mark. "Maybe there were 10 people sorta sympathetic to new wave. Everybody else was just cowboys and jocks. There was an agricultural program—it was super-redneck and hicky."

During the summer of 1981, with Mark back at home after his first year in college, Mr. Epp took some steps towards actual existence. They spent a day sticking "Mr. Epp Is Coming" posters around Seattle, inspired by a Malcolm McLaren-esque *How to Beat the Music Industry* guide Smitty had read. "We started writing fake letters to magazines, talking about how we'd seen this band, Mr. Epp, and how they were so awful," he says. "And it kinda worked, because there was so little going on that people started getting interested in this thing that didn't exist."

One of these letters, written by Mark to the local fanzine *Desperate Times*, saw the first published usage of the word "grunge" in reference to a Seattle band (although certainly not the first ever—the word's derivation can be traced at least as far back as *Creem* rock critic Lester Bangs' 1971 description of garage band The Count Five's "grungy spunk"). The letter began: "I hate Mr. Epp & The Calculations! Pure grunge! Pure noise! Pure shit!" It went on to vilify Epp for not wearing chains or mohawks, for being older than The Grateful Dead, and for loving "Emerson Lake & Palmer (my mother's fave). . . . While my friends listen to Mr Epp & The Calculations, I listen to Mr [Philip] Glass. His music is repetitious, redundant and repetitive. Pure art! It's sooooooo intellectual, like me." After stating he listened to Glass "over and over and over and over again," the author signed the letter "Mark McLaughlin" four times, before adding an editor's note: "Mark McLaughlin does guitar and vocals in Mr Epp & The Calculations."*

The letters and flyposting caught the attention of *Desperate Times*' editors Maire Masco and Dennis White, who also promoted gigs and had their own record label, Pravda. Their offer of the opening slot at a forthcoming show forced Mr. Epp to consider what this would entail:

* *Loser* by Clark Humphrey (Feral House, 1995), 62.

most pressingly, the acquisition of instruments, as well as deciding who would play what. Although resistant to the notion that he should drum for such a terrible band, Darren Morey's ability made him an obvious choice—as well as the fact that all alternative candidates kept disappearing. Having played on an early demo, Peter Wick quit because, much to Mark's amusement, "he didn't want to dedicate his life to music." Wick's tipping point came when Smitty and Mark split the cost of a pawn-shop guitar and a small Peavey amplifier.

"He was like: 'This is becoming real now, and I just can't do it!'" says Mark. "The guitar's A-string tuning peg was broken and rusted. Thank God that string never broke because there would have been no way to change it. Not that we knew anything about tuning or the idea that there was such a thing. We couldn't play—at all. And if it wasn't for punk rock, we would have never thought we could get on stage and do this in front of anybody. We were just doing it for our own amusement."

As well as obtaining equipment, that summer also brought a development that would define one member permanently. One day, the band were helping to build Paul Morey's newest business venture—Second Ave Extension, a hamburger restaurant in downtown Seattle's Pioneer Square district—though according to Smitty their "work" mostly amounted to "talking, listening to punk tapes, and breaking plates and glasses."

"We were all bullshitting and making fun of silly put-downs like 'shit head,' 'fuck face,' and 'dick brains,'" he says. "We posited that one could also say insults of all body parts like 'nose neck' or 'tongue sternum' or 'arm arm.' 'Arm arm' stuck and became 'Mark Arm.'"

Mark's other Epp handles included "Mahavishnu Mark McLaughlin" and "Uppin' Arms," but in an era when having a punk name was almost obligatory, "Mark Arm" transcended cliché while still evoking contrariness. It also happened to be easier to say than "McLaughlin."

"We all changed our names often then," says Smitty, who for Epp purposes was always "Jo" rather than "Jeff." "I don't think any of us were happy with who we were, and punk/art allowed us to be other people."

After canceling several shows—some of them because Darren's bass-playing, 16-year-old brother, Todd, had been grounded by his parents—Mr. Epp finally made their live debut on October 8, 1981, supporting Student Nurse at the UCT, a trade union hall at Fifth and Aloha in Seattle's Queen Anne district—just north of the Space Needle, the 600-foot tower that dominates the Seattle skyline. Though politely received, their 15-minute set made it clear even at this formative stage that Mr. Epp were destined to fulfil a role as irritants. "I Wanna Wash Yr Dog" was a haplessly rendered tribute-cum-parody directed at The Fartz, one of several local bands inspired by two Seattle shows played by Black Flag in 1980 to plug into the gut-wrenching, high-velocity schematics of punk's latest variant—hardcore. That Mr. Epp were in no way competent enough to play so fast didn't matter at all; it wasn't as if The Fartz were so much better.

Satirising a scene to which they ostensibly belonged soon became Mr. Epp's default position—and, in due course, that of Mark Arm too. The band's reputation as suburban snarks was enshrined by "Mohawk Man," the lead song on their debut seven-inch EP, *Of Course I'm Happy, Why?*, recorded in March 1982 at Triangle Studios, in the northwest Seattle neighborhood of Ballard. The band's nerves were assuaged by the fact that John Rubato was present to tell the skeptical engineer that he should let the band do whatever they wanted, despite their inexperience. Darren had finally been prevailed upon to join the band by now, and his assured beats made Epp a relatively plausible proposition.

Delivered deadpan by Arm, the lyrics lampooned the decay of punk's creative anarchy into new clichés: "I'm a mohawk man and I can look real mean/I got a mohawk, man, and I can make the scene . . . I got lots of chains and I'm getting more/I've ordered a dog collar from the local punk store/Now I'm hardcore . . . "

Clearly indebted to *Metal Box*–vintage Public Image Ltd., with scratchy guitars slithering across tribal drums and a troubled bass line, "Mohawk Man" is an authentic period curio. Its quirky appeal made it an unlikely alternative radio hit; the University of Washington's KCMU was an enthusiastic champion, while for one epochal week "Mohawk Man" was the most requested record on fervent Anglophile Rodney

Bingenheimer's KROQ show in Los Angeles (ahead that week of "Anything by The Jam" and Toni Basil's "Mickey"). "I think we were disappointed in how antiseptic 'Mohawk Man' sounds," says Smitty. "But the spirit still comes through."

By the summer of 1982, Mark Arm was done with McMinnville. Despite the skiing, it had been a disheartening experience, epitomized by a moment towards the end of his sophomore year when he and a friend silenced the Linfield College cafeteria by walking in with bleached buzz-cut hair. The entire room fell silent. "Forks and knives drop, everyone's looking—like, *look at those freaks.*"

One of the college football players, who regularly teased Mark by calling him "Devo" (the minor detail that Mark had moved on and was now into hardcore was lost on him), walked up to the pair. "Devo," he said, eyeing Mark's new haircut with disdain, "I'm gonna kill you!"

Mark returned to Seattle, switching his studies in English Lit and Philosophy to the University of Washington, and immediately took advantage of the city's social and cultural vibrancy. On July 4, he witnessed one of the most important shows of his life. Black Flag, the U.S. hardcore scene's catalytic engine as well as its iconoclasts, played at the Norway Center. On their previous visit to Seattle, on August 16, 1980, just four days after Devo, Arm hadn't yet been aware of the band beyond the fact that their name was a popular graffiti symbol. He'd made good during the intervening period and, when Black Flag's epochal debut album, *Damaged*, was released in early 1982, Mark reviewed the record for the second issue of *Attack*, a fanzine edited by Smitty, who was by now also studying literature at UW.

In the first issue, Mark had penned a critique of *In God We Trust Inc.*, the EP by The Dead Kennedys, which saw America's premier punk band endorsing the scene's gear-shift into hyper-velocity.

"I was tapping into the whole American hardcore thing, period," says Arm. "The first record was The Dead Kennedys', and I'm thinking, 'Wow, this music is super-super fast.' And then The Circle Jerks—'Oh shit, this is even faster! How fast can music be?!' And a slew of singles, like the Minor Threat single, and the Flipper single, then the Flipper album and Black Flag . . . it was all happening really fast. A pretty exciting period for me. And that was the general framework for Mr. Epp, but the last thing Mr. Epp wanted to be was a generic hardcore band. When all that stuff first popped up, there wasn't a generic template. But within a year you started noticing, 'Oh, there's another band sounding like Minor Threat . . . '"

Even as they acquired sufficient chops to deliver credible hardcore blasts, Mr. Epp were never didactic, run-of-the-mill speed merchants, thanks to the sheer idiosyncrasy of their constituent parts. It was obligatory for hardcore bands in 1982 to pen songs agonising about the threat of mutually assured destruction or preaching the ascetic delights of a straight-edge lifestyle, but Epp's variants on the form—like "Smile" and "Out of Control"—were far more ambivalent, thanks mostly to droll vocalising from Smitty or Arm's subversive lyrical instincts. "Smile," for instance, suggested that people should embrace nuclear weapons—"be glad we can all die together—nuclear war, it's our friend!"—while Mark's screams on "Genocide" were so unhinged as to blur the song's moral stance. Meanwhile, Smitty's discovery of Albert Ayler impelled his purchase of an alto saxophone, pushing Epp's modus operandi further into the realm of amorphous noise assault. Needless to say, these layers of ironic discourse were lost on the increasingly hostile, identikit "punkers" the band encountered at their live shows.

"We all had a pretty strong vibe of 'people think this is weird and crazy music, but here's something weirder and crazier,'" says Smitty. "Some guy with a mohawk came up to me after a show and went, 'That's not music, that's just noise.' I said, 'Isn't that what your mom told you about The Clash?' People were not nearly as liberal as they thought they were. I definitely worshipped the most extreme thing I could get my hands on. So once I started listening to free jazz and Throbbing Gristle, that stuff made punk rock seem like Blondie. Live, we were basically just trying to blow people's heads off. When we were opening for bands, we were happiest if we cleared out the room."

For his first term (or quarter) at the University of Washington, Mark lived in a hall of residence. But it wasn't long before new friendships forged over discussions about music would prompt a move off-campus into a series of shared apartments near Brooklyn Avenue or the U-District's main thoroughfare, University Way. Some of the characters he met during his initial months at UW would be critical to the impact of Seattle's rock underground. One such individual was Kim Thayil, originally from Park Forest, Illinois, who attended the same modern philosophy class and routinely arrived 10 minutes late, before maddening the professor by sidetracking any discussions via abstruse tangents.

Thayil recalls Arm as intense and initially distant, though they soon found common cause in punk: "The first day in class he had short hair and was wearing a blue button-down shirt with a homemade 'Minor Threat' stencil on the back. Eventually as I got to know Mark, through the comments he made at shows, about bands, he was pretty caustic. And that endeared him to myself even more. He's a pretty witty guy. My wit was more abusive than caustic. So the combination on some levels worked."

Another key acquaintance made during this period was Charles Peterson, a photography student from the Eastside suburb of Bothell, who spotted Mark sitting on his own in the dorm cafeteria wearing a Crass T-shirt. Intrigued to meet another fan of the infamous British anarchist collective, Peterson went over to introduce himself. Soon he and his punk girlfriend were invited back to Mark's room to listen to the first Meat Puppets album. "We became good, fast friends," says Peterson. "We were both from the suburbs, so we had that bonding. But mostly it was the love of punk rock music. When he was done with dorms, we rented a grotty little basement on 11th or 12th [Avenue]. He was still in Mr. Epp then, and the apartment became a hangout for a bunch of our new friends, like Ed Fotheringham."

Although U.S.-born, Edwin Fotheringham had grown up in Australia, moving there with his mother at the age of five following his parents' divorce. After graduating from high school, he returned to his father's home city of Seattle and began studying painting at UW, where he ran into Peterson and, in due course, Arm.

"He was a decent bloke," says Fotheringham, "and we were both into the music of the time—The Birthday Party, The Fall—so we got along. He was a straight guy. Really straight. He didn't drink, and me being from Australia, I was terribly behaved. What amazed me most was when Charles told me Mark was in Mr. Epp, who I remembered hearing on college radio. I thought if they were on the radio they must be a really big deal. And I guess they weren't! But as an 18-year-old from Australia, I was impressed—maybe even star-struck." He laughs. "But then I met him and that soon waned."

In the years to come, Kim Thayil would form Soundgarden, while Charles Peterson's photography and Ed Fotheringham's art would define the Seattle scene's visual aesthetic. Other figures may not have been so noted, but their influence was just as important—people like Dana Greeley, who lived in a notorious party house called the Ski Lodge and introduced Mark to vital records like "Hate the Police" by Austin, Texas, hardcore band the Dicks, or the Fast Product record label's *The First Year Plan*, a key UK post-punk compilation featuring Gang of Four and The Mekons.

In terms of significance, however, one chance meeting trumped all others. In fact it would provide Mark with his musical partner of the next 30 years.

Standing in line to see Public Image Ltd. play The Showbox on November 12, 1982, Mark saw Alex Shumway who, although three years younger and in his senior year at high school, was known to Arm because he lived in the U-District. Shumway was accompanied by one of his school friends, a 17-year-old punk fan named Steve Turner.

"We were introduced as being straight-edge by Alex, who was straight-edge at the time," says Turner. "Me and Mark just rolled our eyes because it was such a stupid term, and it didn't matter. Mark *was* straight-edge, except he took acid! He didn't drink, but he was fine with taking acid. So me and Mark hit it off; we started hanging around."

Arm and Turner had middle-class suburban backgrounds in common, as well as somewhat contrarian sensibilities. Both loved punk but disdained its tribal codes of behavior and dress. Having graduated from high school in the summer of 1983, Turner joined a hardcore band called Spluii Numa featuring Shumway on drums, only to quit after a couple of rehearsals because the other guitarist wanted him to purchase some more professional equipment. Then Arm asked him to join Mr. Epp.

"I loved Mr. Epp," says Turner. "Noisy and weird. They were part of the punk scene, but they had a real sarcastic edge to them. I gravitated to that, definitely. I loved hardcore, but I didn't look hardcore. I had short hair sometimes, but I didn't really adhere to that uniform. No leather jackets, no mohawk. Weird, cool people—those were the people I started hanging out with a lot. And this was 1983, so we had the Metropolis club going. It was the place to hang out and so it's where we were every weekend."

The Metropolis was opened in March 1983 by a Frenchman, Hugo Piottin. He used the money he'd earned from four years fishing in Alaska to turn a derelict space on Second Avenue near Pioneer Square, just south of downtown Seattle, into a welcoming, all-ages hangout. Due to the city authorities' traditionally hostile policy towards entertainment for young people under the legal drinking age of 21, it took a brave or idealistic character to attempt such an enterprise. Piottin was both of these.

Run on co-operative principles for its brief 12-month lifespan, The Metropolis nurtured the nascent Seattle scene, providing a safe haven for young kids as well as a purpose-built venue for smaller touring bands and local outfits to play—and get paid.

"When Mr. Epp opened for The Dead Kennedys, we didn't get paid a dime," says Arm. "We weren't thinking there was any money to be made. So Mr. Epp plays the Metropolis for the first time and we get paid a hundred dollars. Holy shit! What are we gonna do with a hundred dollars?!"

Arm was one of hundreds of punters squeezed into the Metropolis on October 16, 1983, to see local glam-punk peacocks Malfunkshun open for Hüsker Dü, the Minneapolis trio then on the cusp of blasting through the generic straitjacket of hardcore with their new pop blueprint, plus The Circle Jerks, led by former Black Flag vocalist Keith Morris.

Except The Circle Jerks canceled, so Deranged Diction, a local hardcore band originally from Montana—their self-released cassette was titled *No Art, No Cowboys, No Rules*—stepped in at the last minute. Their bassist, Jeff Ament, was already a Metropolis regular; whenever he couldn't afford the admission price, Hugo would offer him free entry in exchange for sweeping the floor at the end of the night. "Deranged Diction were supposed to get 75 bucks for the show," says Ament, "and when we went to get paid, Kyle Nixon, the promoter, looks at me and says, 'I can't pay you guys; we didn't make enough money.' And the place was packed. So he pays Hüsker Dü 500 bucks and then just walks out. I was just totally bummed. And the guys from Hüsker Dü gave me two joints and 25 bucks, then Hugo came in and gave us all the tip money for that night. I was just like: 'We made 50 bucks!'"

It was typically perverse of Mr. Epp that, having recruited an extra guitarist and found a generous patron in Hugo, they played only two more gigs, both at The Metropolis, and never recorded again despite having written a batch of new songs. The band broke up shortly after its final show on February 3, 1984. Essentially, Steve Turner joining Mr. Epp made Mr. Epp a more musically coherent band—and consequently sowed the seeds of its demise. With Turner sharing Arm's admiration for the acid-blasted twist on hardcore deployed by Butthole Surfers or Tales of Terror, the internal dynamic shifted away from Smitty and the Moreys.

"Basically, Mark was propelling the music more towards harder rock," says Turner. "That's obviously what he was into—and me too. I think the other guys wanted to be more experimental than we did, and they weren't loving the direction it was going in. It was still *far* from a regular rock band—we could barely play! We asked them to record, and they weren't interested. One day we were over at Darren's house, where we practiced, and they said they didn't want to do it anymore. Me and Mark were pretty united in what we were trying to do. I guess the dynamic changed a little too much for them."

Like all provocateurs who stick around long enough, Mr. Epp eventually found their own audience of like minds, thereby negating their very *raison d'etre*. Far from clearing the room, their last two gigs saw the Metropolis packed with stage-diving fans chanting, "Art spazz!"—originally an insult hurled by Epp-haters, now appropriated as their own badge of pride.

For their valedictory blast, Mr. Epp realized that if the music no longer had irritant value, the performance had to compensate. Before arriving at The Metropolis, the Moreys went to their father's salon and filled a large rubbish bag full of the day's hair clippings, which was duly deposited over the audience during a 30-minute version of "Flogging a Dead Horse," Epp's traditional set-closer, a tortuous endurance test of feedback, skronk, and Smitty slobbering into the microphone.

"I'm not really sure why we broke up," says Smitty, "apart from the fact that Darren didn't want to do it anymore, and we were smart enough to realize that if we advertised for another drummer we wouldn't get anyone. Maybe we were going in different directions, maybe it was pushed as far as it could go. But Mark and Steve didn't wait very long before starting another band."

By the time Mr. Epp broke up, Mark Arm had just turned 22 years old. He was still at the University of Washington and, although enjoying aspects of his studies on an intellectual level, any enthusiasm he'd felt for academic life was long gone. His energies were almost entirely devoted to music: listening to it, talking about it, watching bands play it, and playing it himself. The Metropolis had been his place of education, not UW; his teachers were Black Flag, or Tales of Terror, or Void, or Butthole Surfers, or Flipper, or Meat Puppets, or The Replacements . . . all bands forged by punk who took its energy as a platform for risk-taking, rather than as a wall to hide behind.

At The Metropolis, Arm was meeting people who shared his obsessive instincts. Like Bruce Pavitt who, in 1979, had moved from Chicago to found his own degree in punk rock at Evergreen College, and now ran Bombshelter, an indie record shop in Capitol Hill, as well as DJing at Metropolis and writing a column called Sub-Pop USA for Seattle's music paper, *The Rocket.*

Fueled by the inclusivity fostered by The Metropolis, the Seattle area was producing a succession of utterly distinctive bands: like The Fastbacks, a pop-punk girl/boy harmonic powerhouse who could drop AC/DC or Sweet covers into their set without blinking, or The U-Men, whose twisted psychedelic garage rock took on a darker edge thanks to the amazing presence of singer John Bigley, or Malfunkshun, led by the flamboyant Andrew Wood, who looked like glam rockers but sounded like punks playing Cheap Trick, or The Melvins, a maniacal trio from the coastal lumber town of Aberdeen.

All distinct entities, these groups shared one common trait: the urge to create fresh vehicles for delivering heavy rock. Mark Arm's next band went a little further, in that it provided a vehicle that helped change rock music forever.

2

Take a Shot at Forever

In Seattle, money heads to the water. You can see the proof whichever way you drive on the twin Interstate 90 floating bridges across Lake Washington that link Seattle to Mercer Island. On both shorelines, discreet early twentieth-century houses struggle for space against an influx of hulking new-build McMansions. You can tell a McMansion from the real thing by its look of flat-pack ostentation—plus the fact that it's too large for the plot it sits on. They began appearing in the wake of the city's new-tech boom during the eighties and nineties, as executives of Microsoft, Amazon, Nintendo, and other drivers of the "clean" Industrial Revolution invested in property to match the size of their profits.

The premium for waterfront addresses is especially apparent on the west side of the lake. Barely more than a mile inland is the Central District, the heart of Seattle's black population, a diverse urban neighborhood that has to deal with some typically diverse urban challenges. But drive east along Yesler Way, cross MLK Jr. Way and head northeast towards Lake Washington Boulevard, and the Central District turns into Leschi and Madrona and Denny-Blaine: all areas synonymous with wealth and exclusivity. Most of the lakeside millionaires have jetties poking out into the water, where luxury powerboats await a joyride around the lake, or perhaps a trip across to Mercer Island, Seattle's waterlocked suburb, an overwhelmingly white, solidly upper-middle class enclave where, once again, the houses get bigger the nearer they are to the shore.

If this seems a world away from Seattle's punk rock heritage, then look again. Kurt Cobain spent the last months of his life holed up in a large, secluded Denny-Blaine house, built with old money in 1902 but purchased in early 1994 with more than one million dollars' worth of grunge lucre. His neighbor on Lake Washington Boulevard East was Howard Schultz, the CEO of Starbucks. Today, a couple of miles south from the former Cobain residence, Pearl Jam guitarists Stone Gossard and Mike McCready live just five minutes apart from each other, on either side of the I-90 bridges. One day, Steve Turner was visiting Gossard when he was tickled to see McCready show up by boat. Turner notes that the guitarists' contrasting temperaments, an intermittent source of tension over the years, are mirrored in their domiciles.

"Stone's house is much cooler: old, small," observes Turner. "McCready's is bigger, fancier. I love McCready—hopping around, throwing guitar picks. It's part of Pearl Jam's appeal, that they exist together and make it work. I was disappointed that as soon as Stone got success with Pearl Jam he mellowed out. He should have been like David Lee Roth, running crazy for just a little while. McCready was! He was out of his mind for a couple of years! It was great!"

Steve laughs at the thought of his old friend getting in touch with his inner Diamond Dave. Although Stone Gossard today is the ascetic, reflective strand of Pearl Jam's guitar weave, Turner remembers a far cockier character when they first encountered each other as fellow pupils at one of Seattle's most renowned private schools, the Northwest School for the Arts, Humanities, and Environment.

"I met Stone and his friend Jeff Covell," he says. "Stone was a year younger than me, Jeff was in my class. They were the two smart-ass heavy metal dudes in the school. Real smart alecks. They flipped everybody shit. But I could handle it; they were actually really funny. We became friends and started hanging out. I also met Alex Shumway—we were both new that year, and the obvious punk kids. It was a small school and everybody was kinda weird. There was one preppy dude and he really stood out as being the normal guy."

Turner arrived at the Northwest School via an impeccable liberal middle-class upbringing, though the journey was not without its bumps. Born on March 28, 1965, in Houston, Steven Neil Turner was the youngest of three children. His father, Robert Neil Turner, worked in international trade development and, when he took a job with the Port of Seattle, the family made the long diagonal move from Texas to the Pacific Northwest.

Initially, the Turners—Robert, his wife, Patricia, plus Steve and elder siblings, Patrick and Mary-Virginia—rented a house in the Capitol Hill area of Seattle, just a couple of blocks away from Stevens Elementary school where Steve attended kindergarten. Today, a house in this corner of Seattle, where the wealthy founding fathers of the city built their homes, would cost upwards of a million dollars. But in the early seventies the locale was a good deal sketchier: the Turners lived near a notorious drug den and the sound of gunfire was not unusual. After three years in the city, Robert and Patricia decided on a move to the select suburb of Mercer Island: all six square miles of it, population 20,000, surrounded by Lake Washington and connected to Seattle and the Eastside suburbs by bridges.

"It was an awesome place to grow up, because it was such a small community," says Steve. "I had total freedom. I was on my bike 12 hours a day, or my skateboard. I had a lot more freedom than my brother or sister had in Seattle."

As Turner takes the exit off I-90, past Mercer Island's modest shopping mall and towards his former family home at 3410 76th Place South East, it soon becomes apparent that some suburbs are more suburban than others. If the Kingsgate development where Mark Arm grew up adheres to the stereotype of suburbia, where uniform dwellings and replicated streets make its sheer pleasantness feel perversely threatening, then this neighborhood in the northern half of Mercer Island looks far less clinical. The houses are slightly older—late Fifties rather than mid-Sixties—the woods and lawns seem a little more naturally outgrown, the ambience less neurotic and manicured. The differences aren't merely physical, for this is a bastion of bourgeois enlightenment: during Steve's time there, Mercer Island High developed an experimental curriculum, with open classrooms and no grades, while the island's council was a pioneer in environmental and green issues. At the age of 13, Steve volunteered to work at his local recycling center.

Liberal values also prevailed within the Turner household. Both his parents were well-educated Roman Catholics, and Steve remembers singing along to acoustic guitars at folk mass at St. Joseph's parish church in Capitol Hill. After the move to Mercer Island, Patricia embraced the new fads for health food and hiking, taking Steve with her on 10-day treks through the wilderness.

In terms of music, although classical records predominated in the Turner household, it was by no means a closed shop—and there were some notable exceptions. "When he was in the army, before he was married to my mom, my dad, for whatever reason, bought a couple of 'jazz' records—one being a Leadbelly 10-inch," says Steve. "So that record was in the house, as well as a couple of Clancy Brothers albums. Then, because she was hip to the feminist thing, my mom bought Dory Previn's first album, *On My Way to Where*, which is still one of my favorite records. So there were four records I listened to as a kid. My brother, y'know, I don't think he knew he was gay yet, but all the evidence was there—he liked show tunes and Liza Minnelli!"

With three years' service in the U.S. Counter-Intelligence Corps during the late fifties, and his subsequent travels with ground-breaking U.S. trade missions to the USSR, China, and the Middle East, Robert Turner looms enigmatically in the family history. Even after leaving the Port of Seattle, his ostensibly above-board new job as Washington State Apple Commissioner still required many trips abroad to sensitive regions amid the chilly depths of the Cold War.

"We never confirmed it or not, but my dad easily could have been a spy," says Steve. "He was going to Russia and China. He was a certified genius on MENSA. He had this top security clearance in the seventies, that in case of nuclear war his family would have access to the deep bunkers. He never talked about it much—he was a very quiet guy. We've built onto his myth after his death. We never thought of it while he was alive to have him explain to us this high security clearance and working in the intelligence corps and him working through the government to advance international trade to very risky areas. He had this telex machine in this office that was going constantly. Why we didn't think of it, I don't know!"

Turner senior's role as a trade ambassador even prompted his youngest son's passion for skateboarding. In 1975, Steve was presented with three prototype examples of what his dad said was "apparently the new trend from California," plus an issue of *Skateboard* magazine to show him how to use them. "So I had a skateboard before anybody did in my neighborhood. It was more of a toy; I was just 10 years old. I got more into bicycles and bicycle racing, and then a few years later these older kids had a ramp and I'd come by and start clowning around on it on their skateboards. Within a month I was better at it than they were. So I decided to get my own skateboard and took off with it," Steve says.

By the time Steve was at high school, his sister had started college and pop music began to filter into his life. The Beatles' "red" and "blue" compilations *1962–1966* and *1967–1970*—as omnipresent a seventies totem as *The Joy of Sex* or *Jaws*—were in the house. But still, for the most part, the appeal of rock'n'roll escaped him. "When I was 11 or 12, my BMX friends were really into KISS. And they tried to turn me onto that. I was like, 'Are you kidding me?! This is stupid! Cartoons!' An opinion I never managed to shake. I must have been a petulant, irritating child in some ways, 'cos I thought that was kids' stuff and below me."

Indeed, had it not been for skateboarding, Steve Turner might never have discovered punk rock—thereby opening up a counterfactual black hole in the history of grunge. In 1979, however, Steve Olson, a 17-year-old from California's Orange County, won the Skateboarder of the Year award and showed up at the ceremony wearing a white blazer and stolen leather bondage trousers. With his hippy Cali locks scalped and spiked in tribute to the new musical wave, he picked his nose and threw the trophy away. Steve stared in amazement at the pictures of Olson giving the middle finger: "It was the shock heard around the skateboard world: 'OK, we're all punk rockers now!' It was that easy."

The following year of 1980 saw the pastel calm of Mercer Island upset by a shocking act of violence, placing the neighborhood in America's national news headlines. During the early hours of June 12, 16-year-old Jason Perrine and his 15-year-old girlfriend, Dawn Swisher, stole her sister's Chevrolet Camaro, cranked Lynyrd Skynyrd's hard-rock love ballad "Freebird" up to full volume on the stereo, and then drove at 110 miles per hour through the gymnasium wall of North Mercer Junior High. Perrine was killed instantly; Swisher, who ducked down at the last second, emerged alive though with severe injuries. Steve Turner's gym locker, meanwhile, was completely destroyed.

"He was a good friend of mine," says Turner. "Both he and his brother were on my soccer team. He was a wealthy kid, going off the rails in high school. He got really into *Jonathan Livingston Seagull* and the idea of reincarnation. I would guess it was the early onset of schizophrenia." Press coverage of the suicide pact typically focused on the apparent disconnect between Mercer Island's affluence and its population of maudlin, alienated teenagers—as if this wasn't a universal phenomenon.

Steve Turner's own version of teenage alienation took root later that summer. On August 12, he went to the same Devo gig at the Showbox as Mark Arm. Four days later, Turner went one better and saw Black Flag too. His 15-year-old mind was blown. Hitherto excellent school grades began to wobble, but he just about held things together for another 12 months. Steve's junior year at high school, however, was an almost total write-off. By now both his parents worked—Patricia was a customer service manager at Boeing—so he could skip school with relative ease. Most mornings he went to Mercer Island Public Library and read about anarchist theory, then came home and went skateboarding.

"Mercer Island is such an upper-middle-class, cliquey, preppy place, and I was the odd man out," he says. "I think all teenagers feel that, but I was literally the only punk rocker, the only skateboarder, the only guy that still rode a BMX bike. I essentially stopped going to school. I didn't have any friends. Jim Bouvet, my best friend for most of my growing-up years, would still talk to me a little bit, but I wasn't in the same classes as him because he was a really good student. I was floundering."

Robert and Patricia sent their angry little punk rocker to stay with relatives in Texas for the summer of 1982, where he was able to put some perspective on his situation. While he was in Texas, his parents called to say that, in order to try and boost his grade point average, they were willing to pay for his senior high school year at the élite Northwest School for the Arts in Seattle. "Basically," laughs Steve, "my parents bought my high school diploma."

During his year at Northwest, Steve Turner formed a band with those smart-ass heavy metal dudes Jeff Covell and Stone Gossard. Named after the murderous Catholic gang in Philip Kaufman's film *The Wanderers*, The Ducky Boys featured Covell on drums, Gossard on bass, and Turner on guitar. They did have a vocalist, Chris Peppard, but he was too shy to sing in front of the others. Consequently, The Ducky Boys' existence amounted to nothing more than a couple of practices in the basement of the Gossards' large family home on Capitol Hill—Stone's father was a successful attorney; his mother worked in local government—where they hung out, played records, and jammed instrumental versions of "Dr. Love" by KISS and The Kingsmen's "Louie Louie."

But although it never went beyond the basement, this short-lived enterprise laid the foundation for a colossally influential chapter in rock history. Simply by bringing together Gossard and Turner, The Ducky Boys proved that a metalhead and a punk could coexist harmoniously in a group context—effectively, the critical mass of grunge.

Both parties came to realize there was merit in the other's dogma. Hitherto, Gossard had disdained all punk rock, but via Turner he came to appreciate the hook-heavy, somewhat streamlined southern California hardcore of Orange County bands like The Adolescents, Social Distortion, and Agent Orange. In return, Gossard pointed Turner towards Alice Cooper and Motörhead, neither of which he might have entertained otherwise due to their overly flamboyant aspects.

"He played me the Motörhead live album," says Turner. "Which of course is amazing. The thing about Stone turning me onto Alice Cooper was he turned me onto *Killer* and *Love It to Death*, which I loved. His favorite was *Billion Dollar Babies*, which was great stuff. And I'd asked him: Did these guys have any earlier records? And he said, 'Yeah but they're horrible; you don't wanna hear them.' So of course that made me want to hear *Pretties for You* and *Easy Action*, and those just blew my mind because they were so weird. And I showed those to Mark—we'd recently become friends—and Mark just loved that stuff too.

"The fact that me and Stone became friends—it was the start of grunge," Turner smiles.

The Ducky Boys ended with Turner's graduation from Northwest. Twelve months later, however, he and Gossard would be playing in a new band—this time with far-reaching results.

★ ★ ★

During the summer of 1983, in addition to playing guitar in Mr. Epp, Mark Arm began playing drums with The Limp Richerds, another more-or-less satirical band of nerds from a Seattle suburb—in this case, the southern outpost of Federal Way. After Mr. Epp had broken up in February 1984, Arm convinced the Richerds' singer, Dave Middleton, that they needed a second guitarist, whereupon Steve Turner stepped up. But with Federal Way inconveniently located an hour's bus journey away, Arm and Turner's joint involvement ceased after only two rehearsals.

By this time, Turner had already dropped out of college. Despite excelling academically in his year at the Northwest School, his grade point average was still too low to get into the University of Washington and so he'd elected to go to Seattle University instead. The choice of this prestigious independent Catholic institution on Capitol Hill pleased his parents—but Turner lasted just one academic quarter (10 weeks).

"I should have taken a little bit of time off," he says, "but I was feeling the pressure from the parents to go straight into college. I had no idea what I wanted to do, other than skateboard and play guitar."

In the spring of 1984, Turner took a job at Raison d'Etre, a coffee shop in downtown Seattle. He needed the money—Seattle University was expensive; three months there had cost $2,000 in student loans—but Steve's primary motivation was to befriend one of the employees and persuade him to join the band he and Mark Arm were putting together.

They had already recruited Alex Shumway to play drums and for a bassist they wanted Deranged Diction's Jeff Ament, having noted both his tasty-sounding distortion box and an ability to jump really high and keep playing. Arm was on friendly terms with Ament, having watched him DJ-ing at the Metropolis one night. Amid a predominantly hardcore set, every now and then Ament would play KISS or Alice Cooper. When he followed Black Flag with Aerosmith, Arm was so impressed at this recontextualizing of his rock adolescence that he walked over to introduce himself.

"He said something like: 'That Aerosmith record is great, but the good song is 'Nobody's Fault'—and I'd played 'Rats in the Cellar,'" says Ament. "After that, whenever we met we'd talk about records."

The difficulty, as far as Arm and Turner were concerned, was that Ament's tastes tended towards the serious, rather foursquare strain of hardcore coming out of Boston: bands like SS Decontrol, whose records were well-produced and proficiently played. They assumed, correctly, that he wouldn't want to play in a band with two former members of Mr. Epp & The Calculations.

"There was a record store in Montana called Urban Renewal," says Ament, "that sold punk rock records and weird clothes. I remember them playing 'Mohawk Man' in the store and thinking it was funny, but I wasn't around a mohawk scene so I didn't fully comprehend. I saw Mr. Epp play twice. Mark and Steve were obviously having an amazing time—but I thought they were awful. Absolutely nonsensical noise."

Ament was hesitant when the new dishwasher at Raison d'Etre began chipping away at him to come and join his latest band. But frustration with his Deranged Diction colleagues, who he felt weren't sufficiently dedicated to the band, soon coupled with Turner's unflagging enthusiasm, and so he trekked out for a practice at the Turner family home on Mercer Island.

"The amazing thing is, it was pretty apparent from the outset that those guys were super-motivated," says Ament. "They wanted to practice, they wanted to write . . . It was great. They already had a couple of songs worked out."

One of these was "Baby Help Me Forget," which actually came from the cache of unrecorded Mr. Epp songs written during the band's final twin-guitar phase. Although Mark Arm's role in this new band was solely as singer—partly dictated by the fact that his guitar equipment hadn't survived Mr. Epp's apocalyptic finale—it wasn't long before he proposed that they get a second guitarist. Intrigued by the potential of a culture clash similar to Ament's punk/metal DJ set, Arm nominated Steve Turner's old sparring partner Stone Gossard. Ament, however, wasn't thrilled by that prospect, having already been on the sharp end of Gossard's wiseacre repartee.

"I'd met him a couple of times; he hung out with this guy Chris Peppard and I don't know if they were taking pills or drinking a lot, but they would go up to the toughest guy in the room—which sometimes was probably me—and basically make fun of him," says Ament. "Everybody called me 'Jeff Diction.' So he's like: 'Ooh Jeff Diction, what a cool name! I heard you're from Montana, do you fuck cows?' All this shit, trying to get a rise out of me. I told Mark: 'You'd better ask him to leave right now, or something bad's gonna happen.' Growing up, I didn't know what sarcasm was. I could deal with it from Mark and Steve because they weren't really making fun of other people, they were making fun of each other. But Stone's whole point was to drive you crazy. I said: 'I'm not playing in a band with that guy.'"

Arm kept massaging Ament's weak spot, which he knew was the bassist's love of classic rock hardware. Gossard may have had a tendency toward being an annoying prick—but he also had a Les Paul guitar and a Marshall amp!

Within a couple of weeks, Ament relented. With Gossard on board, rehearsals shifted to his parents' house on Capitol Hill; the sound immediately became twice as powerful and much, much heavier—certainly not what might be expected from two former merry pranksters from Mr. Epp.

The band's name, too, served notice of an ominous intent. Although "Green River" had perfectly innocent connotations—whether to the 1969 Creedence Clearwater Revival album or a community college in the Seattle suburb of Auburn—given the time and place, people inevitably understood it as a reference to the Green River Killer: an active serial murderer of young women, so called because some victims' bodies were found in the river of the same name, which rises in the

Cascade Mountains and eventually flows into Seattle's Elliott Bay. "It was," Turner reflected later, "a dumb joke."*

Green River's first public performance was on July 1, 1984, at a house party thrown by the band PMA at the storefront where they lived in Seattle's Central District. Oddly, although having joined the band, Gossard chose not to appear, though he did lend Ament his Marshall half-stack. "Stone wanted everything to be perfect with everything he was playing," says Turner. "So he was practicing his solos and he just didn't feel he was ready yet."

This early intimation of Gossard's priorities foreshadowed the differences that eventually tore Green River apart. Initially, however, its disparate components seemed emblematic of Seattle's tolerant musical subcultures. The local underground rock scene simply wasn't big enough for mutually exclusive cliques to be viable and, as a budding anthropologist, Turner in particular could appreciate the theory of metal dudes and punks taking scoops from each other's world and creating a new hybrid from the residue. But the reality of playing in a band where some members were only somewhat ironically extolling the virtues of UK proto-black metal band Venom (whose *At War with Satan* album featured a 20-minute title track and such choice cuts as "Women, Leather, and Hell") began to wear him down, his own passions increasingly manifested in a strain of garage-rock primitivism from the UK.

"Green River started pretty great," Turner says. "It was just like trash rock. Ex-hardcore dudes playing a little bit more complex—a little bit poppier—songs, which was what I liked. One of my favorite bands was The Replacements. I loved *Hootenanny*—and that's what some of the early Green River stuff reminded me of. But Stone and Jeff were more enthralled by heavy metal. They were really into Iron Maiden. I was really turned on by some of the earliest Milkshakes and Billy Childish–related stuff I was hearing. The Milkshakes versus Iron Maiden! Not a lot of common ground there. The songs were getting too complex. The perfect example of a song that was absolutely confounding to me was 'Tunnel of Love.' I don't think I ever knew how that song went."

* "Dirty Deeds Done Cheap" by Damon Wise, *Sounds*, June 30, 1990.

Mark Arm felt more relaxed with Green River's attempts at cultural alchemy. Having grown up in the Eastside suburbs, the heartland of Seattle's metal scene, he was *au fait* with the lumpen elements of hard rock and could see that Ament and Gossard were far more enlightened. "To me it was never an either/or situation: you could like Venom and The Chocolate Watch Band at the same time!" laughs Arm. "Steve didn't see the humor in Venom, just the ridiculousness. And they are totally ridiculous, but they're totally funny, and pretty great. On the very first Green River record we were trying things out just for the sake of trying things out. We wrote 'Tunnel of Love,' which has so many different parts. We never did anything like that again. We were figuring out what we could be."

Knowing Mark from their university classes, as well as from seeing him play with Mr. Epp, Kim Thayil found early Green River performances quite an eye-opener. "I thought that Mark was affecting a rock star persona, which I didn't expect from him having come from Mr. Epp," he says. "But it worked. Green River had an equal part homage to rock'n'roll as they had a mocking attitude towards it. A little bit of parody and a little bit of tipping the hat. Mark may have been pushed towards that rock persona because of the other guys in the band—y'know, a couple of them started using hairspray. The line between parody and self-indulgence is pretty blurred."

Punk and heavy metal, despite shared roots in the UK R&B and garage rock scenes of the sixties, had an oppositional relationship dictated primarily by punk's *tabula rasa* rhetoric. Metal was deemed part of the regressive "old wave," to be swept aside by the new. However, as punk established stifling orthodoxies of its own—hair, clothes, politics, or the music itself—the form's smarter exponents looked for ways to escape.

Having hit the wall of speed with their early records, Hüsker Dü mined sixties pop and psychedelia, compacting hardcore's intensity into singalong nuggets of alienation—a formula Nirvana would later adapt with devastating results. Black Flag, meanwhile, played Seattle on August 7, 1983, and shocked the more lumpen elements of their audience with as yet unreleased songs from their next album, *My War*, that decelerated the signature hardcore psychosis to a seething trudge, over which singer Henry Rollins stared into his own existential no man's land. While the mosh pit wrestled, Mark Arm stood transfixed, in tears.

"They did 'Nothing Left Inside,' a super-heavy, draining song, and that really, really hit me, emotionally," says Arm. "Black Flag relished pissing people off and punk rock people were very easy to piss off. At that show there was a contingent of kids really pissed off that Black Flag were playing slow songs. 'Ooh, they've sold out . . . ' Actually, they were just moving forward and doing whatever the fuck they wanted. That was way more punk rock than people like Stalag 13 who just wanted to be Minor Threat Jr."

After the gig, Arm and Jo Smitty interviewed Black Flag for a never-published fanzine article and asked what music they were listening to in the van. Drummer Bill Stevenson replied,"Dio"—as in the new band formed by Ronnie James Dio, the ex-Rainbow singer who had replaced Ozzy Osbourne in Black Sabbath. As was doubtless intended, the reference was lost on the young interrogators. "Dio? What's *that*?" said Arm. "And Greg Ginn [Black Flag's guitarist and conceptual linchpin] said, 'It's Italian for God.'"*

Suspicious of their own deified status among the U.S. punk cognoscenti, as far as Black Flag were concerned their fans were fair game. It was no accident that Ginn would adopt the bludgeoning hallmark of the most primordial heavy metal band with which to carve out a new direction beyond the speed barrier. Duly intrigued, Arm also began investigating Black Sabbath, aided by Turner who had been introduced to metal by his fellow Ducky Boy, Stone Gossard. Though younger, Gossard fulfilled the "older brother into Sabbath" archetype that neither Arm nor Turner had experienced.

"If I'd had an older brother or sister, I probably would have been familiar with Black Sabbath and Alice Cooper," says Arm. "I'd heard 'Paranoid' on the radio, but that was before I was buying records. I didn't really get turned on to those bands until after I got into hardcore. So Black Sabbath seemed new to me. And I don't know if it would

* *Spray Paint the Walls* by Stevie Chick (Omnibus Press, 2009), 278.

have made as much of an impact if I'd been exposed to that stuff earlier. A lot of the records I listened to before punk rock, I'd sold them and then started buying them again, used. Ted Nugent sounded lame, and KISS, the drumming was so bad and kinda sluggish and just not heavy. Everything was 'not there.' The only band I'd listened to previously that sounded good was Aerosmith—which ended up being part of the Green River equation."

Like Arm, Jeff Ament was reared on AOR radio staples prior to having a punk epiphany—on his first trip to Seattle he'd seen The Clash and X. While in Montana he produced his own punk rock fanzine, *Hicksville Trash*, before moving to Seattle and changing its name to *Grasp*.

By 1984, however, he too was frustrated by punk's reduction to the lowest common denominator. Messing with the formula appealed. Ament had a roommate obsessively committed to following the so-called New Wave of British Heavy Metal, which had sprung from inauspicious working-class origins in the late seventies UK, combining flashy metal hallmarks—technical virtuosity, fantastical lyrics, very tight trousers—with some of punk's grimy authenticity. In commercial terms, the NWOBHM's spearheads were Sheffield's Def Leppard and Iron Maiden, from London's East End. As a result, Green River were given a hotline to the NWOBHM's latest rising stars—hence Venom, or sub-Black Sabbath schlock peddlers like Witchfinder General, a West Midlands quartet named after the notorious scourge of Satanism in seventeenth-century England and whose debut album, *Death Penalty*, had a sleeve photograph of a semi-naked woman undergoing "investigation" from band members.

"It wasn't really part of our world," says Arm. "But there was a weird notion for a moment that maybe metal had changed. Of course there was Motörhead, but then hearing the first Metallica record I was like, 'Oh! Maybe I'll go and check out some local metal shows.' And I went to them and was totally disappointed."

Arm brought to Green River a natural frontman's charisma, albeit at this stage he was rather too self-consciously in thrall to the theatrical outrage of Alice Cooper and Iggy Pop. Given the hostile reception they typically faced as the support act for touring bands, Arm's gung-ho antics would be an asset, though they did nothing to dispel the confusion audiences felt when presented with this exotic new punk/metal cross-breed.

Opening for The Dead Kennedys on October 19, 1984, Green River encountered a 1,500-capacity Moore Theatre in downtown Seattle full of what Arm terms "weekend punkers,"* who threw popcorn, ice, and shoes.** Arm responded by ridiculing both the audience and himself. Witnessing Green River that night for the first time, Jonathan Poneman—who knew Arm from his occasional stints as a DJ at Radio KCMU, where Poneman hosted a show—was bemused. "Mark was very funny," he says, "but it seemed more like comedy rock, parody rock, than actual *rock* rock."

As Ament and Gossard increasingly strutted like surrogate New York Dolls, Arm responded with his own twisted take on glam style, such as wearing dresses over silver tights. From his vantage point down the front, beer in one hand and camera in the other, Charles Peterson saw an astonishing transformation in his friend.

"Mark obviously had a huge fondness for Iggy & The Stooges, so he'd do the total bendy stage performance and jumping into the crowd," says Peterson, "making it seem as out-there and dangerous as you could at the time. He was doing the Eddie Vedder thing before Eddie Vedder, in front of at most 500 people instead of 50,000. Green River was unlike anything anyone else was doing at the time. It all seems so stupid now, what they were wearing, but they were trying to find their own way. There was certainly a rejection of punk. Particularly at that time in Seattle, punk had devolved into just being a fuckup, like this street gang called the Bopo Boys, who would go around fighting at gigs and parties. Punk didn't have any political or social meaning anymore. Green River wanted to see if they could go beyond that."

Thanks to a combination of Ament's hustle and Arm's networking, the prospect of a Green River record actually prompted a minor bidding war among record labels. Their third gig had been supporting Fang, a

* *Grunge Is Dead* by Greg Prato (ECW Press, 2009), 186.

** *Green River Tourbook*, www.ocf.berkeley.edu/~ptn/mudhoney/tourbook/gr.html

punk band from Berkeley, California, whose guitarist Tom Flynn ran a label called Boner and expressed interest in a Green River release. Ament then mailed out some demos, recorded with local engineer Chris Hanzsek just as Gossard joined the band, and was amazed to get an enthusiastic response from Steve Pross, who worked in A&R for Los Angeles–based independent label Enigma.

Meanwhile, Arm's burgeoning friendship with Bruce Pavitt was about to unlock the first of many doors.

By the summer of 1984, Pavitt was running a new record shop in Capitol Hill called Fallout, while maintaining its predecessor's name for his first record label: Bombshelter released the debut EP by Seattle's anarchic garage crazies The U-Men. While traveling around the U.S. in 1980, Pavitt had met Gerard Cosloy in Boston. Then a precociously talented 16-year-old writer, Cosloy produced his own hardcore fanzine, *Conflict*, and would soon graduate to the columns of *New York Rocker*. At the age of 20, Cosloy was running Homestead Records, which by 1985 would have arguably the coolest roster of any U.S. independent label, including Sonic Youth, Dinosaur Jr, Big Black, and Nick Cave. One day, Cosloy called Pavitt at Fallout and asked if he could recommend a good Seattle band. Pavitt responded with two: The U-Men and Green River.

Because all agreed that Pavitt's U-Men EP sounded great, it was decided that Green River should record at the same Seattle studio, Crow. But Crow was expensive at $300 a day and Ament had budgeted for four days to record six songs, which worked out at $240 per member. So they played some gigs, saved their money, and, in December 1984, recorded *Come on Down*, once again with Hanzsek. Although betraying the participants' naivety—Arm's lyrics are filled with clumsy sex-as-violence metaphors; the guitar parts are sometimes bewilderingly over-elaborate—the recording still retains a disconcerting presence. But it was a struggle for all concerned.

"We were trying to do something beyond what we were capable of," admits Ament.

Turner contributed the stand-out riff on the record's stand-out song, "Swallow My Pride," and battled his way through "Tunnel of Love"—

which even Arm had taken to mocking at gigs, introducing it as "a short little operatic piece called '2112,'"* in reference to the seven-part, 20-minute title track from the 1976 album by Canadian progressive rock band Rush. Mostly, however, this wasn't what Turner had signed up for. "It had a couple of cool songs, but the rest of it, I don't even know how to play that shit," he says.

On January 19, 1985, the band opened up Sonic Youth's first ever Seattle show, in the larger of two rooms at a Chinatown club called Gorilla Gardens. Thurston Moore was amazed at the size and enthusiasm of the audience, but thought Green River "had too many musicians on stage." By the time Sonic Youth returned for their second Seattle show, six months later, at the same venue with the same opening band, one of these musicians was missing. Steve Turner had quit Green River in the summer of 1985.

It had been a long time coming. Although at odds with some of his bandmates' musical and visual aesthetics, Turner could appreciate that it was partly what made Green River such an exciting proposition. But the experience of recording their debut EP had emphasized how much he disliked some of the songs—in particular the multipartite noodlethon "Tunnel of Love"—and how little emotional capital he had invested in the whole enterprise.

"Green River just got away from what I thought it was so quickly," says Turner. "They were wearing makeup and stuff, and I . . . I just don't like heavy metal. I never liked it. There was very little middle ground between me and Jeff in particular."

"There were probably things about my personality that drove him crazy," says Ament. "Ever since I was a little kid I was always an organizer, always getting other guys together to play baseball. I guess I took that role in the band. At one point we were going to be doing a photo shoot with Charles Peterson, and at practice I said I thought Steve's hair looked cool. Steve cut his hair the next day. That story right there probably tells you why Steve left. I meant it as

* *Green River Tourbook*, www.ocf.berkeley.edu/~ptn/mudhoney/tourbook/gr.html

a compliment, and he took it as: 'If *he* thinks I'm cool, I'm doing the wrong thing.'"

The photograph is subtly indicative of the group dynamic. Though they are still clad in jeans and T-shirts, Ament and Gossard's hairstyles are showing signs of inflation and there's a hint of steel as they offer the camera full eye contact; Arm and Shumway (who by now had tired of people mispronouncing his family name, adopting his father's middle name of Vincent as his surname) wear shades and hide behind curtain fringes; in his black turtleneck, meanwhile, Turner looks like a surrogate member of Jefferson Airplane. Standing perkily with hands on hips, he's the only member of the band smiling.

Steve Turner freely admits that he had begun deliberately sabotaging Green River's gigs. He would play with his back turned to the audience. He stopped using any distortion effects on his guitar. He even sat down. "I was basically being a dick onstage," he says. "Wasn't loving it at all. And I felt bad about that—clearly this isn't working out and I shouldn't be trying to fuck them up."

The guitarist's decision to leave was accelerated by the fact that Ament was organizing a tour to support the release of the EP. Turner had already paid his share of the recording costs; the prospect of shelling out more money just to be miserable a long way from home clinched the matter. He even nominated his own replacement, Bruce Fairweather, who was both Jeff Ament's roommate and former colleague in Deranged Diction. By common consent, Green River improved as a result of Turner leaving.

"They dropped the more overtly metal and complicated stuff after I quit," says Turner. "I don't know if it was just Bruce coming in or if they rethought it a little more, and got more Aerosmithy. But it was not a band I should be in. I could really appreciate them once I was out of there."

"Maybe Steve quitting made Jeff and Stone go, 'Woah, he's got a point,'" says Arm. "Everybody except for Stoney came from punk bands. We were like, 'Let's try doing this; we've never been able to do this before.' Just because you can do something doesn't mean that you should. But sometimes you have to learn that and put it on a record for everyone else to know."

For all that no one seemed really satisfied with the finished record, *Come on Down* was a lightning bolt to the coalescing Seattle scene. The core elements may have been familiar; but, even at this formative stage, Green River was developing a new vocabulary.

Seattle scene historian Stephen Tow notes that Doug Pray's 1996 documentary *Hype!* features Leighton Beezer, who played with Arm; Turner; and Ed Fotheringham in improvised noise miscreants The Thrown Ups, illustrating on a guitar the difference between "punk" and "grunge." For punk, he plays the riff to The Ramones' "Rockaway Beach"; for grunge, he plays Green River's "Come on Down." Just a few notes apart, the two are strikingly unalike.

Says Beezer: "When I noticed [Green River] playing 'Come on Down' for the first time. . . [I] immediately went, 'God, they're just playing punk rock backwards. Awesome!' It is basically a tribute to Black Sabbath. The augmented fifth [note used in 'Come on Down'] is the classic Black Sabbath sort of 'ominous, slightly discordant but also gets the adrenaline going in a strange way' kind of note. It's a very cool note—and it's not in punk rock."*

A band hewn almost entirely from punk rock, but willing to deal with aspects of heavy metal on nonjudgmental terms: what Green River were doing may not seem revolutionary now, but that's because the motifs they introduced have since been refined umpteen times over and assimilated into mainstream rock culture. At the time, however, with punk's absolutist repudiation of the past providing the new orthodoxy, to delve into hard rock's murky origins was in itself transgressive behavior.

At Sonic Youth's second 1985 Seattle show, Thurston Moore found himself marveling at Green River's power and audacity. "They were focusing on rock moves that predated punk, without losing the punk aspects," he says. "These moves belonged to sixties garage bands but also longer-haired sub-metal bands, be it Deep Purple or Sabbath. It was spearheaded by Black Flag saying, 'We're into music that predates 1977.' I was fascinated by that, having experienced that music before punk, to

* *The Strangest Tribe* by Stephen Tow (Sasquatch Books, 2011), 96.

the point where, in 1979 and 1980, I found those dinosaur records like Pink Floyd in my mother's basement and had this sense of almost weird sadness about it, seeing them sitting there, knowing that I actually had invested some merit in them—because I'd excised them from my life to such a degree. They'd been blown away by the excitement of the new. So years later, to have underground bands referencing Black Sabbath, it was a tricky and radical thing to do. I saw Green River coming out of that, and Seattle being the first place to really buy into it: 'OK, we're growing our hair and doing some metal moves, but we're still gonna be smart and we're still gonna be punk.'"

However, when Green River finally embarked upon their long-planned U.S. tour, they found such enlightened attitudes in short supply. Indeed, scarcity was the tour's defining characteristic. Most of the scheduled 16 gigs were canceled and, as the band hauled their way fruitlessly across the USA, tempers frayed or were lost altogether.

By the time they made it to Ohio, they'd only played two gigs and one of those had been in Missoula, Montana, where Ament went to college and which was close to his hometown of Big Sandy. Another former Missoula resident, Steve Albini, offered them a couple of gigs supporting his band, Big Black, the first of which was in Newport, Kentucky, just across the Ohio river from Cincinnati, at a punk rock dive called The Jockey Club. Having anticipated Big Black pulling a large audience, Green River were crestfallen to walk onstage before no more than two dozen people.

This was not what they'd become accustomed to in Seattle, where their opening slots for touring bands took place in front of hundreds and upwards, and club gigs were real events. When a blown fuse silenced their set, Arm assumed the plugs were being pulled deliberately and went berserk, smashing one of the club's microphones.

"They were threatening not to pay us, and I remember Steve Albini going, ''Course they don't want to pay you—you just fucking destroyed a mic,' and me feeling admonished, and rightfully so . . . Maybe I was spoiled by being able to get away with really stupid shit in Seattle."*

* *Everybody Loves Our Town* by Mark Yarm (Faber & Faber, 2011), 84.

In spite of this, Shumway says Albini gave them some of Big Black's payout and they escaped unscathed: "The guy who ran the club was gunning around town trying to find us. Some girls at the show... knew he was not a good fellow. So they hid us out of town in one of their fathers' cabins . . . Nothing happened, except that Jeff learned to properly tease his hair."*

The tour reached its nadir in Detroit. Any romantic notions that the home of The Stooges and The MC5 was going to welcome Green River as a new embodiment of the city's stentorian rock heritage were painfully disabused. The fact that they were supporting former Misfits singer Glenn Danzig's band Samhain on November 1—the pagan Celtic New Year festival that lent the band its name—might have been a portent of ill tiding, but as the band confronted a hostile crowd amid the desolation of downtown Detroit, reality hit home soon enough.

The locals were possibly unimpressed by some increasingly cocksure displays of effeminacy: in addition to ballet shoes and his now expertly teased coiffure, Ament sported a lavender T-shirt bearing the words "San Francisco." In his silver tights, Arm braved a torrent of spit from one especially irate girl, until Ament placed his foot inbetween her and his bandmate. The girl's boyfriend, however, assuming that Ament was trying to kick her in the face, hauled the bassist off the stage and began beating him up.

"I remember being face down on the ground just getting pummeled," testifies Jeff. "I could hear my bass the whole time going, 'WHOORRGH! WHOORRGH!' against the floor. Security came and dragged the guy off me and then I had to get back up on stage. I thought, 'This is the worst feeling. I just got my ass kicked and now I have to play two more songs.'"

It got worse. At the end of the night, Ament visited promoter Corey Rusk to get paid. As bassist in hardcore band The Necros and the founder of Chicago's renowned independent label Touch & Go, Rusk was a legendary figure to him.

* *Green River Tourbook*, www.ocf.berkeley.edu/~ptn/mudhoney/tourbook/gr.html

"I was so nervous at meeting him. He was back there counting the money out, and Danzig had made a thousand dollars, maybe even more. We were supposed to get a hundred dollars, and he looked at me, and said: 'Man, you guys sucked, I can't pay you anything.' So I had to put my head down and go back and tell the others: 'Hey guys, we didn't get any money . . .'"

Indeed, even if they had got paid, the whole tour was being funded out of the band's pockets anyway. The budget permitted one night in a hotel—in Boston, where they were booked to open for the latest incarnation of British punk warhorses The UK Subs. Unable to find a hotel in Boston for less than $100, they drove out into rural Massachusetts, through Salem, until they found a $60 room in the town of Tewksbury. They then drove the 20 miles back into Boston, only to arrive at the club to find a notice pinned to the door: "Show canceled."

Permanently clouding Green River's perspective was Homestead's nonrelease of *Come on Down*, the record the tour was scheduled to promote. Having plumped for the cachet of Sonic Youth and Nick Cave as labelmates, the band began to realize that it didn't matter how cool your record company was if it couldn't actually release your record.

Finally, the EP came out in early November, almost two months late, as the band arrived in New York where Gerard Cosloy had got them a gig at CBGB. The thrill of playing the legendary Lower East Side punk club overrode the fact that they were in the cleanup slot at 2 a.m., with only the staff, some drunken businessmen, and four Japanese tourists for company.

On one level, playing just seven gigs in a three-week transcontinental slog made no sense at all. Yet for Green River to venture beyond the Pacific Northwest in the first place was a remarkable achievement. There was no infrastructure to supply organization; rather, the tour was entirely self-planned, mostly by Ament with a copy of hardcore fanzine *Maximum Rock'n'Roll*—ending postcards with tapes to labels, begging favors from friends of friends—and financed by each band member to the tune of $500.

It wasn't entirely unprecedented for a Seattle underground band to tour the U.S.; The U-Men had done so earlier that year. But in the words of guitarist Tom Price, "You could barely call [that] a tour. It was more like a migration for the summer."* As with Green River, most of The U-Men's gigs fell through. Having made it down the West Coast to Los Angeles, the band struggled across to Austin, Texas, where they essentially lived for the entire summer, enjoying the hospitality of the local hardcore scene, even getting part-time jobs. Likewise, Green River's American odyssey was more of a grueling holiday than a tour—but in their case without the sunshine.

"In retrospect it seems ridiculous," says Ament, "but we were a bunch of kids motivated enough to save a few bucks and make our way across the country. None of us had ever been east of the Mississippi before, so it was a cool trip. We saw the Badlands, New York City . . . Big Black were amazing, so powerful. On one of the nights off we saw The Necros and Minutemen—turned out it was the third to last Minutemen show. All sorts of great things happened on that tour. Just to be out there in the middle of it was amazing."

★ ★ ★

In 1985, the notion that, only five years later, Seattle might enjoy international status for its insurgent rock'n'roll scene would have seemed ludicrous. For sure, the city and its hinterland was steeped in musical history, with Seattle producing or nurturing some of twentieth-century popular music's most important figures. But few people beyond the Pacific Northwest thought of Jimi Hendrix, who attended the Central District's landmark Garfield High School, as a Seattle musician. The same could be said of another Garfield student, Quincy Jones, who as a teenager played with Florida *emigré* Ray Charles on the city's vibrant jazz scene. In today's marketing parlance, Seattle suffered from "poor brand recognition."

In the eighties, the historical templates suggested that Seattle musicians should either leave town to make their mark upon the wider world or stay put and linger in obscurity. Among the local musicians scrabbling

* *Everybody Loves Our Town*, 75.

around The Metropolis or Gorilla Gardens, the textbook example of the former was Duff McKagan. After dropping out of Roosevelt High School when he was 15, McKagan had played in a string of bands either as drummer or guitarist, including The Fastbacks and The Fartz, following the key members of the latter into Ten Minute Warning as they slowed down their hardcore aesthetic.

McKagan's decision to quit in 1984 came as a surprise to many, though not to Bruce Pavitt. "In 1983, shortly after I first moved to Seattle, I got a job as a prep cook in a restaurant and Duff McKagan was working there as well," says Pavitt. "After a few months he told me he was gonna move to LA and try to get a job as a rock star down there, because there was no way he could make a living being a musician in Seattle. I wished him good luck with that!"

On June 8, 1985, Duff returned to Seattle with his new band to play a gig at Gorilla Gardens. The flyers advertised, "Guns and Roses—featuring ex-Ten Minute Warning member Duff McKagan." Only 13 people watched, curious to see their old friend. "I don't remember much except they butchered a couple of Stones songs," said Mark Arm. "I couldn't believe that Duff quit Ten Minute Warning and moved to LA for this."*

Increasingly, however, Seattle was off the map for many touring bands, who either couldn't justify the expense of traveling there or were deterred by the city's peculiarly restrictive attitude towards youth entertainment. Shortly before Green River embarked on their 1985 tour, the Seattle city authorities introduced the Teen Dance Ordinance, which effectively made all-ages rock shows illegal. Gorilla Gardens became one of the first casualties, losing its licence following a Hüsker Dü gig on October 26, at which a number of people quite likely still in their teens were observed to dance (or an approximation thereof). Clark Humphrey's history of the Seattle underground** notes that the building's landlord shut the doors after the authorities told him he was leasing the space to a "known teen dance promoter."

* *Grunge Is Dead*, 66.

***Loser*, 97.

Historically, the Pacific Northwest has witnessed persistent conflicts between the liberal imperative of its outlaw heritage and the conservative strictures of local politicians. When it came to enacting Prohibition legislation, Washington state got there in 1916, several years ahead of the rest of the U.S. Prospects of Seattle emerging as a countercultural hub to rival New York or San Francisco in the Sixties were inhibited by the city's licensing restrictions on "teen dances." In 1985, the Teen Dance Ordinance was rushed through the city council as a compromise to a proposed curfew on minors amid an atmosphere of moral panic about violence, sexual activity, and drug use at two all-ages discos, Skoochies and The Monastery. The legislation placed unfeasibly onerous demands on the licensing of live music events open to anyone under the age of 21. It seemed that the combination of alcohol and loud music could whip Seattle's city fathers into an unholy sweat: if the liquor board didn't prevail, then the police would turn up randomly with volume meters and shut down gigs that breached noise restrictions.

Pernicious legislation though it may have been, Mark Arm has argued that the Teen Dance Ordinance had a positive side effect in compelling bands to find new venues, places like The Ditto Tavern and The Vogue in Belltown, the slightly tatty northern adjunct to downtown Seattle that was crucial in fostering the nascent underground scene. Meanwhile, the bigger all-ages shows went to other towns beyond the city's jurisdiction, such as Tacoma.*

Seattle's isolation, whether it be geographical or psychological, had fostered do-it-yourself attitudes born out of a classic fatalism: if you have nothing, you have nothing to lose. Moreover, Green River's debut U.S. tour had proved beyond doubt that being a sizeable cheese in Seattle meant little beyond the Pacific Northwest.

So there was a real can-do spirit behind recording engineer Chris Hanzsek's latest enterprise, which got under way in the summer of 1985 and would have repercussions far beyond its initial impact. Hanzsek, along with his girlfriend, Tina Casale, decided to start a record label—C/Z Records: the "C" for Casale, the "Z" from Hanzsek—and wanted

* *Everybody Loves Our Town*, 64.

Green River for its first release. Impressed by Soundgarden after seeing them open for Green River, Hanzsek revised his plan into a split record: Green River on one side and Soundgarden on the other, which duly turned into a multiband compilation documenting the metal/punk hybrid evolving in the Pacific Northwest.

Arm and Thayil thrashed out the other participants in a single phone conversation. Malfunkshun and The Melvins clearly fitted the template; The U-Men didn't really sound like anyone else, but everyone liked them and, as the scene's most popular band, their omission would be folly; the last band to be added was Skin Yard, featuring local engineer Jack Endino and future Soundgarden drummer Matt Cameron.

"It could just have been our two bands on the record," says Thayil. "But Mark said, 'Hey, there's The Melvins and Malfunkshun out there—get them and The U-Men on, and you've got a great Northwest compilation.' Chris had no hesitation. It was a strong gesture to associate these bands together."

All six bands recorded their tracks with Hanzsek: the first ever Melvins, Skin Yard, and Soundgarden recordings to be released on record, and the only Malfunkshun recordings released during the band's lifetime. Titled *Deep Six*, the album slipped out, to little fanfare, in spring 1986. But some key figures took notice.

A few months earlier, in a Capitol Hill restaurant called the Surrogate Hostess, 18-year-old drummer Dan Peters was taking a break from his dishwashing shift when a friend from Garfield High walked past. Peters mentioned that Bundle of Hiss, one of two bands he was playing in at the time, had a gig coming up at The Ditto Tavern. Also on the bill were Soundgarden and Skin Yard.

"You should come," said Peters. "It's going to be good." These were words a Seattle musician might not have uttered a year or two previously.

Peters' friend was Nils Bernstein, a year his junior and one of the younger members of the Metropolis-era all-ages crowd, whose father ran the Eagles Hippodrome club where Mr. Epp had opened for the Dead Kennedys. From Bernstein's perspective—a teenager deeply embedded in the local scene—things were changing in Seattle.

"Just in this passing conversation it was like Dan was saying: 'Doesn't it seem like our bands are getting better?'" he now says. "And it did. Around '85, it started to feel more exciting. *Deep Six* was a physical manifestation of that. There were always local compilations that had bands that you liked on them, but *Deep Six* said: 'These bands have something in common.' And it was really dramatic, and theatrical, and heavy."

Essentially, *Deep Six* defined Seattle's underground music identity. In his April 1986 "Sub-Pop USA" column for *The Rocket*, Bruce Pavitt caught the prevailing mood:

> *Deep Six* LP. You got it. It's slow SLOW and heavy HEAVY and it's THE predominant sound of underground Seattle in '86. Green River, Sound Garden [sic], The Melvins, Malfunkshun and even Skin Yard prove that you don't have to live in the suburbs and have a low IQ to do some SERIOUS head banging. As an extra bonus you also get one cut by local sex gods the U-Men. [It] sounds quirky and out of context (a fat slab from skull thumpers My Eye would've made more sense). But enough slack, THIS RECORD ROCKS.*

Pavitt's appraisal noted both the slightly anomalous presence of The U-Men and the fact that other bands could just as easily have been included on *Deep Six* without compromising its sonic coherence: My Eye, for instance, who were formed out of Eastside metal band Overlord, or Bundle of Hiss, or Feast, who were Dan Peters' other band as well as a regular pull at The Ditto Tavern and The Vogue.

More importantly, however, his April column signified a light bulb exploding in Pavitt's brain. Soon after starting his degree in punk rock at Olympia's Evergreen College in 1979, he had become enthralled with the specific regional traits of post-punk scenes across the U.S., to the extent that he began to devote one night a week of his radio show on Evergreen's KAOS-FM to this very phenomenon.

Pavitt's show was called *Subterranean Pop*, which was also the title of the fanzine he first published in May 1980, further exploring the

* Quoted in *The Strangest Tribe*, 120.

phenomenon of independently released music in the U.S. After the 'zine's second issue, published in November 1980, Pavitt elected to shorten its name—to *Sub Pop*. After four issues, Pavitt started alternating print versions with a compilation cassette of music featuring examples of regional scenes all over the USA, which thrived despite being ignored by the traditional music media. He sought to prove that what was happening in Boise, Idaho—or Albuquerque, New Mexico, or Louisville, Kentucky—was just as valid as anything from the major population centers and traditional rock'n'roll hubs of New York, Los Angeles, or San Francisco. Indeed, Pavitt suggested that, thanks to developing in a state of splendid isolation, these regional scenes might offer something better.

In 1983, Pavitt left Olympia and moved to Seattle. Having released a final *Sub Pop* tape, in April he began writing his "Sub-Pop USA" column for *The Rocket*, maintaining focus on the fathomless variety of American independent music. It was this nationwide scope that underpinned the evolution of Sub Pop into a record label, with the 1986 release of *Sub Pop 100*, a 13-track compilation album that featured artists from all over the U.S. (as well as one each from Japan and Mexico).

A statement on the spine of the record sleeve hinted at a more grandiose, specifically regionalist ambition: "The new thing: the big thing: the God thing: a mighty multinational entertainment conglomerate based in the Pacific Northwest."

Such rhetoric seemed far-fetched, not least to Pavitt's friends in the Seattle punk clubs, a coterie of several dozen people whose ambitions went little further than attending each other's shows, drinking beers, and snacking on MDA (the psychoactive drug, closely related to Ecstasy, enjoying huge popularity in Seattle at this time).

Yet even before *Sub Pop 100* reached the shops that summer, Pavitt was acting upon the realization that had been percolating throughout his three years of immersion in the Seattle underground scene, and which *Deep Six* brought to the boil: of all the local scenes across the U.S. he had been monitoring, it was that of his hometown that was the most vibrant. Pavitt decided that Green River would be at the vanguard of his mission to sell Seattle to a wider world.

"I got really excited by *Deep Six*," he says. "When *Deep Six* came out, it hammered home the idea that there was a scene happening. So, we agreed to put out a Green River single on their own label, Tasque Force, and I sent that out as a promotional item when I sent out the *Sub Pop 100* albums—with the intention that there was going to be follow-through with an EP."

★ ★ ★

Bruce Pavitt may have been excited, but Mark Arm was having no difficulty keeping a lid on his expectations. Towards the end of 1985 he'd started going out with Emily Rieman, a Roosevelt High contemporary of Duff McKagan and The Fastbacks. The details of their meeting are fuzzy in Mark's mind: "We met probably at a party or a show. I don't remember the exact circumstance, but there was a lot of beer and MDA around at the time."*

A couple of weeks into 1986, Emily dumped him. Mark could see her point: "I didn't really have much going on. I was sleeping on an air mattress in Jeff Ament's apartment. She gave me shit for not having a job. So I got a job as a janitor. It was one of the worst things ever, because they paid by what got done and not by how much time you spent doing it. So basically it was a lot of work for a very little amount of money."

Mark's life prospects in 1986 were a far cry from what his parents must have envisaged when they sent him to Bellevue Christian High. They had hoped he would follow his father into the air force or take a steady company job. Instead, he emerged from the University of Washington two semesters late with a degree in English Literature and hadn't even bothered going to the graduation ceremony.

He lived in a succession of party houses, where like-minded people gathered to drink, take drugs, eat tinned macaroni, and play music. He was the singer in a rock band, albeit one that didn't seem very

* "Mark Arm Wears Gravity Boots" by Lacey Swain, *Sub Pop Blog* (www.subpop.com/channel/blog/mark_arm_wears_gravity_boots), February 5, 2008.

successful. None of this bore any relation to the lives his mother and father had known: Calvin had grown up the youngest of 10 during the Depression, escaping a life in the dirt-poor middle of nowhere by joining the military, where he served 20 years and got his pension, before joining Boeing for the rest of his working life and getting another pension; Anita had been a young woman in Nazi Germany, living amid perpetual fear and suspicion, who saw her Jewish friends disappear and whose hopes of a singing career were destroyed, along with her family and her country, by war. They had made sacrifices and worked hard so that Mark could grow up in a middle-class suburban neighborhood, eating three square meals a day and enjoying an expensive education.

And he told them he was bored! They didn't understand him at all. Could this be their son?

"They must have thought I was an ungrateful little shit," says Mark. "They would try to explain their hardships, and I had none of that. My mom told me this story: apparently my grandma was no fan of Hitler. When it was announced on the radio that German troops had invaded Czechoslovakia, my grandma actually said, 'Good, that's the end of him . . . ' She assumed that the rest of the world would come down on him super-hard. My mom shot her a look: 'What do you mean by that?' And my mom could tell that her mom suddenly got frightened and shut up. Because she realized: 'My daughter could turn me in for saying what I think in my own home.' Another time, there was a holiday gathering at my grandma's house and the Nazi block captain came in and presented her with a picture of Adolf Hitler. He could tell she wasn't enthusiastic, so he went: 'This would look good right here'—and hung it up on her wall. She had to sit there and take it."

Anita also told Mark of the time she was on her way to a bunker with a friend during an air raid and went back home to fetch something, ending up in a different bunker. The next morning, the bunker she originally intended to go to was bombed and all the people inside were killed.

Anita's father had been gassed during World War I, losing a lung, and never lived to see World War II. Her mother died of cancer before the war's end. "My mom was on her own by the time she was 19. I can't even imagine the stuff she went through. I'm sure they thought of me as really undisciplined, which I was, and impulsive. I remember her saying: 'You don't know how good you have it—studying English and philosophy and playing in a rock band.' By that point, Green River had just gone on our second disastrous tour!"

He laughs, adopting the petulant tones of the archetypal Generation X dropout: "'Fuck you, it's the new reality, Mom! I'm suffering from ennui over here!'"

Green River's second U.S. tour, in November 1986, collapsed in farcical circumstances entirely consistent with the spirit of their first. Although scheduled to last almost a month, with a run through Oregon into California, across to Texas, then back to California and finally back up the West Coast, the old school bus the band had bought from Jeff Ament's father barely made it as far as Los Angeles before conking out.

They never made it to Texas. Mark was forced to phone his parents and beg a plane ticket home. But with a second show in Los Angeles scheduled after the Texas leg of the tour, they were forced to hang around LA for two weeks with barely any money. Although most of the band stayed in Hollywood, Mark accompanied Bruce Fairweather to the guitarist's parents' house in Laguna Beach, 50 miles to the south. "They were super-nice, but two weeks is a long time to stay at someone else's parents' place."*

Even in its truncated span, the tour was not short of incident. At the Satyricon club in Portland, Arm split his head open after colliding with Ament's bass and ran to the bathroom to clean himself up. There he was confronted by a young member of a local skinhead gang who had been abusing the band. The skinhead saw Mark's bloodied face, said, "Oh, I guess they already got to you," then left. "It seemed to me that this guy was new and his initiation was to beat up one of those 'hippies' from that band."**

* *Grunge Is Dead*, 123.

**Ibid.

Thanks to Mark's extravagant showmanship, there was always the chance of random mayhem at Green River gigs—it was one of the reasons the band became a popular attraction in Seattle. Yet there was little momentum otherwise. As per Bruce Pavitt's masterplan, they recorded an EP during the summer of 1986, but lack of financial wherewithal meant it wouldn't appear until the summer of 1987.

There was no sense among any of the *Deep Six* generation that releasing records could sustain a career. Nor touring—Green River's calamitous jaunts had proved that. So the procession of club gigs at The Ditto or The Central Tavern continued, without much in the way of tangible purpose or payback.

In terms of entertainment infrastructure, the Pacific Northwest's long-term lack of visibility in the popular media had bred an inferiority complex. Promoters would automatically relegate local bands to support slots, even when the likes of The U-Men or Green River were a demonstrably bigger attraction than an out-of-town headliner—a band like The Sea Hags, for instance, who hadn't yet released a record but enjoyed the virtue of coming from San Francisco, a city with a recognized rock heritage.

"Soundgarden or The U-Men would open for a national act, and you'd get 500 people showing up to see the local band and then leaving the club," says Kim Thayil. "At least the Seattle audiences were actually applying value and merit to their own backyard."

Although none were exactly content with their situation, some members of Green River began to bridle at it more than others. Jeff Ament resented what he saw as the discrimination against local bands by local promoters. "Seattle bands had always been second-class citizens," he says. "We could pull hundreds of people into a show, but we still weren't getting any real respect. And I think that probably led to Mark taking the piss."

Mark Arm at least had the escape valve of The Thrown Ups, the wilfully bad improv outfit he began drumming with in late 1985 as a means of staying in touch with Steve Turner, who joined shortly after quitting Green River. Even as Turner revived his student career in January 1987, by enrolling at the Western Washington University in

Bellingham, The Thrown Ups continued with their occasional gigs, which typically involved gross-yet-ingenious costumes—such as Ed Fotheringham's plastic "zit pants," from which he squirted shaving cream into the audience.

Through Turner's friendship with Tom Hazelmyer, a U.S. marine stationed on Whidbey Island near Bellingham in the far northwestern corner of the state, The Thrown Ups had even released a single, "Felch," on Hazelmyer's record label Amphetamine Reptile.

"The Thrown Ups was a social experiment—what can you get away with and be really shitty?" says Fotheringham. "How bad can you be and make a record? Apparently you can be pretty bad. There were a lot of bands in Seattle *trying* to make a record, and they were pretty serious. We *were* making records and we couldn't even play!"

Yucky stunts became an increasing part of Mark Arm's onstage armory with Green River too. While opening for The Butthole Surfers at the Central Tavern shortly before the 1986 tour, he stuffed cooked spaghetti in green Jello-O, which was then placed in a cooler and hurled into the crowd, much to the displeasure of the club's staff. Fish were a favorite gambit, secreted down the front of his trousers and then whipped out at an opportune moment.

"There was a trashy, performance aspect to certain punk bands," says Arm. "The first time I saw The Butthole Surfers they did all kinds of wacky things. Gibby Haynes was wearing clothes pins in his hair, maybe 50 of them, and at some point he starts shaking his head rapidly and all the clothes pins fly off in all directions—how did he even conceive of that?! So I was like: 'What can we do to outdo the Butthole Surfers?'"

Arm didn't always have something untoward up his sleeve (or down his pants), but this certainly wasn't the behavior of someone impelled by his band's commercial potential. One key figure in his future had seen the light, however. Jonathan Poneman was booking bands at a bar just south of the U-District called Scoundrel's Lair, where Green River played the record release party for the long-delayed EP *Dry as a Bone* on July 5, 1987. That night, Poneman suddenly appreciated what made Green River unique—and decided that the band's staunchest advocate, Bruce Pavitt, was a man he could do business with.

"To this day it's one of the five best rock shows I've ever seen," says Poneman. "It was absolutely and utterly mesmerizing. Before then I had booked Green River at various shows and it almost seemed like it was parody, but the crucial difference [now] was that they had an audience that was all theirs and completely got it. Sub Pop's relationship with Green River early on was really what cemented the label. Bruce had this undying belief in all things Green River, whereas I had an undying belief in all things Soundgarden. In many ways, in retrospect, Green River were the smarter band, in that what they were doing was a lot more sophisticated. Or what they were *trying* to do. At the time it was all about the live shows, and Green River was much more multi-dimensional because you had all these different characters onstage."

Almost immediately thereafter, Pavitt and Poneman agreed to get together, initially to release a Soundgarden EP and then to run Sub Pop as a joint record-label enterprise. Independently of each other, the pair had come to the same realization: the Seattle scene had all the requisite elements of a social phenomenon, building its own momentum amid the communion of like-minds, with performers and spectators both turning up the volume. "Subterranean pop" indeed.

Poneman had eloquently appraised the situation in a December 1986 article in *The Rocket*:

> The town right now is in a musical state where there is an acknowledgment of a certain consciousness. A lot of it has to do with our geographical isolation: for once that's paying off in that the bands here are developing with their intentions staying pure . . . Something's gonna happen.*

Pavitt's fervent belief in the vanguard qualities of Green River was such that he borrowed $2,000 from his father to finance the release of *Dry as a Bone*, while cranking up the hyperbole in his June 1987 "Sub Pop USA" newspaper column:

* Quoted in *Loser*, 107.

> The next few years will see the ultra-heavy rock of Seattle rival the Motor City scene of the early seventies. I believe that bands like Green River and Soundgarden are every bit as great as The Stooges and The MC5.*

(The notion of Seattle as a mythical rock Valhalla, the post-hardcore generation's equivalent of Detroit, would be a favored strand of Sub Pop propaganda in the years to come.)

Produced by Skin Yard guitarist Jack Endino at Chris Hanzsek's new Reciprocal studio, *Dry as a Bone* offered the most vivid representation of the Green River sound—a trebly, fissile assault bound together by a glowering low-end, reminiscent of The Dead Boys, the Cleveland punks whose negaholic anthem "Ain't Nothing to Do" was covered on the B-side of the Tasque Force single.

By his own admission, Endino had been a "rank beginner, and hardly knew what I was doing," yet he helped Green River realize a taut power that gives a taste of how powerful a proposition they could be. It was Ament and Gossard, Endino notes, who seemed to call most of the shots during that 1986 recording session—but a year later, as Green River assembled to make their next record, their first full-length album, the same pair's ambitions had begun to outpace the band's capabilities.

"There were various things driving me, one being my family telling me that this was absurd and I should be going to college," says Ament. "But in Stone I found a guy who was similarly motivated. That's when the thing split open a little bit. In some ways I went from being Mark's ally to Stone's ally. We had bigger things planned. It certainly didn't seem like there were a lot of options in Seattle at that point."

After recording demos with Endino on Reciprocal's eight-track recording machine, it was decided the songs would benefit from being recorded in more upscale facilities. So Ament cut a deal with the $800-a-day Steve Lawson Studio in downtown Seattle to record in the middle of the night at a cheaper rate, with his friend Bruce Calder producing.

* Quoted in *This Ain't the Summer of Love* by Steve Waksman (University of California Press, 2009), 246.

Though Pavitt and Poneman wanted to release the album, Ament was not so keen. Sub Pop had no money. He booked a string of West Coast dates specifically as a calling card to record labels, culminating in a Los Angeles gig at the Scream club supporting Jane's Addiction, who were already a cult phenomenon and capable of filling the 2,000-capacity venue. Prior to the tour, however, Ament and Gossard's self-improvement kick overstepped a line: they suggested to Mark Arm that he take singing lessons.

"I'm sure we meant it in the best of ways," says Ament. "But I'm sure it didn't come out right! I can only imagine how that felt—you've been in this band for three or four years and then all of a sudden the band says, 'Hey, have you ever thought of taking vocal lessons?' That's grounds for divorce right there. I can totally understand why maybe he started pulling away from us at that point. But again, that was just the mindset we were in: we wanna make this thing *great*, how do we make it great? Y'know, he was a college student—he'd been to writing classes. So from my standpoint I figured why wouldn't he want to learn to sing better? I don't think that conversation went well—in fact, I think it went super-quiet."

"Stoney and Jeff—Jeff in particular—I think they really wanted to make a career of music," says Arm. "I think they rightly thought they weren't going to get anywhere with me as a singer."

Mark Arm had no quibble with bands that were popular—he would most likely never have seen Devo if they had not enjoyed a modicum of commercial success. But he had read enough about music to know that popularity involves a tradeoff, usually in terms of artistic control. And more than anything else, he wanted to maintain control over the process, to dictate how it might happen—which didn't entail learning how to sing "better."

His attitude was also a function of Seattle's entrenched underdog mentality. For Arm and most of his contemporaries, the idea of playing music as a career—especially the music he wanted to play—was ridiculous. Notwithstanding the fact that it seemed to have worked, the "Duff McKagan option" was little better than a lottery ticket.

The alternative to skipping town was Bruce Pavitt, by now covertly running Sub Pop from his day job as a tape returns coordinator for

Muzak, purveyors of soft background music to the world's restaurants and elevators. "I had the factory ship the records directly to Muzak," says Pavitt. "And I stored them underneath my workspace. The distributors would call me at work to place orders. So when they called, the receptionist would go, 'Hello, Muzak.' And the distributors would go, 'Err, is Bruce there?' They'd hook me up and I'd go, 'Yeah, yeah, that's my friend, Muzak.' Then I would ship it out via Muzak's shipping system."

By this point, Mark Arm was also working at Muzak, on the lowest-rung grunt job available: recycling tape cartridges so that they could be sent out looking like new. He and his coworkers, invariably fellow musicians recruited via the Pavitt connection, would play tapes on a ghetto blaster cranked to full volume so that they were audible over the noise of the cartridge cleaning machines.

"Seattle wasn't any kind of musical epicenter at that point," says Arm. "And the idea that it would become one was just so far-fetched. The assumption was that you would have to leave town to make 'it' happen, and play whatever games it took to get signed to a label, which was something I didn't have the patience for figuring out how to do, or didn't care enough about it."

The day before the prestigious engagement with Jane's Addiction in LA, Green River played a riotous gig at San Francisco's Chatterbox, a tiny dive bar in the Mission district. "It was just a totally crazy, wild, great great show," says Arm. "In fact, I blew out my voice that night."

Prior to the Los Angeles show, Ament and Arm had clashed over the guest list. Ament had invited some record company A&R representatives to come early and check out Green River—he wanted to use the band's allocation of 10 free tickets for them. Arm argued that they should put their friends on the list instead. Ament prevailed, but, unfortunately, out of all the A&R people he invited, only Anna Statman of Slash Records showed up—and even she arrived too late to see them. The dispute exemplified the philosophical rift within Green River, who that night delivered a lackluster, disconnected performance with Arm barely able to sing by the end.

"I remember driving back from LA and we had a tape of the show and it just wasn't very good," says Ament. "I think everybody knew on that drive back that the band was at an end. I don't remember there being a whole lot of drama."

Exactly a week later, on Halloween, 1987, Arm and Shumway were getting ready for a band practice. "Bruce and Jeff and Stone walked in," says Arm. "They're like, 'Y'know, the band's broken up.' It wasn't really a surprise. To me, it was a relief—I had been somewhat frustrated with the direction, with the impulses that they had. I just didn't know what I was going to do next."

Ament, Fairweather, and Gossard had already been playing with Malfunkshun singer Andrew Wood and drummer Regan Hagar, in a covers band called Lords of the Wasteland, so it was no surprise when they reemerged with Wood as the singer of a new band: Mother Love Bone. Since Wood's engaging stage persona had always suggested a role as the singer in the ultimate arena-rock band, he seemed the perfect fit for the commercial tendencies that Ament and Gossard had struggled to insinuate within Green River. Landing a major record deal within a year, Mother Love Bone would follow a brief, intense, frustrating, and ultimately tragic course.

It's tantalizing to wonder what Green River might have become, had Mark Arm been just slightly closer to Ament and Gossard either personally or philosophically. Others would very soon demonstrate that the band's musical contradictions were hardly irreconcilable. As Jonathan Poneman noted, what Green River and Soundgarden were doing wasn't so different—but Soundgarden ultimately proved more effective because the band's attack was more focused.

It's also true that Soundgarden were able to subsume their personality foibles for the collective good—and in Chris Cornell they had a frontman who had no problem with taking vocal lessons. For Green River, the fissure that was exposed when Steve Turner left was never truly repaired. As the couture turned glammier and the tour bus ambience was provided (without irony) by seventies hard rock like Whitesnake, Mark Arm could only go along with so much before his ambivalence ultimately became a deal-breaker.

"I remember Green River were about to play a show at the Rainbow," says Kim Thayil. "Alex went up to the stage to check his drum set, and then he grabbed a can of Aquanet, which was a hairspray popular in the Sixties, and he starts spraying his hair. I thought—that's gotta be a joke! But he seemed serious. He adjusted his drum set, fixed his hair, and then was like, 'OK, what now?' I think, given that context, Mark went along that direction and Steve left the band. When Steve left Green River, that left that band to Jeff and Stone, and when that band broke up they formed Mother Love Bone to further the direction they were going. Steve wanted to maintain more of a pure approach to playing guitar in a hard rock band without any of the artifice. Without the scarves and all that rock'n'roll stuff. He just wanted to play his guitar loud."

The Green River album, *Rehab Doll*, was eventually released by Sub Pop in 1988. When Jack Endino heard it, he was appalled at the new "professional" versions of songs he'd initially recorded. "I thought then, and I still think, that *Rehab Doll* sounded like dogshit," he says. "I listen to it and can hardly recognize it's the same band. I was kind of aesthetically offended, but on the other hand, it was a confidence builder for me as a budding record producer, you know: 'Sheesh . . . so *that's* my competition?!'"

"It is a terrible recording," agrees Ament. "We had all sorts of crazy ideas, trying to get experimental with sound, but it comes off like a bad Eighties rock record."

Tellingly, the best song on the album was also the best song on *Come on Down*: a rerecorded "Swallow My Pride," now augmented with an excerpt of Blue Öyster Cult's "This Ain't the Summer of Love," after Kim Thayil pointed out the unwitting similarity between the two songs. Two years on, Green River still couldn't get over the absence of Steve Turner.

"The greatest situation would have been if Steve had written three or four songs for us a year!" says Ament. "He wrote such cool, simple riffs. We'd got to the point where we were almost prog, the riffs were so complicated and the arrangements were so complicated, and the songmanship was out the door. That was the element that was missing by the time we were making the last record. There was just way too much wanking and not enough good songs. Mark was still writing pretty great lyrics, but the music suffered. I think we probably played better and we got more done when Steve wasn't there, but the songs were not as good."

It didn't take Mark Arm very long to figure out what his next move should be. But before calling Steve Turner, he went out and got completely hammered. At The OK Hotel, a club near Pioneer Square, he saw Dan Peters waiting to use the bathroom.

"Green River broke up!" he repeatedly exclaimed, before asking if he could jump the queue. Peters nodded. Arm ran in, then vomited all over the toilet. He didn't know it at that precise moment, but Mark Arm and sickness were soon to become important twin elements in Dan Peters' life.

3

Drag You through the Mud

The view is magnificent as the Honda Odyssey crests the I-5 Bridge over Portage Bay. Way ahead, late afternoon sunshine shimmers against the reflective glass panes of the downtown skyscrapers, while in the foreground yachts bob on Lake Union and a seaplane prepares to take off. It could be embarking on a sightseeing trip around the city, or a scheduled flight to one of the remote San Juan islands near the border with Canada.

To our left, the houseboats of Eastlake look as friendly as their immortalized images in *Sleepless in Seattle*; behind them rises Capitol Hill. To our right, the Space Needle peaks out above Queen Anne Hill and just visible in the far distance is the snow-capped, 14,000-foot volcano Mount Rainier, crowning this incredible panorama. The city of Seattle—built on hills, between lakes, and upon land reclaimed from the sea—is a display of man's perseverance in the face of nature's indomitable might.

"Y'know all that stuff about this place being gloomy and depressing?" says Dan Peters, nodding at the skyline. "Bullshit. That's just one of those myths, and I'd say it's been mostly put around by people who've never lived here. Just look at all this—we're surrounded by mountains and lakes. I think Seattle is a beautiful city."

He has more perspective than most. Daniel Joe Peters was born on August 18, 1967, in Lynnwood, a featureless segment of the northern Seattle suburban sprawl, where he lived until the age of three when his parents, Pete and Maureen, divorced.

Thus began a nomadic, unhappy childhood. Along with brother Jim and sister Cappie—the children from Maureen's previous relationship, respectively two and four years his senior—Dan moved with his mother, herself just 24, to the neighboring suburb of Edmonds and then to the port city of Everett, 20 miles further north.

Maureen had ambitions to pursue a career as a lounge singer. While performing with her regular guitarist at a bar in Everett one night, a promoter from the South offered her some gigs in Arkansas and Mississippi. Along with her guitar player, his wife, and three children, Maureen and her own three children drove across the U.S. from Everett to Little Rock, Arkansas, where they lived for three months in a mobile home before moving to Oxford, Mississippi, for a further three months, enrolling the children in new schools at each new place.

After Maureen's anticipated big break never materialized, the two families crammed into a single station wagon and drove all the way back to the Pacific Northwest, where the Peters found themselves homeless due to Maureen having defaulted on the mortgage. They duly moved into the basement of her guitarist's house near Sea-Tac airport. "So that was my fourth school that year," says Dan. "Then my mom and her guitar player had a huge falling out."

The family's next move was courtesy of Peters' father, who let them occupy his parents' recently vacated house. So Dan saw out his second grade and began his third living in north Seattle. Maureen resumed singing around town, performing contemporary MOR hits—Barbra Streisand, The Captain & Tennille, *Jesus Christ Superstar* medleys—with a new band, working the bars on Seattle's notorious Aurora Avenue.

"For lack of a better term, my mom was a 'partier,'" says Dan. "She liked to have fun." It was while singing at The Ribber, a steak restaurant on the strip, that Maureen met Nick Berkovich, who was working there as a cook. Shortly after, she took nine-year-old Dan to meet her latest boyfriend. "I remember I looked at him and I freaked out, crawled under the table. I just had this weird feeling. And that was the beginning of fucking hell."

In 1977, Maureen and Berkovich married and moved to the Totem Lake area, not so far from where Mark Arm lived. Shortly afterwards, Berkovich hit Dan for the first time. "It was in the driveway of the house we lived in. Soon after they got married, he got pissed off with me about something and smacked me. I went, 'You fucking dick.' And from then on it became a regular scenario. Any time I irritated him it resulted in a massive slap on the side of the head. Being the youngest and something of a mama's boy, I think he looked on me as competition for my mom's affections and so became incredibly, horribly abusive to me—he never touched my brother and sister. I said, 'I hate you!' He went, 'I hate you too.' At that point I thought, 'I guess I'm on my own here.'"

Twelve months after moving to Totem Lake, the family uprooted yet again. A 90-minute drive north of Seattle, Camano Island is situated in the Puget Sound and linked to the mainland by a bridge across a narrow channel known as Davis Slough. Maureen's parents had lived there since the late sixties, and in 1978 they helped purchase a parcel of land for Dan's family and Bob Miller, Maureen's older brother. After clearing the property of fir trees, two mobile homes were installed.

The island is a beautiful place to visit—you can watch orcas swim in the Saratoga Passage that separates Camano from the much larger Whidbey Island—but its remoteness soon compounded Dan's ongoing persecution at the hands of his stepfather. The contrast between his increasingly constricted island life and Steve Turner's suburban dream on Mercer Island is stark. There were no schools on Camano then, so Dan had to take the school bus 10 miles to Stanwood, a "town" of 2,000 people comprising two main roads, several bars, a couple of grocery stores, a bowling alley, and the area's main employer, the Twin City Foods processing factory.

Maureen had stopped singing on a regular basis and took a job behind the bar at the American Legion, while Berkovich commuted to Seattle where he worked as an industrial painter. "Life became fucking grim," says Dan. "There's no public transportation. I used to hitchhike home after football practice because my parents would never pick me up. My stepdad went to town on me on a regular basis. And of course by this point I'm zoning out, smoking pot. I was a horrible student. I felt I had no options in my life whatsoever. The only thing I wanted to do was to be a drummer."

Dan had fixated upon the idea of becoming a musician ever since the drummer in his mother's band gave him a pair of sticks when he was five. He'd listen to music with his brother Jim, pretending to play along. The most important influence came from his uncle Bob—not only was he a drummer himself, who coached Dan's air-drum flailing in the finer points of timekeeping, but he had a large collection of exotic-looking records. Thanks to his uncle, out of all the future members of Mudhoney, Peters was the first to hear the sacred texts.

"In 1975 I was listening to The New York Dolls and The Stooges. It was funny—when I was a teenager and getting into punk rock, people would say: 'Have you ever heard The Stooges?' 'Pffhht! Yeah, about 10 fucking years ago!' My uncle would give us records every year as a Christmas gift. So in 1977, I got Roxy Music's *Greatest Hits*. He took me to my first rock concert, which was King Crimson in 1980. Anything weird and out there, he was into and therefore I was privy to. But he was also into stuff like Blue Öyster Cult . . . his taste was pretty wide."

Once Bob had set up his mobile home on the Camano Island property, he moved in a couple of roommates who were equally devoted to collecting records. Dan remembers them playing a newly released copy of *Gravest Hits*, the 1979 debut EP by The Cramps. He listened repeatedly to "Human Fly." fascinated by the pounding rhythms, then went back to his room where he acted out the drum parts. "My brother would always make fun of me: I had my drumsticks and an invisible drum set. It was the only place I felt comfortable."

★ ★ ★

Dan frowns as he drives over the Camano Gateway Bridge, the sole access route to the island from mainland Washington. It's the first time he's been here in over 10 years and he's noticing some major changes.

"This is crazy, none of this was here—this stop light never used to be here!" The bridge itself is new, having replaced the Mark Clark Bridge in 2010, while the island now has two elementary schools, so the younger children don't have to go to Stanwood.

But some things haven't changed. At the junction of NW Camano Drive and Vista Drive, Dan points to a signpost. "That's where I used to wait for my school bus—I would sit there and drink Mason jars full of booze before I went to school. I was in seventh or eighth grade."

We turn right into Vista Drive, which soon turns into Laguna Vista. Dan slows the car, peering around at the road where he grew up. He gives a slight grimace and shakes his head. The mobile home where Dan lived with his family is still there. Keeping the engine running, he parks up opposite the property.

"So that house up there was built by my uncle. And next door, the gray mobile home was mine. A lot of bad activity happened in that house."

He puts the car in gear and drives away.

In 1980, on the way home from her bar job at the Legion, Dan's mother suffered critical injuries after her car left the road, flipped over, and landed in a ditch. Paramedics performed an emergency tracheotomy at the scene of the accident and she was in a coma for four months.

"At this point," says Dan, "my stepfather took control—and his hatred raged hard. Mom's in a coma and it's basically everyone for themselves."

Berkovich would hide food in his room so that the children couldn't have it. One day he told Dan to clean his bedroom; Dan complied, making his bed, smoothing down the sheets and going over every inch of the floor with the vacuum cleaner, even taking care to place the rubbish bin on top of his bed so he could clean underneath it.

He was just finishing off when his uncle dropped by. Bob wanted to borrow the vacuum cleaner and also wondered if Dan wanted to come and hear a new record he'd just bought. So Dan took the cleaner over to his uncle's, leaving behind a spotless room.

"My uncle put on 'Generals and Majors' by XTC, cranking it while he was down the hall vacuuming. So I'm sitting there listening to 'Generals and Majors,' going, 'Hey, this is cool,' and then my stepdad comes busting in the door. He looks at me: 'I told you to clean your room, you motherfucker.' Then he grabs me, throws me out the door, and proceeds to kick me and beat on me all the way to next door—because the garbage can was still on the bed."

Even at Stanwood Middle School, which he attended between the ages of 12 and 14, Dan wasn't beyond his stepfather's grasp. Berkovich sent letters to the teachers, giving them permission to hit his stepson if they deemed it necessary. No such assaults by proxy occurred—Dan found the letter thrown in a bin by his home economics teacher—yet school offered little respite from his misery.

"A depressing place," says Dan. "I played football for my seventh and eighth grade years, and on the first day of practice, even before we got geared up, we were doing pushups and the coach stops and looks at me: 'Peters, why do you wanna play football?' That's how encouraging people were."

Whenever he got into trouble, Dan was sent to the school office. He and the vice principal, Mr. Lewinsky, saw a lot of each other. "One time Mr. Lewinsky calls me into his office, and says, 'Dan, I hear you've got a drug and alcohol problem.' I'm like, 'Really? Who told you that?' 'Your stepdad. Well, hopefully things'll work out for you.' And he sent me on my way."

Five months after her accident, Maureen returned home. Confined to a wheelchair, her presence did little to curb her husband's excesses. One Friday, Dan and Jim came home from school to be told by Berkovich that they would be spending the weekend digging a ditch in the driveway. Jim told him to dig his own fucking ditch. For the first time ever, much to his disbelief, Dan saw his stepfather hit his brother.

"I reach for a phone and go, 'I'm calling the cops,'" says Dan. "And he stops. The words are: 'Now it's your turn.'"

The brothers scattered in opposite directions, Jim out the front door, Dan out the back in bare feet, running down the street. Reaching the safety of some bushes, they hid and watched as Berkovich threw the entire contents of their bedrooms onto the yard.

"We waited until my uncle came home," says Dan. "He parked in his driveway and we circled round him, going, 'We need help!'"

After this, all three children moved in with their grandparents, six miles to the south, where they stayed for the best part of a year. Then came another crisis—Cappie ran away to California. Dan and Jim moved back in with their mother and stepfather, but the situation was no less toxic. Or violent.

"I think I knew that it wasn't right," says Dan. "At one point my stepdad turned to me, in front of my mom, there was some row going on, and he said, 'You're nothing but a little cunt, just like your mother.' And at that point I realized, 'This isn't my problem. It purely has to do with you.' I tried to realize as it was going on that none of it was my fault."

Music remained the only real escape. In the summer prior to enrolling at Stanwood High School for his ninth grade, Dan met Kurt Danielson at a party in his uncle's house: there was a keg of beer out on the lawn, while live entertainment was provided by Bob Miller's band, The Modified 5, Stanwood's very own roughhouse rockabilly heroes. Dan knew of Danielson, who had just graduated from high school, for two reasons: first, his father edited the local newspaper; secondly, and most pertinently, he played in The Mod 5's local rivals, a band called Bundle of Hiss. Dan was intrigued, not least because Bundle of Hiss looked quirky and had exotic tastes, such as Joy Division, Public Image Ltd., and Gang of Four, which marked them as outsiders in Stanwood terms. At Miller's party, Danielson was impressed that this 14-year-old kid was drinking, and no one, least of all his relatives, seemed at all concerned.

"He was wise beyond his years," says Danielson. "This I knew immediately. It was probably around this time that Dan earned his nickname, 'the Grog Boy,' given for obvious reasons: he always enjoyed drinking."

By now Dan had acquired his first drum kit. Bob Miller bought it from The Modified 5's frontman, Mike Borseth, and helped sneak it into his nephew's room bit by bit. "When my stepdad found out that I'd brought it into the house, he said, 'If I hear that drum set within 150 yards of the house, I'm gonna beat the shit out of you.' I didn't know what to do. And my brother told me, 'Dan, you gotta go, you gotta get out of here.'"

In desperation Dan begged his father, who remarried in 1978, to let him come and live in Seattle. Pete Peters agreed, on condition that he ask his stepmother's permission too. "My stepmom drove up here in a car and I packed what little clothes I had, and a box of records and my drums. I remember my mom at the time, sitting there on the day I left, getting her hair done by my uncle's wife. And I just went, 'OK, see ya.' And I left."

He returned twice in the following months to see his brother, and noticed that his bedroom was padlocked. "I said, 'Jim, what's up with my bedroom?' He says, 'Once the parents go to bed, I'll show you.' And my brother grabs the key and opens it up—and my stepfather's growing weed! He's turned my bedroom into a huge grow-room to make money. But that was it. I was 15, and I never came back."

Outside the house in Cove Place where his since deceased grandparents lived—the property, owned by his uncle Bob, sits vacant—Dan gazes beyond the woods, towards the beach, the bay, and the orcas, where summer tourists boost the island's population and the area's beleaguered economy. "You're probably thinking this is a beautiful place," he says. "And I wish I could say that. Because it is. I understand why people would think that. But it reeks of pure evil to me."

As he leaves Camano Island again, the mere act of crossing the bridge over Davis Slough seems to ease the stress lines on Dan's face. Soon, however, he indicates left and pulls up outside the Stanwood Hotel. "We're gonna have to go there for a beer," he says. "This was *the* big place, the bar that everybody would go to. And I've never been."

Built in the 1890s and now restored after decades of neglect, the once-notorious Stanwood Hotel is a cozy and amiable saloon, albeit with one detail that's particularly disconcerting for Dan: the draught beer comes served in Mason jars, the very utensil from which he supped as an unhappy teen while waiting for the school bus. It's a little eerie, sitting at the bar, knowing that the man who was his violent nemesis doubtless came here during the bad old days.

"My brother was the key to me leaving—it was always in the back of my head that I wanted to leave, but I needed to be pushed," he says.

"Jim never left. He stuck it out until the bank took the mobile home. The thing is, my abuse was immediate; it was physical. My brother and sister watched. They've both had major psychological problems, struggles with drugs and alcohol. I've certainly got my own issues—but I like to think I came out of it relatively unscathed."

Although he felt relief at leaving behind this violent, dysfunctional situation, adjusting to life in Seattle was far from easy. In terms of education, Dan went from a small school in a tiny rural town to a large school in the heart of a city. Garfield High was predominantly black. There were any number of reasons for him to feel like an outsider, and, after a few weeks, he decided that he wanted to go back to Camano Island.

"Because it was all I knew. I didn't know anybody in Seattle. I was alone and I freaked out. But one of the things I can thank my dad for is he sat me down and said, 'You can't go back to that. Give it time, it'll get better.' After the first year of living in Seattle I started to meet people and hang out—and I joined Bundle of Hiss. That was the big thing. I joined Bundle of Hiss when I was in the eleventh grade and started playing music. I never looked back after that."

Dan had no experience of playing in a band, but, despite being four years younger than bassist Kurt Danielson, singer Russ Bartlett, and guitarist Jeff Hopper, he fitted in well. There was the Stanwood connection, of course: The Modified 5's Mike Borseth had recorded some Bundle of Hiss demos and, on learning that the band needed a new drummer, recommended Bob Miller's nephew. At first Danielson couldn't place him, until Borseth jogged his memory: "You know him—the Grog Boy! He's an awesome drummer! Way fucking better than Bob! He'll be great for you guys. Killer!"

Having also recently moved to Seattle, to study at the University of Washington, Danielson called Peters and arranged to pick him up for an audition. They greeted each other dressed to impress: Danielson in his home-kntted American flag sweater and ill-fitting platform boots, Peters in a Dead Kennedys T-shirt, both with homemade buzz-cuts. Immediately it became apparent that the self-taught Peters, even at 15 and a half, was a prodigiously able drummer. This quality, as much as his youth, would soon be noted as Bundle of Hiss appeared as the opening act in punk clubs around town.

"His style was intuitive, soulful, direct," says Danielson. "And whatever he did, he did it far better if allowed to do it his way instead of in the manner of another drummer. Everything we did after Dan joined us was influenced by Dan, and was either adopted or rejected because of how it fit with how Dan played with us."

This extended even to Peters' after-school job delivering the *Seattle Times*: the other Bundle of Hiss members would take it in turns to drive him around his route because it gave the band more time to practice. Peters rarely talked to his bandmates about his traumatic upbringing. "There was pain and alienation in him," says Danielson, "but he hid it pretty well. He fueled it into his drumming."

Initially, Bundle of Hiss were somewhat mismatched with the Metropolis hardcore scene, but they thrived on the audience interaction and soon garnered a good reputation among local promoters. Peters in particular made a lasting impression on Jonathan Poneman, who had begun to book bands for KCMU showcase nights at The Rainbow Tavern in the U-District. "I knew Dan Peters as this underage guy who had to come covertly into these places to play," says Poneman. "He was an extraordinary drummer. And an incredibly gracious and good-humored person."

After Hopper quit to move to Bellingham, Danielson recruited a new guitarist, Jamie Lane, who he'd met in one of his UW poetry classes. Once a week they would practice at the Peters' family home in the north Seattle neighborhood of Green Lake. There was no soundproofing, but the noise was just about tolerable because the bedroom Dan now shared with his brother, Jim, was right at the very top of the house.

Following Bartlett's departure in 1986, Lane doubled up as vocalist, and the trio's sound shifted into line with the prevailing mood circa *Deep Six*: slower, heavier. They began appearing with Green River or Soundgarden at The Ditto Tavern, or The Central, or The Rainbow—and were by no means the lesser attraction. For a brief period, Green River were banned from The Ditto following one of Mark Arm's fish-related incidents, and Peters sweet-talked the venue into putting them

Green River Mk 2: (from left) Jeff Ament, Bruce Fairweather, Mark Arm, Alex Vincent, Stone Gossard. CHARLES PETERSON

Mr Epp & The Calculations, Seattle's Central District, 1982: (from left) Darren Morey (a.k.a. Darren Mor-X), Mark McLaughlin (a.k.a. Mark Arm), Jeffrey Smith (a.k.a. Jo Smitty), Todd Morey (a.k.a. Todd Why?). MARK ARM PRIVATE COLLECTION

Only one man is smiling at the last ever Green River Mk 1 photo shoot: (from left) Stone Gossard, Mark Arm, soon-to depart Steve Turner, Jeff Ament, Alex Vincent. CHARLES PETERSON

The Thrown Ups as Queen, 1986. (top pic, from left) "Roger Taylor" a.k.a. Mark Arm, "Freddie Mercury" a.ka. Ed Fotheringham, "Brian May" a.k.a. Steve Turner. (bottom pic, from left) "John Deacon" a.k.a. Leighton Beezer, Fotheringham, Turner.
MARK ARM PRIVATE COLLECTION

Charles Peterson images from Mudhoney's first summer, 1988: (top) the Central Tavern, Seattle and (bottom) the I-Beam, San Francisco. "It was tight and loose," says Sub Pop's Jonathan Poneman. "Menacing yet playful . . . with these amazing songs. They were instant classics. Every single song: it was like, this is fucking great." CHARLES PETERSON

Team bonding on the Sonic Youth/Mudhoney U.S. tour, 1988. "They're probably the most fun-loving band I ever toured with," says SY's Thurston Moore. "They were like a gang who'd found this thing and it was brilliant." MICHAEL LAVINE

Sweet young things. Dan Peters, Steve Turner, Mark Arm, and Matt Lukin, Seattle, 1988. "They seemed like a 'group' in the best sense," says producer Jack Endino. "There was a chemistry there. They meant business but they were there to have fun too." CHARLES PETERSON

On the couch during the infamous nine-week European tour, spring 1989. "Between week six and week seven we lost our minds," says Turner. MARK ARM PRIVATE COLLECTION

Mark Arm at Toronto's Apocalypse club, October 24, 1989. DEREK VON ESSEN

Steve Turner and Mark Arm enjoying a tender moment backstage at the Reading Festival, August 24, 1990, amid uncertainty over the band's future in the wake of Turner's decision to return to college. STEVE DOUBLE

During the three-night residency at the Fulham Hibernian Club, London, June 20, 1990. PAUL SLATTERY

Krist Novoselic, Dan Peters, and Kurt Cobain. For a brief moment, this was Nirvana. From the *Sounds* photo shoot at Novoselic's house in Tacoma, September 23, 1990. IAN TILTON/RETNA

Peters, Turner, Lukin, and Arm mud up in homage to The Slits *Cut* album sleeve, spring 1989. CHARLES PETERSON

on a bill with Bundle of Hiss. "We were all hanging out and doing the same thing," says Peters. "You can't help but be influenced by what's going on around you."

Having spent so long thinking about playing drums, and then initially doing so in isolation, Dan relished the social communion of being in a working band. He was particularly keen to study other players at close quarters and wasn't shy about taking notes. One of the first gigs Bundle of Hiss played at the Ditto was with Skin Yard, whose drummer, Matt Cameron, dealt in asymmetrical time signatures and spacey grooves. Not only was Cameron clearly influenced by the fusion style of Bill Bruford—Dan's favorite drummer at the time—but the comparison in no way flattered him.

Dan was hugely impressed. "Skin Yard actually did a King Crimson song!" he says. "That was amazing, to see some people you know pull that stuff off." Around the same time, Peters also began playing with another band, Feast, who dealt in post-punk melodrama with a six-axle crunch. "I met them at a party and they said they needed a drummer. I had never seen or heard them, but I wanted to play as much as I could."

Peters had the time and energy for more than one group. By now, music was his sole focus—much to his father's dismay. Pete Peters owned his own company, designing and installing fire protection systems, and was hoping his son might join him in the sprinkler business once he realized there was no future in rock music.

In the meantime, there had been provisional discussions about enrolling in the graphic arts program at Seattle Central Community College. Two weeks before his high school graduation, however, Dan had a jarring conversation with his father. Peters senior demanded to know how he could afford to go to college if he didn't have a job. Then Dan was informed that, as of graduation day, he'd be charged $147 a month rent to stay at home.

"He basically pulled the rug from under me," says Dan. "He's like, 'If you can find some place cheaper, go for it.' And I found some place cheaper. I found some place for $92 a month. And I left. Never came back. After that, every time I'd see my dad, he'd be like, 'So, still playing in the rock band?' 'Yeah, still playing in the rock band.' He says, 'When are you gonna give that shit up and get a real job?' The only time that my dad has said he's proud of me is when I bought a house. And I'm like, 'You're proud of the fact that I bought a house, but you're not proud of the way I went about buying a house; you're not proud of the fact that I actually did what I wanted to do and I actually made it happen—I bought the house because I play music.'"

★ ★ ★

In the autumn of 1987, the idea that playing music might one day buy him a house would not have detained Steve Turner beyond a brief laugh. His long-term plans were based around education. Upon graduation from high school, Steve informed his parents quite seriously that he hoped to be out of college by the time he was 30. He foresaw a long road to his eventual attainment of an anthropology degree, with breaks along the way for six-month archaeological digs, foreign travel, and other new adventures.

He certainly wasn't envisaging a career in rock'n'roll when he told his parents that he'd be calling his first time out after just one year in Bellingham. The Thrown Ups were hardly a commercial proposition, after all. But on his occasional weekend trips to Seattle, where he'd hook up with Mark Arm and see shows, Turner had begun hankering for a band that, while not motivated by the illusory prospect of success, might actually get together and rehearse now and then—maybe even write some proper songs.

Steve didn't really know Dan Peters, beyond seeing him at gigs and parties around town. At one drunken midnight revel, they found themselves jamming in a basement on some equipment that had been lying around, while Ed Fotheringham screamed into a microphone. Turner suggested they get together again, and, much to his surprise, both Fotheringham and Peters agreed. They met for one rehearsal, at which Steve came up with a catchy guitar riff that sounded like a drunken hillbilly tune; it would later become the Mudhoney song "You Got It (Keep It Outta My Face)," while a version was also recorded by The Thrown Ups entitled "Bucking Retards."

But the concept of rehearsal was anathema to Fotheringham. "I'm not a musician," he says. "I really like music, but I just can't do it. I don't have the ability. I don't deal with effort really well. So that jamming thing was not a major deal."

Thus Ed Fotheringham quit the embryonic ensemble after just one practice. Shortly afterwards, Mark Arm called Turner to tell him Green River had broken up . . . and did he have anything going on? Arm was astounded at what he heard next.

"Somehow, Steve had convinced Dan Peters to get together with him and Ed Fotheringham," says Arm. "Dan was a *great* drummer around town—one of the three best drummers we knew, alongside Matt Cameron and Greg Gilmore. I'm like: 'How did you get him to play with you?!' Steve said Ed wasn't interested, but maybe the next time him and Dan got together I could join in."

Arm, Peters, and Turner rehearsed several times over a couple of months, while deliberating who they might ask to play bass. They considered Jim Tillman, formerly of The U-Men: a great bass player, but no one knew him very well. On the other hand, The Melvins had recently disposed of their bassist, Matt Lukin, in peculiarly contentious circumstances.

After being told that the band was breaking up because leader Buzz Osborne was moving to San Francisco to live with his girlfriend, Lori Black (who happened to be the daughter of Hollywood child star Shirley Temple), Lukin subsequently learned that drummer Dale Crover had also moved to San Francisco and that The Melvins were, in fact, alive and well, with a new bassist: Lori Black.

Widely admired for his intricate playing, Lukin was familiar on the scene from his trips into Seattle from Aberdeen to watch bands, often in the company of his exceptionally tall friend, Krist Novoselic. So the trio chose Matt Lukin—but he didn't exactly jump at the offer.

"Mark called me up," he says. "Obviously I was still living in Aberdeen, a two-hour drive away. So I said, 'Weeeeell . . . I dunno. Maybe I'll give it a try. I'll come up and jam next time I'm in town—but I'm not ready to move to Seattle right now.'"

Lukin was next due in Seattle on December 31. He had a ticket to see Alice Cooper and Motörhead at the Seattle Center Coliseum, although on the day itself Motörhead were detained by U.S. immigration officials and never made the gig—so Matt saw Alice and LA glam merchants Faster Pussycat instead ("which was a bummer").

Nonetheless, on New Year's Day 1988 he climbed into the rear seat of Steve Turner's mother's car and greeted his potential new bandmates. He noted to himself that Dan Peters was wearing a beret, but any initial awkwardness was assuaged when the drummer excitedly suggested they stop and buy some beer en route to the practice space. The only flaw was that, at 20, Peters couldn't yet legally purchase alcohol.

"So Matt walks over to the beer cooler," says Peters, "and grabs a half-case of beer: 'I've got mine!' So I grabbed one too and had to get him to pay for it. I was like, 'This is excellent! He's going to drink a half-case of beer to himself—I'm gonna do that too!'"

From such auspicious overtures grew a firm friendship. The practice too was a success, though Arm has no memory of it whatsoever. As they ran through various riffs the trio had been working up, Lukin was impressed at how straightforward this material was compared to the logarithmically complex song structures of The Melvins. But mostly he was impressed because the beer didn't seem to impair his ability to perform. "I'm like, 'Jeez, if I can get this drunk and still play the songs, it seems to be a pretty fun band to be in,'" he says.

★ ★ ★

Freewheeling through life thus far had suited Matthew David Lukin well enough. Born in Aberdeen on August 16, 1964, he grew up in Montesano, 10 miles up the Chehalis River, which flows into Grays Harbor, the large bay upon which Aberdeen sits. The small towns in this remote, lush corner of the Pacific Northwest exist because of either fishing or timber, once-thriving industries now in decline, and the communities bear the deep-set scars of economic depression. Matt's father, David, spent years in the logging industry before becoming a fireman. His mother Kay was an optometrist's secretary, then took a job as a school lunch lady. Whenever he went to see bands in Seattle, such as Black Flag's September 25, 1984, gig at the Mountaineers Hall (with Green River opening), the teenage

Matt would subsist on a bag of leftover pizza slices that his mother had brought home from the school kitchen.

Matt did have an older brother, Mark, though he wasn't "into Sabbath." But his older sister, Jody, was; she liked Ted Nugent and KISS too. "That was cool enough for me at the time," says Lukin. "I didn't know any better. Plus, my mom was into Neil Diamond. I love that shit—it still reminds me of being a kid."

Usually along for the ride on those trips to Seattle, 100 miles to the northeast, was Roger "Buzz" Osborne, whom Matt had met at Montesano High School. With his big helmet of curls, upon arrival into a tight-knit community as a 12-year-old, Osborne looked, and was made to feel, different.

"He was a freak and no one liked him," says Lukin. "He played guitar and he knew I had a guitar, a crappy second-hand thing I bought when I was 14. I was listening to Cheap Trick and Van Halen, that kind of shit. But for some reason I couldn't make my guitar sound the way those guys did! But then I met Buzz and he showed me how to play power chords. I didn't know what I was doing until I met Buzz."

At 16, Matt pooled some money he'd been given for his birthday and bought a Les Paul guitar. This considerable investment convinced Osborne that Lukin should join him and drummer Mike Dillard in a band. But as Osborne was already the guitarist, they wanted him to play bass instead. Lukin was so keen to be in a band that he agreed.

"It was not that I was talented, it was just: 'Here, you play that,'" he says now. "At the time I didn't know very much about either the bass or the guitar, so I approached playing bass the way I approached playing guitar. I did that for years, thinking that was the way to do it: strum it, play chords. Even into Mudhoney days I was doing that. And then after a while I realized less is more."

Osborne named the band The Melvins, after a hated fellow employee at the Montesano Thriftway where both he and Dillard worked. For a long while they just jammed on cover versions, mostly by The Who and punk bands, and eventually got to play a high school dance. "I'm sure everyone thought we were playing original material," says Lukin, "because nobody at my high school was into The Clash, or The Sex

Pistols, or The Ramones—no one had heard that shit. Realistically, the school dance was the peak of our ambitions. There wasn't anywhere to play in the Grays Harbor area if you were a punk band, or anybody writing originals. If you were one of those bar bands that would do nothing but covers that everybody wanted to hear, you could make a pretty good living. But you weren't going to go anywhere. And we definitely had ambitions to get out of town. We knew there were scenes going on in the big cities: Seattle, or San Francisco. It just took a while to finally get there."

Clever and intense, Osborne had been emotionally ripe for a punk conversion. Once he'd heard the Pistols and The Clash, he began delving beyond the obvious with the help of a sympathetic Aberdeen record shop employee, Tim Hayes, who would recommend the latest Cramps or Black Flag records to Osborne and Lukin whenever they dropped by. Much as a firebrand preacher would spread The Word to his congregation, Osborne took it upon himself to spread the word of punk to his social circle, a group that soon included Krist Novoselic and a young former baseball teammate of Lukin's, Kurt Cobain. The Melvins became Osborne's soapbox—and his getaway vehicle.

"Buzz was so important, because he was the one who brought the punk rock to Grays Harbor and Aberdeen," says Novoselic. "He understood the sensibility, and he was so advanced musically. I remember he wrote a story for the Montesano newspaper, *The Vidette*, and it said, 'I don't wanna go to some big rock concert in a coliseum where I need binoculars to see the band, I go to punk rock shows where I can be right there in front.' He made this defense, this advocacy, this plea for punk rock. So he was an evangelist for it. And that's how I fell into it."

Osborne realized that a band could only escape the stultifying environs of Grays Harbor by finding its own distinctive voice. One look around at their contemporaries, playing hack rock covers of hack rock bands like Loverboy, proved that.

"Those guys thought once they made it to Seattle they'd be playing the Coliseum, opening up for Van Halen," says Lukin. "And they would laugh at us—they would think we were the idiots. 'You guys with your silly punk rock . . .' Well, we were getting out of town and getting gigs—those guys weren't playing anywhere beyond the Harbor, except Elma. Which was only 10 miles closer to Seattle than we were."

Initially a hyper-velocity punk band—albeit one that played KISS covers—The Melvins took a handbrake turn in 1984, perhaps not coincidentally around the time of Black Flag's *My War.* They began playing at enervated tempo, but with the fervor of hardcore and the discipline of speed metal, evolving an abstract, sensual form of heavy rock that was uniquely theirs.

"The Melvins went from being the fastest band in Seattle to the slowest, almost overnight," says Kim Thayil. By now playing regularly in the city, the band were powered by the precision bludgeoning of Dale Crover, a friend of Krist Novoselic with whom Osborne had replaced Dillard. Or rather, he had persuaded Lukin to spin Dillard a line about Osborne quitting The Melvins and starting a new band with Crover on drums and Novoselic on bass.

"Apparently, Novoselic didn't work out so I got a call to rejoin the band," says Lukin. "Which never really happened. That was just a story to get rid of Dillard without having to hurt his feelings."

Or indeed, without having to confront Dillard with the uncomfortable news that Osborne had found a drummer he preferred—exactly the same gambit he used to fire Lukin from The Melvins, but this time with Crover delivering the message. (A similar passive aggression would hallmark Nirvana's treatment of a succession of drummers until they found Dave Grohl, whose piledriver style was very similar to Crover's.)

Regardless, Dillard bore no grudge and, with Crover onboard, The Melvins swiftly came into their own. Although the least popular of all the *Deep Six* bands in terms of crowd-pulling power in Seattle—significantly, they were the only band without a charismatic lead singer—their contributions to the album are a tribute to their relentless drilling by Osborne. The band would rehearse every day at Crover's mother's house on Third Street in Aberdeen, with Kurt Cobain and Krist Novoselic in attendance, taking note of their friends' dedication.

"You could listen and hang out, but it wasn't a party scene," says Novoselic. "They basically would go through the set list forwards, then they would go through the set list backwards. Those songs Buzz would write, those twisted, heavy tunes, they were difficult to play. It was really compelling. Kurt and I saw that if you want to be in a band like The Melvins you need to be serious about playing."

Crover and Lukin assented to Osborne's strict work ethic, as Dillard's lesser commitment had contributed to his exit. If Lukin's subsequent renown as Mudhoney's party-hearty clown prince might seem at odds with his pivotal role in The Melvins' tightly wound machine, that's partly due to a disconnect between image and reality. Behind the bravado, Lukin was more serious than he might have been comfortable admitting. Nonetheless, the efficacy of what he terms Osborne's "dictatorial" leadership became clear, as The Melvins began to play gigs beyond their locality, whether it be in Olympia, Tacoma, or Seattle. In 1987, the band would also release its debut full-length album, *Gluey Porch Treatments*, via the San Francisco record label Alchemy. Osborne's vision had not only taken the band beyond Grays Harbor, it had actually produced a bonafide artifact.

"Buzz was definitely the Hitler of the band," says Lukin. "I mean, he always encouraged us to write songs, but nothing me and Dale came up with was ever good enough. He was the guy with all the opinions. Which was good because I was always just along for the ride: 'Show me the notes to play . . . ' Our main goal was to tour and not have to pay to do it. To make enough money to get enough gas to get to the next town. I never had any idea that I would make a living out of it, though obviously that would be nice. I didn't have any other prospects. I wasn't planning on college. After high school I just figured I'll get a job somewhere doing something. About the time I was getting out of high school I figured: 'What can I do? Well, I *can* do carpentry—maybe I'll go into that.' I'd taken the woodshop class in high school and we would sometimes go out and build a deck for somebody in the community. I had some experience of building shit. And I liked it. But still to me it was a job—it wasn't what I wanted to do my whole life."

So the fact that he had a job as a carpenter in Aberdeen—where he shared a house with Kurt Cobain for a few months—was little comfort to Lukin when The Melvins relocated to San Francisco without him.

Beyond the fact of his escape route out of Aberdeen being closed, what really hurt about the episode was its devious execution.

"Buzz never stood up and said, 'I don't wanna play with you anymore and I'm moving on.' I could probably respect him as a human if he did that. He probably figured that once he's out of town and in San Francisco he'll never have to see me again, y'know—'That loser's never leaving Aberdeen, he's gonna be there the rest of his life.'"

Soon after his dismissal, a friend was making a trip to San Francisco and Lukin went along for the ride. He was hanging out with Strephon Taylor, bassist in Bay Area thrash metal band Sacrilege BC, when the new model Melvins unexpectedly dropped by.

"I'm like, 'Hey, so you thought you'd never see me again!'" says Lukin. "Then I turned into a wimp and started crying . . . it was a cry-fest. I bitched at Buzz for a while and then we went our separate ways. But I was bummed. What the fuck am I gonna do now? Live in a small town, or on farmland, with cows and chickens?"

Lukin felt conflicted: he had a steady job, with a boss who was happy to give him time to fulfill band commitments, and life in Aberdeen was comfortable enough. It was what he knew, after all. But even on The Melvins' brief trips to Seattle and California, he'd glimpsed alternative possibilities.

Mark Arm's phone call came at just the right time. The two-hour drive to Seattle would be a pain, but at least he'd be on the move to somewhere. Could he one day make a living from playing music? The only way to find out was to join another band.

"I don't think there was ever an official 'You're in' conversation—I just kept showing up," says Lukin. "All of a sudden I guess I was part of the band, but officially they never really asked me to join. I just figured, 'This was fun, let's do it again.' Next thing I know I'm in a band again."

Lukin soon discovered that the drunken hoopla of that first New Year's Day practice was a one-off—for him anyway. As the only member of the band with a car, he was tasked with driving around town to pick up everyone else, then to south Seattle's industrial district where the Dutchman rehearsal room was located, which he had already driven past on the two-hour schlep in from Aberdeen. All this after a day's work—and then, after practice, Lukin had to drive the other three to their respective houses. The imminent two-hour return journey home meant he couldn't get drunk either.

"At about 1 a.m., I'm fuckin' finally on my way back to fuckin' Aberdeen—*and* I gotta work in the morning! Unlike those assholes!" To keep him company on the long drive, Lukin would sometimes bring along his friend Scott McCormick.

"He would just sit on a stool in the corner, take his shirt off, and rock out as we were playing," says Mark Arm. "Not a lot to do in a small town!"

The new band was called Mudhoney, after a 1965 film by boobaholic exploitation movie director Russ Meyer. The film itself, a hard-boiled melodrama set in a poor rural American backwater, is much bleaker than Meyer's later, infamously camp flesh-fests; indeed, when scheduled between *Up!* and *Faster Pussycat! Kill! Kill!* on a 1987 Meyer triple bill at the U-District's Neptune Theatre, Arm had given *Mudhoney* a miss in favor of getting something to eat. But he thought the title sounded cool and mentally filed it away.

Combining dirt and sweetness, the name Mudhoney would prove the perfect fit—not that anyone was placing too much significance in anything at this point. "It was a really mellow thing," says Turner, "we were just thinking of it as a short-term project, for real, because we were the third band Dan was in at the time, I was just taking another sabbatical from college . . . Just come up with some songs and bash 'em out."

The band's only ambition was to release a single. Arm took a boombox recording of one of these early 1988 sessions to play to Bruce Pavitt in the cartridge cleaning room at Muzak. The recording quality was very poor, but Pavitt both recognized and trusted his friend's excitement at his new project. He gave Arm a couple of hundred dollars and told him to go record with Jack Endino at Reciprocal. Mudhoney felt certain that they could at least get a single out on Pavitt's label, or perhaps Tom Hazelmyer's Amphetamine Reptile. What they absolutely did not want was to just start playing gigs and get stuck on the treadmill of Seattle's club circuit.

"Because there was no real hope of getting anywhere," says Turner. "I wanted a record out, [to] at least leave behind an oddball artifact, like all of the records I like so much. Obscure, weird things for someone to discover 20 years later. That's really all I was thinking."

It might well have been the sum total of their achievements were it not for a couple of factors. Firstly, Bruce Pavitt and Jonathan Poneman were about to act upon the hyperbole of the *Sub Pop 100* spinal message: "The new thing: the big thing: the God thing: a mighty multinational entertainment conglomerate based in the Pacific Northwest." Then, two weeks after Sub Pop became a bonafide company and opened the doors of its first office, Mudhoney recorded some songs at Reciprocal. Among them was a throwaway ditty called "Touch Me I'm Sick."

4

An Inside Job

In one of its creators' few unintentionally ironic strategies, Sub Pop became a legitimate business on April 1, 1988. Bruce Pavitt and Jonathan Poneman had quit their day jobs—Pavitt at Muzak, Poneman at a Kinko's copy shop—and rented the penthouse of the Terminal Sales Building, a dowdy tower block at the seedier end of downtown Seattle's First Avenue.

Sub Pop was on the 11th floor; the elevator only went as far as the 10th. The inauspicious portents didn't stop there: so limited was the floorspace that the bathroom had to double as a stockroom; Sub Pop's initial roster amounted to a band that no longer existed—Green River—and one that had just quit the label. For despite Poneman's anguished entreaties, Soundgarden had elected to give Greg Ginn's SST their debut album before taking the corporate route with A&M.

Pavitt and Poneman almost went bankrupt during that first month. With virtually no capital investment, Sub Pop endured a precarious hand-to-mouth existence with its two founders and a skeleton staff (mostly comprising their friends) hustling and scamming from one month to the next. In July, Pavitt and Poneman attended the New Music Seminar in New York, a three-day industry showcase where labels touted their wares at a convention hall during the day and at night bands played in clubs all over the city. Barely able to afford a booth and without any promotional records, nonetheless they set up a Sub Pop stall. Instead of music to give away, the intrepid duo brought a stash of large-format Charles Peterson photographs and a box of Jeff Ament–designed Green River T-shirts, emblazoned with the words: "Ride the Fucking Six Pack."

"We had these three foot by four foot photos and we had an easel," says Pavitt. "Every few minutes we'd change the photo. People would walk by and see this huge Charles Peterson picture. They'd go, 'You guys got any records?' And we'd go, 'Yeah we got this Green River record . . . ' But we didn't actually have anything. Except we did have the Ride the Fucking Six Pack T-shirt. And we were selling those. Every single booth there was giving stuff away; we were the only booth bringing money in. Next thing we knew, all the security people at the New Music Seminar are wearing the Green River T-shirt—and they paid for it! So all these major label people are wandering round going, 'Who is Green River?' It was brilliant." By the end of three days, Sub Pop had sold all the shirts.

Had things gone to plan, the curious visitors to the Sub Pop booth ought to have been presented with the debut Mudhoney single. The release was delayed in order to accommodate a special brown vinyl pressing, and yet just knowing they had Mudhoney on the label was enough to fuel Pavitt and Poneman's optimism in defiance of the financial realities.

From the very first live performance on April 19, as unannounced openers for the New York band Das Damen at The Vogue, it was clear that any anxiety felt about Green River's demise would be blitzed by the sheer euphoria of Mudhoney's assault. "Seeing Mudhoney play that first time at The Vogue—it was tight and loose," says Poneman. "Menacing yet playful. There was a fuck-all attitude, this air of degeneracy, but with these amazing songs. I mean, they were instant classics. *Every single song*: it was like, this is fucking great."

Mark Arm felt very nervous before that debut gig, mostly because it would be the first time he'd played guitar live since the very early days of Green River. His return to the instrument came at the behest of Steve Turner, who sought to limit the potential for his friend resorting to fish down the trousers and other such antics.

"One of the reasons Steve wanted me to play guitar was to rein me in, and not [have me] constantly jump into the crowd, or roll around on the floor," says Arm. "Although we did play rolling around on the floor and jump into the crowd—but with guitars."

While Arm was most definitely the frontman, at the outset Mudhoney were strongly defined by guitarist Turner's aesthetic preferences. Having left Green River, unable to reconcile love of The Milkshakes with his bandmates' appreciation of Iron Maiden, he remained unrepentantly grounded in the garage.

In late November 1986, with 18 months of community college under his belt and preparing to resume full-time study at Western Washington University in Bellingham the following January, Steve enjoyed a three-week holiday in London, courtesy of Robert Turner's free air miles. After staying at a swish hotel on Grosvenor Square for a couple of days before his father left on a European business odyssey, Steve moved into a bed and breakfast/boarding house near Hyde Park and spent the rest of his stay watching bands and buying records from Rock On, a garage and rockabilly specialist market stall in Soho.

The high point of his trip was a gig by Thee Mighty Caesars, the latest vehicle for Billy Childish, the Medway poet, artist, and garage rock puritan who had previously led The Milkshakes. Unsure of south London's geography, Turner arrived far too early for the gig—at The Cricketers, a renowned pub venue next to the Oval cricket ground—and so he went for a wander. In a nearby pub, he was startled to see Childish sitting alone, drinking Guinness and writing in a notebook. Steve had bought a couple of Childish's poetry books soon after arriving in London and was shocked at the unflinching depictions of sexual abuse. But he couldn't summon the nerve to say hello: "I thought, 'If he's a dick I will not enjoy the show!'" He needn't have worried: the Caesars were everything he'd imagined they should be—minimalist R&B, raw emotion, and humor.

Upon returning to the U.S., Turner packed his bag and headed north to Bellingham. In the course of his year there, he continued to delve deeper into the grot of sixties garage, via the *Pebbles* and *Back to the Grave* compilations ("the crudest music ever made!"), as well as investigating the seamier fringes of seventies punk. A vital ally was

Tom Hazelmyer, the punk rock U.S. marine who hid his fledgling Amphetamine Reptile record label stock in a grenade box under his bed in the Whidbey Island barracks.

Hazelmyer introduced Turner to feedtime, a no-frills Australian trio whose debut album Steve then found in Bellingham's one record store, playing it to Mark Arm on his next weekend visit to Seattle. On another trip home, Turner was browsing in Seattle's Tower Records when he found a cheap import copy of The Scientists' *Blood Red River.* On the basis that any record that looked so much like a Stooges album had to be good, he bought it. Turner played his latest discovery to Arm and both bands became key Mudhoney touchstones.

These Australian groups had a unique malevolence, clearly shaped by punk but driven by a desire to locate that music's deeper sources. The grinding, slide-guitar urgency of feedtime, in particular, sounded otherworldly, like the blues being poked by those neurotically disgruntled punk theoreticians Wire.

Turner's archaeological antennae would continue to twirl whenever he entered a record shop. "If a single came from Australia, I would stare at it and try to figure out if it was going to be any good or not, or ask the guys at Fallout, 'What's this one?'"

Like all keen record collectors, Turner looked for key record labels—in his case Citadel and Au-Go-Go—and became adept at tracing bands' lineage to the first generation of Australian punk. "Obviously we loved The Saints," he says. "I was not such a big Radio Birdman guy; I liked what Rob Younger did with The New Christs much better. But you had the weird side of it, with Lubricated Goat and, if you will, the post–Birthday Party bands, the crazy art-skronk sound, and then that blazing, awesome Detroit-based sound—and we liked them both. The Scientists skate right the way through the middle of that. Me and Mark were definitely turning each other on to the harder, grungier stuff that was hanging around."

Arm eagerly devoured the fruits of his friend's excavations. He felt utterly disenchanted with the wan complexion of the post-punk landscape, which posited an increasingly consensual route as the only option for nonmainstream artists. Both Hüsker Dü and The Replacements had signed to Warner Bros., and made albums which, to

Arm's ears, sounded denuded of the qualities that had made both bands exciting in the first place.

The UK, meanwhile, had remained in thrall to the same post-punk blueprints for almost a decade: be it the industrial/art attack of Joy Division or Throbbing Gristle, the meta-jangle pop of Orange Juice (which begat The Smiths) or the ethereal ambience of Cocteau Twins. The *n*th generation retreads of these core texts sounded pretty wretched.

Australian punk, however, had evolved amid extreme geographical and cultural isolation, with very limited possibilities for commercial crossover—not dissimilar to the Pacific Northwest. No wonder the subterranean sounds from Down Under resonated on an instinctive, primal—indeed, groinal—level. "It seemed like in Australia they still knew how to rock," says Arm.

Mark had felt exhausted by trying to counter his Green River colleagues' drift towards an unironic embrace of classic rock clichés. Nils Bernstein remembers sitting with Arm one night in a mutual friend's truck: "[He said] that he was going to form a band with Steve again, and it was going to be the greatest band in the world."*

During the spring and summer of 1987, Arm and Turner had soaked up the elements that would comprise Mudhoney's musical DNA. They loved the manic economy of early eighties Portland punk trio The Wipers. They dug the volcanic assault of The MC5 and also the gonzoid proto-metal of Blue Cheer, a San Francisco trio who enjoyed a brief late sixties flowering, dealt serpentine blues-guitar figures that moved far too bizarrely to be termed "solos" and proclaimed themselves "the loudest rock band in the world." Mark had been introduced to Blue Cheer at Linfield College by John Mini, his lone punk pal in McMinnville, with the words: "Check out the crazy shit these hippies did in the sixties!" Also prominent in Arm and Turner's minds was a strain of U.S. post-hardcore that favored irreverence over cool, as epitomized by Texas punks The Dicks, whose song "Hate the Police" would become a Mudhoney staple, and fellow Austin rabble-rousers The Big Boys. The latter evolved into Poison 13, whose self-titled 1984 album found particular favour with Arm.

* "Mudhoney: Superfuzzy Memories (An Oral History)," *Magnet*, May 20, 2008.

"There was a time when I listened to Poison 13 nonstop," he says. "There are three records; I think of them as the triumvirate of trash: the first Redd Kross album, *Born Innocent*, the Tales of Terror album, and the Poison 13 album. They're just super-sloppy, super-fun, great records that sound like the bands were totally drunk when they were recording. That was how I preferred my rock'n'roll."

The filter through which everything else dripped remained the brutish simplicity of The Stooges. By now, Mark's yogic onstage suppleness was widely acknowledged as indebted to Iggy Pop, but in terms of pure sonics Green River had been too shrill and complex to truly evoke Iggy's greatest band: the original Stooges lineup featuring guitarist/drummer brothers Ron and Scott Asheton and bassist Dave Alexander. Mudhoney would come much closer in that regard, so much so that, even when actively copping someone else, they still somehow emitted a Stoogean aroma. The key attribute was minimalism.

Tellingly, Steve Turner's favorite Stooges album is the self-titled debut, where the performances are primally stark when compared to the turbo-charged mania of *Fun House* and the almost ludicrous pugnacity dealt by the James Williamson–era band on *Raw Power*. "The first Stooges record sums up that defeated teenage wasteland of suburban America," says Turner admiringly. "They can't even put into words how bored they are. They just sound like total wastoids; they have this weird feeling that something's not quite as good as it should be."*

* Iggy himself also favors the first Stooges album. In a 2007 interview with the author, he said: "I think it's the most powerful of the three. Because it made the freshest amalgam of what was available to us before we started. There was nothing that sounded quite like that until we did that. It's very fresh, and it has a lyricism about it in certain places. And it's very succinct. Whereas the next ones, *Fun House*, as a whole, that holds up, sure—you're there, it's alive, it's like a big snake, and it's got a head and a tail, it's more like a capital 'W' Work of Art to me. But it hasn't got the song values. The more anthemic ones, that people sing along with, or yell along with, are on the first record. And the third record [*Raw Power*], it's more aggressive. That's its great strength. More aggressive and a little more advanced, and a couple of the lyrics are real grabbers. But it's built on the other two."

When Arm and Turner conceived Mudhoney, they wanted a wild yet compacted rock'n'roll band shorn of all egotistical flourishes. Guitar solos would resemble impressionistic spasms rather than any coherent route to gratification. Whereas Green River were guilty of flamboyance for its own sake, this new group dealt a hard-rock meld that owed its lack of inhibition to the pre-punk era, yet was hardened by the spartan purity of hardcore. "It was all about getting stuff down to its essence," says Arm. "And I don't know that we ever completely attained that goal. Though we do have a couple of very, very simple songs."

They would arguably write better material, but few bands can claim to have evoked their essence with such perfection as Mudhoney did with "Touch Me I'm Sick." The fact that they delivered a definitive hand with their debut single is more remarkable still; moreover, it was recorded before the band had ever played live. For some bands this might have been the result of a carefully rehearsed set of plans, but as the quartet had practiced only once a month over the three months prior to recording, it was more a case of instinctive harmony among the four players.

As individuals, they all enjoyed a certain renown on the local scene. When Pavitt and Poneman told Jack Endino that their new band comprised the original guitarist and singer from Green River, the bassist from The Melvins and the drummer from Bundle of Hiss, his sincere response had been: "Seattle supergroup!" But it was by no means certain that players of such pedigree would work well together.

"They really seemed like a 'group' in the best sense," says Endino. "There was a chemistry there, that was obvious. Everyone totally respected everyone else, yet there was no pussyfooting around with opinions either. They meant business, but they were there to have fun too."

Although he knew what sounds he liked, Endino was still figuring out how to get them. Not that the band minded having a novice producer. "If he says he didn't really know what he was doing, we certainly didn't know that he didn't know what he was doing," says Peters. "The recording process was fairly new to everybody. That was the exciting part of it. You'd go in, set up and bust it out, make a record in one day. Jack was there to capture the raw tones coming out of the amps. Certainly, I think later records have better drum sounds, but he was really great at capturing the *shittiness* of the guitar sounds and that was the key thing. Those guitar sounds are pretty damn crappy—but they were intended to be pretty damn crappy."

April's two-day session on Reciprocal's eight-track machine yielded six songs. The band gave one of them, "Twenty Four," to their friend Tom Hazelmyer for the first edition of an Amphetamine Reptile seven-inch single compilation series—named in homage to The MC5's insurrectionary manifesto: *Dope, Guns 'N' Fucking in the Streets*—which, thanks to the delay in pressing the brown vinyl of the Sub Pop single, would actually be the first Mudhoney song released. Three more were demo versions of songs that would appear towards the end of the year on *Superfuzz Bigmuff*, the band's debut mini-LP. But no one left Reciprocal in any doubt that the tracks destined for Mudhoney's debut single were "Touch Me I'm Sick" and "Sweet Young Thing Ain't Sweet No More." Nor was there any dispute over which song should be the A-side—and it wasn't "Touch Me I'm Sick."

"We didn't think much of it really," says Peters. "We'd relegated it to the B-side. 'Sweet Young Thing' was what we considered the A-side, and 'Touch Me I'm Sick' was a nice tidy little B-side."

Sub Pop shared the band's opinion. As far as Pavitt and Poneman were concerned, with its slobbering, sludgy grind and Arm's sinister vocal about a teenage girl OD-ing on mommy's pills and vomiting into the toilet—her queasiness echoed by the jarring glissandos of Arm's slide guitar—the vivid "Sweet Young Thing Ain't Sweet No More" should have been Mudhoney's opening salvo to the world. Their opinion changed, however, when Pavitt sent a tape to Thurston Moore, who had expressed interest in Sonic Youth recording a split single with Mudhoney, whereupon each band would cover one of the other's songs. "They didn't wanna cover 'Sweet Young Thing,'" deadpans Poneman. "So, OK. Sometimes you need other people to tell you what's cool."

Thus spake Thurston. But it wasn't just Sonic Youth, preeminent taste arbiters that they were, who loved "Touch Me I'm Sick." Crowd reaction at Mudhoney's earliest gigs revealed the qualities that are now obvious but that eluded the band at first. Here was a ready-made anthem, simple enough to encourage participation by audiences of all ages in practically any state of disrepair and, at two-and-a-half minutes, just long enough to beg instant replay—in other words, the perfect single.

Turner's riff, a skittery little motif, owed a debt to Rob Vasquez, guitarist in a local garage band called The Nights and Days. "He had a great guitar style, kind of stuttering," says Turner. "He has a much cleaner sound—he didn't really use distortion boxes so much; he had a nasty-sounding amp, he wasn't so much a fuzz guy. So it reminded me of that a little bit. It was a fun riff to play. Usually, when I come up with riffs I try to think what it reminds me of, to see if it's aping something too much—if I can figure out exactly what it sounds like then maybe it doesn't need to exist."

Mark Arm highlighted the song's kinship to Iggy & The Stooges' "I'm Sick of You," which itself derives from The Yardbirds' "Happenings Ten Years Time Ago." "You might as well steal from the best. The frequent use of 'c'mon' and 'yeah' was in homage to The Saints." The lyrics, he insists, are nothing more than his characterization of "a creepy guy."

Arm typically deflects attempts to divine some deeper (or personal) meaning to his words, offering short shrift to Bruce Pavitt's theory that "Touch Me I'm Sick"—"I won't live long and I'm full of rot/Gonna give you girl everything I got"—is sung from the perspective of a predatory AIDS carrier. "If it was a song about AIDS, I think I would have said something about AIDS in there."* Like all the best pop songs, what it's about is less important than how it affects the listener. As proven by the catalytic response of Seattle audiences during the summer of 1988, its immediate acceptance foreshadows its eventual legacy. "Touch Me I'm Sick" marks the ignition point for the Seattle underground.

"I remember Bruce and Jon, early on, being unsure about this band Nirvana," says Nils Bernstein. "Like, OK, these guys are friends of The Melvins, they *might* be good, whatever... But *MarkandSteveandMattandDan*

* *Everybody Loves Our Town*, 138.

have a band, it's called Mudhoney—that's gonna be amazing! They figured we're definitely gonna be good for this year if we can put out a record by Mudhoney. There was no question about Mudhoney. Because 'Touch Me I'm Sick' is—*ta-da*! If any song defines late eighties Seattle music, then that does it. Nobody really remembers the first songs by Skin Yard or Soundgarden or Malfunkshun—but 'Touch Me I'm Sick' everybody knows. Mudhoney was really a magical coming together."

In the same month that Mudhoney stepped out at The Vogue, Nirvana made their debut live performance in Seattle. It was an inauspicious affair. Effectively their Sub Pop audition, Kurt Cobain, Krist Novoselic, and then drummer Dave Foster played The Central Tavern, empty save for Pavitt, Poneman, the doorman, and bartender. Pavitt wasn't convinced, but Poneman, having experienced a jaw-on-the-steering-wheel moment upon first hearing the band's January 1988 demo, persuaded him they should at least do a single with the band.

Nirvana's first proper Seattle gig, at The Vogue on Sunday April 24, wasn't much better. Before a small gathering of mainly Sub Pop bands and associates, including Mark Arm and Dan Peters, they nervously ran through their set, having started playing before the PA was switched on. So underwhelmed was Charles Peterson that he didn't bother to take any photographs.

Even at their peak, tension remained Nirvana's defining characteristic and it would take time for the fledgling band to learn how it could work to their advantage. Mudhoney, by contrast, emerged fully formed. The local groups they supported during these early months knew the game was over after hearing "Touch Me I'm Sick" for the first time.

"Well, I guess this means Mudhoney aren't going to be opening for us anymore,"* one member of Cat Butt sagely noted. By the time of their first headlining shows, on August 19 at Squid Row on Capitol Hill and then at The Central Tavern a few days later, Mudhoney were the scene's new sensation, with people queuing down the street to see them. These gigs were wild affairs, as audiences responded in kind to the onstage mayhem. Giddy with excitement, Arm and Turner would slam

* *Superfuzz Bigmuff Deluxe Edition* (Sub Pop, 2008), sleeve note by Jay Hinman.

their guitars and bodies onto the stage and into each other. Peterson's lens cap was most definitely off when he finally saw his first Mudhoney show.

"I missed their first gig; I think I was out of town," says Peterson. "So until I saw them at the Central I hadn't heard anything. I was just blown away. It was so different from Green River, for one thing, and musically so much more what I was into, which I also knew was what Mark and Steve were into. Taking that great synthesis of punk and sixties garage rock, but making something new of both. The show seemed so high energy. Even though a lot of the time Mark and Steve would be just falling into each other and jumping, it had this tightness, this performance aspect to it that hadn't really been seen with a debut band before."

Ed Fotheringham was equally taken aback at the transformation of his friends and erstwhile Thrown Ups bandmates into a Seattle rock phenomenon. Just as The U-Men became the most popular local live band by virtue of the fact that their shows were unfailingly great fun, so too Mudhoney swiftly earned a reputation for consistent performance and guaranteed entertainment. There was a palpable tingle on the streets as people queued to see this new band.

"They were young, they moved around a lot—they were certainly not shoegazers," says Fotheringham. "It was raucous! It was a beer-drinking, sweaty *event.* I just thought, 'Wow, this is a really fun rock band.' They had a sense of humor. They looked like they were having a good time. When I see someone's having a good time, I tend to have a good time. Green River did become a bifurcated band: there was this bizarre tension between the glam-metal thing and then the punk-Stooges-y thing, and it became confusing—I didn't know what they were trying to do. In Mudhoney, it was absolutely nailed. There was no question. Mudhoney sounded very complete to me. I don't mind avant-garde stuff; I just don't like to be confused. And I think that's why people enjoyed them early on. People were going crazy. Those shows were explosive."

Unlike The U-Men, who never really managed to evoke their onstage vivacity in the studio, with the release of their debut single in

August, Mudhoney already had a classic record to their name. "Touch Me I'm Sick" became the clarion call for a revolution simmering in the Pacific Northwest—and thanks to Sub Pop's vision, the message was soon traveling way beyond the local environs.

In 1988, the patronage of Sonic Youth ensured that the New York City area's coolest record store was Pier Platters, in the New Jersey town of Hoboken, just across the Hudson River from Manhattan. One of its staff members was Susanne Sasic, who also worked as Sonic Youth's merchandise seller.

"Susanne was a very important advocate on the East Coast for what was happening with Sub Pop," says Thurston Moore. "She made sure that anything Bruce Pavitt did they would have in the window."

When she heard the tape of "Touch Me I'm Sick" that Pavitt had sent to Sonic Youth, Sasic got on the phone to Sub Pop and ordered 100 copies—one eighth of the entire brown vinyl pressing.

"So when 'Touch Me I'm Sick' did come out, the whole front window of the record store was lined with all these brown vinyl seven-inches with no sleeve," says Moore. "She was so excited by this record—like, 'This is it, this is the news!' And it was a really great record. So I was excited to see Mudhoney."

Even before Sasic's extraordinary display of faith, one Pier Platters customer had caught wind of something special going on in Seattle. In the pre-internet era, obsessive followers of any niche movement had to nurture their devotion via active physical engagement. They went to gigs or record shops; they wrote letters using pen and paper to send in the mail, or they spoke to people. Maybe, in their quest to find the right person to speak to, they would look at a record sleeve, find a telephone number, and dial it.

This is what Ed McGinley did in the summer of 1988. Jonathan Poneman was taking a breather from cold-calling record retailers when the Sub Pop phone rang.

"I picked it up and this guy started talking to me, about Soundgarden in particular," says Poneman. "But then the conversation branched off into TAD and Mudhoney and Sub Pop and Seattle in general. Ed was a pretty archetypal New Jerseyian, in that he was a very passionate rock'n'roll fan, but there was no pretense to him. And I said, 'Come on man, you gotta come to this show'—I think it was The Fluid, Mudhoney, and Soundgarden at the Central Tavern. He said, 'Y'know? I think I'm going to.' And the guy literally got on the bus in New York City and took a Greyhound bus clear across the country to see this show."

Having traveled cross-continent for a Sub Pop gig, McGinley was so affected by what he saw that he didn't leave. He moved into Bruce Pavitt's apartment for a while and was a fixture at Seattle shows.

"Ed McGinley was my hero," says Poneman. "How can you not admire somebody who gives it all up for rock? Because that's basically what he did."

The show that McGinley drove 3,000 miles to attend happened to be The Fluid's Seattle debut. A quartet from Denver, The Fluid came to Sub Pop's attention via a German label, Glitterhouse, which had licensed the band's debut album. Eager to get European distribution for Green River's *Rehab Doll*, Sub Pop did a swap deal with Glitterhouse: the Germans got Green River, Sub Pop got The Fluid. Peddling a somewhat more conventional amalgam of punked-out blues riffola, The Fluid were a savage live prospect and the Seattle audience welcomed them like one of their own. Walking into a packed Central Tavern, Fluid drummer Garrett Shavlik gasped at the contrast with his hometown.

"The Seattle audiences were somewhat isolated so they supported everybody; there was no factions or bullshit like there was in Denver," says Shavlik. "Tom Price and all those U-Men cats came up and said, 'We can't wait to see you play!' Amazing support. The kids went apeshit and they'd never even seen us before. It was lovely. I was just psyched to see Mudhoney live, because Pavitt had been sending me demo cassettes. They did not disappoint. The Fluid had always prided ourselves on our live show. Boy, after Mudhoney, we were like, 'We really have to step up to the plate now.' The abandon coming off the stage was just unbelievable. Controlled chaos. Everything you want in punk rock. Like the first time I saw Black Flag or The Circle Jerks—holy fuck, but *with a groove*. It was pretty incredible."

Given how long he'd known the protagonists, Kim Thayil's perspective on Mudhoney that night was particularly telling. He especially appreciated seeing Arm in a band that eschewed hack-rock clichés.

"Mark took off that artifice that he'd required with Green River," says Thayil. "From the opening chords Lukin would be throwing his bass around and Mark and Steve were jumping up and down and sideways. They were very animated, very wild. Kinda how a rock band should be: out of control. It was rawer, wilder. It had the element that so many rock'n'roll people are afraid of, which is chaos. What makes heavy metal unattractive to me is the fact that they have to put every note in the right place. It's so informed by their mother's classical music collection. They're so afraid of doing anything wild—even though Hendrix was that way, The MC5 was that way and The Stooges were that way, and Blue Cheer were somewhat like that. Heavy metal and punk share roots, but heavy metal's fascistic fixation with order sucked the life out. Mudhoney were an antidote to that."

Mudhoney's startling impact did result in one casualty. With the release of "Touch Me I'm Sick," Dan Peters had quit Bundle of Hiss. He realized Mudhoney was going to involve more commitment than was possible to share with another band, and suggested Kurt Danielson start a new project with Tad Doyle, a music scholar and part-time butcher from Boise, Idaho, who joined Bundle of Hiss for their final few months. An arresting blend of gentlemanly charm, ribald humor, and 300-pound physical intensity, Doyle had already made a solo single for Sub Pop and the label sensed his star quality. Thus the eponymous TAD was born.

Meanwhile, having established themselves as an instant hit in their own backyard, Mudhoney made plans to spread the sickness further afield. Thanks to the hustle skills of Pavitt and Poneman, however, they were about to venture much further than seemed logical. While in New York at the New Music Seminar, the pair met with Reinhard Holstein, the owner of Sub Pop's new European partner label, Glitterhouse. A plan was hatched whereby Mudhoney would represent both labels at the Berlin Independence Days, a German equivalent to NMS—sales seminars in the day, rock'n'roll shows at night, networking throughout.

So the band flew to Berlin to play a single gig to an audience of music industry professionals. It was only their 12th show. They hadn't even toured the U.S. yet. In 10 months of existence, the furthest Mudhoney had gone beyond Seattle was Portland, a mere 200 miles away. Now they were on a different continent.

"Me and Steve had never left Seattle as far as playing music went," says Peters. "Just going down to Portland was crazy! We were shitting our pants. And there were people at the show! I think we did an interview! It was great. But the Berlin Independence Days—*that* was crazy. We get to go to Europe and play one show? Hell, I'd never been out of the country! And it went really well."

Footage of the Berlin gig (belatedly discovered and released on DVD in 2012) hints at the loose-limbed frenzy of a Mudhoney performance from this period, though the spectacle of the band hurling themselves around is slightly diminished on realizing they're playing in a large room to relatively few people. At one point, Arm invites the audience, "Pull down your pants if you like us," before concluding: "No one likes us."

The significant action was going on behind the scenes. As the band discovered the near infinite variety (and strength) of German beer, Pavitt and Poneman were wooing Europe's booking agents, promoters, and distributors, fixing up an infrastructure that would transport their Seattle rock revolution to an international audience.

Although not conventionally schooled businessmen, Pavitt and Poneman had personal charm and chutzpah that went a long way to keeping their company alive in some precarious cash-flow situations. On an early visit to the New York offices of their East Coast distributor, Caroline Records, the pair donned T-shirts emblazoned with the message "You owe me money," then casually walked around and chatted to staff. At no point was the subject of money raised—but on leaving they were handed a check.

At times, their behavior went beyond the realms of the strictly legal. One day in the summer of 1988, Pavitt took a call from the company printing the sleeves for the Green River album, *Rehab Doll*—a vital release for the label, even though the band no longer existed. The printing company wanted payment in advance. Pavitt knew Sub Pop didn't have the money; he also knew that if the record didn't come out, they would go out of business.

"So I sat down and I wrote a check and sent it," he admits, "and I knew it was going to bounce. We got the jackets and we got the record out, and a couple of months later we paid him for the jackets. But that's the kind of stuff we would do. Ethically, I probably shouldn't have written the rubber check."

Immediately on returning home from Berlin, Mudhoney embarked on their first tour, a three-week trip starting in Salt Lake City and winding up on the East Coast. Their chariot was a baby-blue Dodge van costing $600. Sub Pop's coffers couldn't fund such extravagance, so Bruce Pavitt drained his personal account yet still came up short. Remembering that The Vogue owed him $40 from a recent Sub Pop label night, he headed across the road to the club, got someone to write a check, and made it to the bank with just enough money, five minutes before end of business.

The van was not exactly in its first flush of youth. The heating vents were missing and a crack ran along the length of the floor, condemning whoever sat towards the rear to inhale exhaust fumes. But it got them across the U.S. and back again in one piece. The gig at Maxwell's in Hoboken won a rave review from the *Village Voice*'s influential rock critic, R. J. Smith—which, as far as Pavitt was concerned, meant it was $600 well spent.

In purely financial terms, the tour exceeded expectations. "We came home with 10 bucks each," says Dan Peters. "It didn't cost us anything. Success!"

Although their threadbare van offered little respite from the bitter cold, the band maintained high spirits throughout the trip. Some gigs were better attended than others, but audiences everywhere responded to their unbridled enthusiasm. Plus Mudhoney were actually getting paid. Compared to the travails of touring with Green River, this was a breeze.

"We played our asses off no matter what," says Mark Arm. "We did a show in Lexington, Kentucky, and we played in front of six people—maybe 10 including the staff. They paid us in cigarettes and soda pop. No money raised! A six-pack of Pepsi! Thank you!"

The merriment factor was heightened by the presence of a figure who would loom large in Mudhoney's story during the coming years. Bob Whittaker was the son of mountaineer Jim, the first American to climb Mount Everest; though ostensibly onboard as roadie-cum-tour manager, he chose not to soil his hands with much of what traditionally passes for roadie-ing or tour management. When it came to mundane tasks like stringing guitars or running a PA, Whittaker was clueless. Nor was he about to indulge any fantasies the band may have harbored about rock-star pampering.

"Bob would say stuff like, 'You know what your amp looks like, you fuckin' carry it!'" says Turner. "But he was good at meeting people and finding us places to stay."

Something of a local celebrity, thanks both to his illustrious family heritage and his graffiti-strewn punk-rock party house in West Seattle, Whittaker had just dropped out of Evergreen College and was working as a restaurant cook in the evenings. During the day he was at Sub Pop on the phone, haranguing record shops and radio stations.

"I didn't know what I was doing," says Whittaker, "but I think Bruce and Jon were just keen on my boisterous personality. I got a couple of tiny checks from them, so I was actually a paid employee at some point. Then Mark had said, 'Do you wanna come on the road with us?' Basically to sell merchandise and help out. I jumped at the chance: see the world in a crappy van with four stinky, zit-faced guys? Oh yeah, sounds amazing."

With his eruption of blond curly hair adding to an already formidable physical stature, Whittaker's exuberance amply compensated for his lack of technical knowledge. He certainly helped cement the tight social bond that was forming between the four band members, two of whom had never met until Mudhoney's first rehearsal.

"I didn't know Bob—I knew of Bob," says Matt Lukin. "In fact, I was quite excited. 'That guy's coming on tour with us?! That guy's a maniac; I want to get to know that guy!' We all became good friends. We had a good sense of humor and we could laugh at each other. There wasn't an official singer in the band, so no one had too huge of an ego!"

Whittaker came home with a few bucks in his pocket and a big decision to make. The band was due back on the road in just over a week. He'd asked Sub Pop if he could do the Mudhoney tour and then have his job back, but Pavitt and Poneman said no, they wanted to keep him at the office full-time. Whittaker elected to join the traveling circus—only to realize he didn't have enough money to pay his rent. When Mudhoney had divided up the proceeds from that debut tour, they included Whittaker as an equal, but $10 was still only $10.

"I immediately sold my Elan skis for about a hundred bucks," says Whittaker. "So the joke is that I turned my back on my family's outdoor history—and I invented grunge!"

With Whittaker firmly embedded, on November 11, the band played Seattle's Union Station, the first night of a two-week tour supporting Sonic Youth down the West Coast through Oregon and California, and then across Arizona and into Texas. Sonic Youth had just released *Daydream Nation*, their double-album masterpiece, a visceral elegy to the underground rock community that the band were soon to transcend by signing to a major label—a record deal that would eventually have repercussions way beyond the individuals concerned.

For Sonic Youth, the tour was the beginning of the end of their age of innocence. Mudhoney, on the other hand, were like schoolkids unleashed on permanent vacation. Prior to the tour, Mark Arm quit his job at Muzak—"I didn't have to work another day job for over 10 years"*—much to the envy and amazement of his musician colleagues. Amused at Mudhoney's drunken high-jinks and relishing the opportunity to see them play every night, Thurston Moore found poignancy in the contrast between the groups' respective situations.

"To this day they're probably the most fun-loving band I've ever toured with," he says. "They loved what they were doing so much. They made each other laugh all the time. They would show up at the clubs, and we would be there—and wherever we were in our head space, be it dour or whatever, they would just show up laughing. Spilling out of their van, wrestling each other. They were just like a gang who'd found

* *Grunge Is Dead*, 181.

this thing and it was brilliant. I liked Dan Peters a lot. His sense of humor was very dry; he seemed very grounded. One of those people who was unflappable. Like all he needed was a good day's work and a beer and a cigarette. Real working-class bliss. I always loved that about him."

Dan had been laid off from his job as a motorcycle courier several weeks prior to the Berlin Independence Days trip, after his shoulder was damaged in an attack by a U-District street gang. At 21, he was now on the brink of realizing his life's dream of becoming a professional musician. He had no expectations of getting rich, but making a living playing drums seemed suddenly possible. And it had happened without any apparent effort or planning on the band's part.

"The fact that we were able to have a tour booked, travel around the country playing shows, be it to nobody or to 10 people, was crazy," says Peters. "Knowing we'd got picked to do a tour with Sonic Youth—who to us were rock stars—to meet them and have them take the band on was amazing. Every show was a gas. When you're playing with them, you're playing to a sold-out venue. So that was a kick in the pants for us. We just had a blast, partying, it couldn't get any better. It felt like everything I'd ever worked for was being vindicated."

Mudhoney's mini-album, *Superfuzz Bigmuff*, came out at the very end of the debut tour, after the usual Sub Pop delays that had already become a tradition. So keen were the band to share the fruits of their labors that they had handed out cassettes to reward the few people who'd shown up for the gig in Lexington. But any feelings of irritation vanished as audiences on the Sonic Youth tour began to respond to material they were familiar with.

Produced and mixed by Jack Endino in seven days during the summer, the six-song record served notice that the debut 45 was no fluke and, indeed, that Mudhoney were not wholly defined by primevally lo-fidelity sonics. The upgrade from Reciprocal's old eight-track tape machine, on which the debut single was recorded, to a newly purchased 16-track helped maximize the nuances, as well as the power that the band already wielded.

While attention had been drawn to the single's phenomenally distressed guitar textures—partly a consequence, says Arm, of the sheer saturation of sound on the eight-track tape—the mini-LP had a much clearer palette, much wider scope, and emphasized the contributions of all four members—in particular the rhythm section, who benefited from Endino's commitment to representing a band's engine room. As he once stated: "I like the low end on my records to have shape, rather than just being a wash of sound. I like the low end to be this machine that rolls over you and just crushes you."* From the moment Lukin and Peters arrive on opening track "Need," busting in upon a notably distortion-free guitar and vocal intro, Mudhoney's crushing credentials were established.

Part of *Superfuzz Bigmuff*'s impact was down to its format, with less chance of momentum sagging over six tracks. But the sheer power of the songs could probably have sustained some filler.

Contrary to conventional wisdom that suggests rock records load their strongest material into the front half, *Superfuzz* holds its aces until side two: "No One Has," with Peters' pummelling floor-tom switchback torque and Arm's lacerating screams; the lulling tension, build, and release of "If I Think;" and the epic "In'n'out of Grace," prefaced by a sound sample from Roger Corman's outlaw biker movie, *The Wild Angels*, and featuring a drum-and-bass breakdown, a deranged out-of-phase twin guitar solo, and one of the all-time great double—or is it single?—entendre lyrics: "Oh God, how I love to hate/Sliding in and out of grace." Built from a riff that Lukin brought to one of the band's first practices, "In'n'out of Grace" managed to simultaneously evoke Blue Cheer and The Butthole Surfers as a ready-made set-closer, affording equal scope for the band's contrasting/complementary magnesium-flare vehemence offset by unselfconscious goofability. Whether in the flesh or on record, the response was the same: inevitable submission.

"*Superfuzz Bigmuff* hit the mark," says Thuston Moore. "It was Mudhoney's *Never Mind the Bollocks* . . . like six seven-inch singles on an LP record."

* "Jack's Juggernaut" by Adam Tepedelen, *The Rocket*, June 1992, 29; quoted in *This Ain't the Summer of Love*, 248.

Equally important in creating its definitive aura were the title and artwork. Naming their record after two distortion boxes was just as much a respectful acknowledgment of inspiration as any musical homage. Both introduced in the late sixties, the SuperFuzz and the Big Muff were adopted by rock's premier division guitarists—the former most notably used by Pete Townshend, the latter by David Gilmour—but had long since fallen out of fashion by the mid-eighties and, as a result, were cheap but only rarely available.

Mudhoney's endorsement was certainly an act of retro-fetishism (that the title also carried a whiff of sexual innuendo was a bonus), but their association with the boxes ran deep and originally came about quite by accident. Way back in his days as a Ducky Boy, Steve Turner had got talking to a colleague named Jerry at the restaurant he worked in, who was also an ex-member of Vancouver hardcore band Bludgeoned Pigs. Jerry was interested in the budding guitarist's equipment; Steve told him he played a Peavey with a Sunn amplifier but couldn't get the guitar to sound like any of his favorite punk records.

"And what about your distortion box?" asked Jerry. Turner had never heard of distortion boxes.

"The next day [Jerry] came to work with a smile on his face and handed me a SuperFuzz and told me to plug this thing in," says Steve. "And it was literally life-changing! Oh, *that's* how they get that guitar sound! That got me into old fuzzboxes. You could get them for $5 in downtown Seattle. The Big Muff, I discovered that a little bit later, probably just before Mudhoney started. I was living in Bellingham—I'd heard of them being really cool and some shop had a pile of them on sale out on the floor, literally a stack of Big Muffs. I got one for $25. So on *Superfuzz Bigmuff* I used the Big Muff, Mark used the SuperFuzz. The Big Muff has gnarlier tones, and the SuperFuzz is . . . fuzzier."

Specifically crediting Arm and Turner with their respective fuzz weapons, *Superfuzz Bigmuff*'s artwork was the record's final stroke of genius. The photograph of Arm and Turner was taken by Charles Peterson at the Central Tavern show on August 23, 1988, one of many defining images he shot that night. The typography is an Ed Fotheringham woodcut—the letters appear to be crushed together, just like the two figures in the picture. Clearly mindful of archetypal late sixties covers like the debut 13th Floor Elevators album or Blue Cheer's *Vincebus Eruptum*, the design concept was Peterson's own.

"The Central is like any sort of bar venue," Peterson says. "The stage is knee-height and there were 100 people there, maybe 150 tops. So I believe that shot was when they come out of the drum bit in 'In'n'out of Grace' and fall into each other. I wanted the image to be something that captured the energy but was somewhat abstract: that wasn't just Mark or Steve screaming into the microphone, or a full band shot where you had to get every member in the photo. I wanted to be a little more ambiguous. You don't see either of their faces; it's just hair and beads. And what are they doing? Wrestling? Embracing each other? It's very home-made, but I like that aspect to it."

An epochal impact of hair, beads, and vintage riffology, *Superfuzz Bigmuff* both looked and sounded like some long-lost relic from a mythical psychedelic-punk era, where good times were guaranteed and nobody was afraid to rock out. In fact, the only possible inference to be drawn from this record was that rocking out could be an act of revolution. You could actually identify the spark of rebellion in the record's grooves: the point where Peter Fonda's *Wild Angels* dialogue—"We wanna be free! To do what we wanna do! We wanna be free to ride! We wanna be free to ride our machines without being hassled by the man! And we wanna get loaded! Yeah!"—is cut short by the opening power chords of "In'n'out of Grace," crashing one by one like the Lord's commandments at the feet of Moses on Mount Sinai.

Aware of this music's potential to move hearts and blow minds, Bruce Pavitt and Jonathan Poneman realized they needed to export it. They made arguably the smartest decision in the history of Sub Pop when they added "Touch Me I'm Sick" to the European version of *Superfuzz Bigmuff* and made it the opening track. Then they made sure John Peel got a copy of the record, also sending the legendary DJ a copy of *Sub Pop 200*: a grandiosely packaged vinyl box set including Mudhoney, Soundgarden, Tad, Nirvana, The Fluid, Fastbacks, et. al, whereby Sub Pop explicitly identified itself as custodian of the Seattle scene.

Not only did Peel begin playing the records on his influential BBC Radio 1 show, but, writing in *The Observer* at the beginning of 1989, he declared: "It is going to take something special to stop *Sub Pop 200* being the set of recordings by which others are judged for some time to come . . . Mudhoney and Soundgarden tour this year. The distant roar is the sound of queues forming."*

Less than six months later, Mudhoney caused a friendly riot in London.

* *The Olivetti Chronicles* by John Peel (Bantam, 2008), 394.

5

Our Future of Fun

In 1989, *Money* magazine declared Seattle the "Best Place to Live" in a survey of 300 U.S. cities. The local economy was bubbling nicely once more, almost 20 years after the Boeing bust. The aviation giant, still the area's biggest employer—its staff had included both Mark Arm's father and Steve Turner's mother—was enjoying a resurgence, with record orders for its 757 and 767 passenger aircraft. In nearby Redmond, computer software producer Microsoft was on its way to becoming the world's biggest corporation and its influence was bringing other high-tech companies to the Eastside suburbs. The previous year, Washington state bucked the national trend and posted a trade surplus. Meanwhile, a local coffee retailer called Starbucks had just begun expanding operations beyond Seattle.

The reaction of some locals to *Money*'s accolade was negative. "Did they do that to us?" complained veteran *Seattle Times* columnist Emmett Watson, who for decades had criticized the malign impact upon the city's character of high-profile urban renewal projects and the influx of outsiders. "It frightens me and appals me that everybody thinks they're coming to paradise. After you come here, you still have the problems of paying off your credit cards and moping about the schools and getting stuck in the traffic jams."* And he hadn't even mentioned the weather.

One newcomer to Seattle that year was Megan Jasper, originally from Northampton, Massachusetts, who noted the developments both on the city's skyline and in its vibrant young music community. For all its great music, her native East Coast was still hurting from the economic recession, and she was impressed by how many young people were setting up music businesses—people like Nils Bernstein, who opened his own record store, Rebellious Jukebox, in late 1989, aged 20, doubtless inspired by relative veterans Bruce Pavitt and Jonathan Poneman.

Having previously met Pavitt on a visit to Seattle in March 1989, while selling merchandise on tour for her friends Dinosaur Jr, Megan went to Sub Pop for a job. Sat behind the red main reception desk at Sub Pop's office on the 11th floor of the Terminal Sales Building, bossing the switchboard and greeting visitors, it didn't take long for her to sense which band was the most valued.

"It was different when Mudhoney came in," she says. "They were the flagship band. So many people have this notion that it was Nirvana at that time. And it wasn't—although what Nirvana did was super-exciting; it was Mudhoney. Sub Pop was always referred to as the house that Mudhoney built. So when those guys came in, they were the priority, no matter what was happening. Bruce and Jon stopped what they were doing to make sure those guys had whatever it was that they needed. There was an understanding that it was really important for them to be able to accomplish whatever they were doing, whether it was a tour or a new record or money for a studio session—because that was Sub Pop's future."

Mudhoney had returned from their European tour in May with a greatly enhanced reputation, as well as many hair-raising tales—not just of the riot in London, though it certainly brought the final leg of the tour to a suitably hysterical conclusion. The band had been on the road

* "*Money* Magazine Places Seattle Top Place to Live Among 300 Cities" by Rory Marshall, Associated Press, August 24, 1989.

for nine weeks; in retrospect, it was an insanely long itinerary that at various times had driven each member mad.

"We were pushing it pretty hard," says Steve Turner. "After that tour, we did know one thing: a nine-week tour was too long for us. By the end we were scrambled and beat, and we made a rule: OK, the most we can do is six weeks. It was between week six and week seven that we lost our minds. We were punch drunk."

The trip began on March 17, 1989, on an all-time high: Mark Arm walking directly from the dressing room onto the stage at Newcastle's Riverside club and then onto the upstretched arms of the audience: "The crowd was packed so tight, I thought, 'I'm going to run on top of these people'—not to hurt them, just to be propped up, just like that photo of Iggy at the Cincinnati Pop Festival. That was my goal for that show—and it was met!"

What made the gesture so impressive was that Mudhoney were not even the headline act: once again the band were opening for Sonic Youth, now on a seven-date UK tour. At this particular gig, however, Mudhoney were as much an attraction as the headliners; Newcastle was the British public's first taste of Seattle rock and anticipation levels had hit red. In addition to John Peel playing Sub Pop records on a nightly basis, the label's latest risky business strategy had paid dividends.

Having grown up in the relative cultural isolation of the Midwest, both Pavitt and Poneman were fans of the UK music press. Pavitt would travel to Reckless Records in downtown Chicago and Poneman to Boogie Records in Toledo's Westgate Village Shopping Center, where they pored over the month-old copies of *Melody Maker, New Musical Express*, and *Sounds*, marveling not only that three magazines were covering all the happening music every week but that each did so with a passion and irreverence that chimed with their own sensibilities.

Thus, some 10 years later, when Anton Brookes, the publicist at Sub Pop's UK distributor, asked if the label might pay for a *Melody Maker* journalist to fly to Seattle in exchange for a Mudhoney cover story and a followup piece on the scene in general, Jonathan Poneman felt a sudden emotional pull back to the racks of Boogie. Of course, Sub Pop had no money—but if they could somehow make it happen then the potential benefits were considerable. The great historical precedent was Jimi Hendrix, who had left Seattle unknown, made his mark in London, and was eventually imported back to the U.S. as a star. Could Sub Pop make something similar happen with one of their scuzzy punk rock bands?

"We hadn't really thought in terms of national designs," says Poneman, "but rather, 'What would make a Mudhoney record sell 10,000 copies in Seattle?' And Seattle at the time was a city that is impressed if something's accepted by New York—*Woooh*! And London?! *Woah*! So we were thinking, if we can get the British music press writing favorably about Mudhoney . . . There was something like 250 in our music community, and we were trying to expand that and reach people who we thought would dig this music if they could get around certain preconceptions. We were thinking of this from a pure sales and marketing perspective. The mountain was going to come to Mohammed. We knew the music was potent and that people would dig it, but so often there are certain cultural arbiters—and at the time, it was all about the British music press."

Pavitt and Poneman had visions of a future so at variance with the present that no one else involved really took it seriously. Certainly, Mudhoney were bemused when *Melody Maker* writer Jerry Thackeray—who worked under the alias Everett True—arrived in Seattle along with photographer Andrew Catlin and was treated like visiting royalty by Sub Pop. A blur of gigs, interviews, and many, many beers later, True returned home and realized he needed more material. So he got on the phone for Pavitt and Poneman to feed him their very droll, highly mythologized, definitely label-specific version of the Seattle scene. *Melody Maker* ran it word for word—and the readers bought it.

"I remember this drunk British guy hanging round Seattle for a while," says Mark Arm. "It was a crafty move on Bruce and Jonathan's part, because nobody else would have done that, no other label of that size. They would have just thought, 'That's a ridiculous waste of money.' And it turned out to work for Sub Pop."

Mudhoney arrived in the UK a week after True's interview had graced the center pages of *Melody Maker*. In contrast to the subsequent week's article, which ramped up the hyperbole and spun a vision of

Seattle as a kind of hard-rockin' Brigadoon, where men were men and so were women, the Mudhoney piece was a relatively thoughtful analysis of the band's roots, hinting at the blend of individual characters who balanced caustic wit—Mark Arm: "We say fuck the kids! Except the kids who buy our records. Then they're fucking themselves."—with plain-spoken logic about their motivations.

" [As a kid] I decided I had to look for what I wanted to hear, instead of accepting what was given to me," said Arm. "I had this sound in my head that was a lot louder and a lot noisier than anything I'd ever heard . . . Mudhoney is the closest anyone has yet come to that sound."*

More than any glib stereotypes or overheated theories, it was curiosity about evidently normal guys making extraordinary music that brought people to see Mudhoney on their first UK tour. The gigs were fierce fun for band and audience alike, and a fillip for Sonic Youth, by then weary after almost five months on the road.

"Those shows were a blast," says Thurston Moore. "That was where people were saying, 'What is going on with Sub Pop?' A lot of people saw this as something that's gonna be explosive, and that if anybody was gonna burst out of the scene, it's going to be Mudhoney. As opposed to Nirvana, which came later."

After the Sonic Youth support dates finished in London, with both bands joining forces for a version of The Stooges' "I Wanna Be Your Dog," Mudhoney played their first UK headline gig at The Greyhound, a legendary sweatbox dive on the Fulham Palace Road, where Mark mock-scolded the excited stage divers ("We're tired of all you overactive young people. Let's get some old people in the front row"**). The band then crossed the English Channel for two more shows with Sonic Youth in Belgium and Holland.

Afterwards, however, things began to go awry. Supporting their underground rock-star friends meant guaranteed audiences and no

* "Mudhoney: Sub Pop, Sub Normal, Subversion" by Everett True, *Melody Maker*, March 11, 1989.

** *Mudhoney Tourbook: 1989*, www.ocf.berkeley.edu/~ptn/mudhoney/tourbook/1989.html

obligation to play for longer than 40 minutes. But as Mudhoney undertook their own gigs—beginning in Germany where audiences typically expected a headline band to play for 90 minutes—the realization dawned that they simply didn't have enough material.

"Our whole repertoire was maybe 12 songs," says Arm. "In Frankfurt, there was no other band. We were done with our 40 minutes and people were like, 'Play more!'"

Koblenz was worse: the route to and from the stage was through the audience, who refused to let the band leave. As a result, some songs were repeated, "In'n'out of Grace" was ludicrously extended and a cover version of Spacemen 3's recent single, "Revolution," was attempted for the first time.

A mere three weeks into the tour, it all got a bit too much for Mark Arm.

In Hamburg, Steve Turner was walking through a parking lot when he tripped and impaled his hand on a broken car aerial. By the time he was discharged from the hospital with a large roll of gauze round his hand, it didn't look as if they would be able to make the next gig—another Sonic Youth support, in Nijmegen, just over the border into Holland.

As tour manager-cum-soundman Erik Mans thrashed the van across Germany, someone cracked open a bottle of vodka, which Arm, Lukin, and Peters demolished in swift order. Much to their surprise, Mans got them to the gig 10 minutes before they were due to play. They set up and rushed on, though Turner could only play sitting down.

For any number of (possibly valid) reasons, the audience greeted them blankly. In his compromised state, however, Arm considered this reaction an affront.

"It was an arrogance of youth sort of thing, but after playing all these shows in the UK where we would go on and people would go crazy, and were familiar with the band, all of a sudden we're in Holland with a very stoic audience who had probably never heard of us and were just waiting for Sonic Youth—God knows what they were thinking, because they were just standing there with their arms crossed. If I wasn't that drunk, it probably wouldn't have been anything: 'OK, that's how they do it here.' But I took it personally! I ran into the crowd and threw some waterlogged punches. People were just like: 'That's weird, what's that guy doing?' Then I stormed off. I had a mini-meltdown."

It got worse. Having expected the others to follow his lead, from backstage Arm could hear the rest of the band carrying on without him. Eventually, he slunk back onstage and finished the set.

Meanwhile, from side of stage, Thurston Moore was wondering why Turner was sat on a chair. "I presumed he'd broken his leg. There was always shenanigans. They liked to get really, really *drunk*. I said, 'What's with you guys?!'"

Thereafter the itinerary meandered through Austria, Italy, France, Switzerland, back to Germany, back to Holland, back to Germany, back to Holland yet again ("Our booking agent was Dutch," explains Arm), before returning to the UK for one final week.

The lowest low was in Paris, where, after playing through dilapidated equipment at the Gibus club, the gig's promoters left them outside a building with a key and no explanation. It might once have been a hotel, but the place was now quite clearly an abandoned squat. In the shared bathroom, the toilet bowls had been trashed—it was literally a shithole, with human feces smeared on the walls.

Arm and Turner's room wasn't much better. "It stank of urine," says Mark. "We slept in our clothes, on top of the bed, with the windows open."

In the adjacent room, Lukin and Peters had also opened their window. Leaning outside, they saw two streams of water issuing from next door. Arm and Turner were peeing out of the window because they couldn't face the prospect of visiting the bathroom.

At least in the UK, the insanity was as it should be, mostly attributable to the overamped audiences. The "friendly riot" at the London School of Oriental and African Studies was just the most extreme example. Three days later, after being supported by Soundgarden for a second (and last) time, Mudhoney played the Knights club in Chester.

Fan recordings and video footage from Chester show just how nonchalantly powerful the band had become. During the climax to "In'n'out of Grace," Arm began thanking the audience while processing his voice through echo and delay:

> Thank you, thank you, we love you. Thank you, thank you, thank you, you're the best audience ever. You're beautiful. Thank you . . .

As far as the audience was concerned, the emotion was real and reciprocal. People loved Mudhoney for their utterly vehement performance while appearing so disarmingly casual. No wonder Leila Kassir, the 18-year-old girl who watched the SOAS gig sat on top of the PA stack, would see the band upwards of 10 times over the next couple of years.

"Mudhoney were very charismatic and also very accessible," she says. "Although they didn't take a lot of things very seriously—themselves especially—they were definitely serious about the music. I think that's what came across: that they loved what they were doing, but they weren't all pretentious or up themselves; they were very natural. Quite earthy, and quite hilarious. They were larger than life."

* * *

Three weeks after Mudhoney arrived home from Europe, it became apparent that Sub Pop's gamble in bringing the mountain to Mohammed was paying off. In Seattle, their grand plans had hitherto provoked skepticism. Indeed, the scene's default inferiority complex meant its protagonists were unaccustomed to thinking big, instinctively frowning upon anything that could be construed as aspirational.

So it was that booking the 1,400-capacity Moore Theatre for a Sub Pop showcase on Friday June 9, 1989, seemed ridiculous—not least to the bands due to play the so-called Lame Fest. "I remember thinking Jon and Bruce were crazy for booking the Moore," says Mark Arm. "Because local bands never played the Moore. It was too big."

Although he had actually played the venerable auditorium with Green River, it was only as the opening act to The Dead Kennedys. To Arm, despite all the acclaim Mudhoney had received overseas, the prospect of an equivalent response on his own doorstep did not quite compute. Such opinion wasn't confined to the local musicians. The theatre's management also harboured low expectations, hiring fewer stage security guards than usual.

"They said, 'We're not expecting a whole lot of people tonight,'" says Bruce Pavitt. "It sold out. People went crazy."

With equal parts irony and self-aggrandisement, Sub Pop's bill posters proclaimed: "Seattle's lamest bands in a one-night orgy of sweat and insanity." Unusually for Seattle at the time, Lame Fest was an all-ages gig, so for many members of the audience it was their first live rock show—and no ordinary show at that.

Nirvana opened up—the gig was doubling as the release party for their debut album, *Bleach*, freshly pressed and on sale in the foyer—followed by TAD. It became obvious during both bands' sets that security was unprepared for such a large and energetic crowd. By the time Mudhoney took to the stage, introduced by Ed Fotheringham as "Mudhanky," the skeleton security crew was blatantly beating up stage divers and the atmosphere had turned ugly. Mark Arm kicked a security guard in the back, while Matt Lukin poked one crew member in the backside with his bass.

In the midst of the chaos, Bruce Pavitt and Jonathan Poneman felt a mutual surge of vindication. "It was the turning point in the scene," says Pavitt. "Terry Pearson, Sonic Youth's soundman, was there, and he said: 'You guys got something going on here.' The whole place was shaking. Next day, word hit the street that the Moore had actually sold out a show of local bands. Then the local media really started taking the music a lot more seriously."

Mudhoney playing the Moore Theatre also represented personal validation for those concerned. As well as his brother Jim, both Dan Peters' parents attended, at their son's insistence—indeed, much of the surviving video footage of Lame Fest was shot by Dan's father.

"The funny thing about the footage from that show is you can see this dude trying to get up on stage, stumbling and falling—that's my brother," says Dan. "My dad was doing the filming and that's why he gets focused on. My brother had stopped drinking, he was clean and sober for a year up until that point, and then had fallen off the wagon. He didn't know Dad was there. I remember playing the show and looking down and going, 'Oh fuck, that's Jim—and my dad's filming!'"

Mark Arm would always present his parents with a copy of the band's latest record—which, in the autumn of 1989, was Mudhoney's first full-length album, hastened onto the shelves by Sub Pop a mere three months after it was taped. It's hard to imagine the finer points of, say, "You Got It (Keep It Outta My Face)," or "Here Comes Sickness," or "Dead Love" going down a bundle with the pastor at Our Redeemer Lutheran Church in Kirkland.

These three songs were all set-list fixtures during the European tour, along with several others that made a painless transition from stage to studio when the band reunited with Jack Endino at Reciprocal in July. But, just as the songs had to be stretched to pad out their live set, in the studio Mudhoney didn't exactly have a vast cache of material to draw upon.

"By Her Own Hand" was a leftover from the *Superfuzz* sessions ("I loved the break in the riff," says Arm, "but I don't think it's a super-strong song overall"). In need of a B-side for "This Gift," released as a single alongside the album, they had to resurrect "Baby Help Me Forget," the Mr. Epp song that fleetingly appeared in early Green River sets. Inevitably, given that their best material had been loaded onto *Superfuzz Bigmuff* and the band were touring almost permanently thereafter, inspiration was at a premium. One especially perfunctory new song was called "Flat out Fucked;" even the album's title, simply *Mudhoney*, smacked of a rush job.

There was some great material, but also an aura of ennui—a possible by-product of eight months on the road, according to Endino. "By then they were a much, much tighter band. If anything, they were too tight! It's almost too perfect a record, like they knew the songs too well."

Tellingly, an earlier version of "You Got It," recorded shortly prior to the European tour and released as a single in the spring, was rawer and sounded better for it.

"I think some of *Mudhoney* sounds already-been-there-done-that," says Turner. "Maybe not right at the time, but pretty quick to me it was a little one note-ish. And I think a lot of the songs are really great. I guess we didn't really push anything. But I don't know if it was our job to push anything. Really, I think part of our appeal and our Achilles' heel was the fact that we didn't try very hard. And I actually believe that should be the approach we should take. I don't necessarily believe effort makes something better. It can, but sometimes it kills the magic too. So how do you navigate through that? At that point we were going on the if-it-ain't-broke-don't-fix-it mode."

Turner's ambivalence was born out of the very narrow aspirations he'd had for Mudhoney at the outset. His one-single-left-for-posterity model seemed a long way off now. "The success we were getting, it could be argued that we should have taken it more seriously, but we sure didn't," he says. "I didn't give a shit about it. I was still going back to school soon and this would be this funny weird chapter."

Aside from "Baby Help Me Forget," only one other additional song was recorded at the album sessions—the cover version of Spacemen 3's "Revolution." It proved highly contentious.

From the prosperous Midlands town of Rugby and driven by the increasingly combative duo of Pete "Sonic Boom" Kember and Jason Pierce, Spacemen 3 evangelized a psychedelic rock pantheon with which Mudhoney had obvious kinship: The Stooges, MC5, 13th Floor Elevators, and Suicide were all directly referenced in the band's music. Spacemen 3 had also been frank in their advocacy of drugs as a route to personal enlightenment: their second album, *The Perfect Prescription*, was a vaguely conceptual set of anthems for blown minds, ending with the haunted OD hymn "Call the Doctor"; their weave of euphoria and damage reached a sensualist peak with 1989's *Playing with Fire*, where, as one critic observed, the songs were no longer merely about drugs but had in fact become drugs.* A case in point was "Revolution," a repetitive solar flare blast of guitars and drums, over which a soporific Sonic Boom declared himself "sick, so sick" of people "tryin' to tell me what I can and can't do with my life." He then exhorted his audience to "get off their arse" and "better this society—'cos it's shit."

* "God Only Knows" by Ralph Traitor, *Sounds*, March 11, 1989.

The comedic aspect of a self-professed heroin addict advising his audience that the time was right "to start thinkin' about, a little . . . revolution!" was not lost on Mudhoney. While retaining the music's incendiary aura, their version almost completely rewrote the lyrics, satirizing the narrator's perspective and lampooning the banal routine of junkie life. "I'm sooo tired, of getting up in the morning/For that long, uphill walk to the methadone clinic," Arm drawled. In the third verse, which quotes the MC5's "spiritual adviser" Brother J.C. Crawford's famous observation that "it takes five seconds of decision," Arm notes: "It takes . . . just five seconds to put a morphine suppository all the way inside." Despite their music's often profound beauty, there was always a hapless countenance to Spacemen 3, which Mudhoney exploited brutally with their take on the band's most famous song.

Nonetheless, the tomfoolery might have passed relatively unnoticed had it not been for Sub Pop's plan to release it as a split single—with Spacemen 3 in turn covering Mudhoney's "When Tomorrow Hits," the brooding highlight of the new album. By now, artistic rivalry had poisoned Kember and Pierce's relationship to the extent that they were recording songs for the next Spacemen 3 album separately; in October, they set aside their animosity just long enough to work up the Mudhoney cover. It would be the last time the pair recorded together.

Shortly afterwards, however, Sonic Boom heard Mudhoney's version of "Revolution"—and was not amused. He told Jonathan Poneman that such flippant disregard for his song's critique of the UK drug laws meant Spacemen 3 could no longer proceed with the project. The offending "Revolution" was instead released on the 12-inch edition of "This Gift." Spacemen 3's take on "When Tomorrow Hits," meanwhile, lay in the vaults as the long, agonized dispute between Kember and Pierce unraveled over the following 12 months. It eventually appeared in February 1991, on the final Spacemen 3 album, *Recurring*, occupying the demilitarized zone halfway through a segregated track sequence that had Kember's tracks grouped together in the first half and Pierce's in the second.

Unlike Sonic Youth's somewhat perfunctory galumph through "Touch Me I'm Sick," the S3's "When Tomorrow Hits" was a revelatory treatment of an already outstanding song, with bottleneck guitar intensifying the sickly blues pallor of the original—though the distracting flicker effect on Kember's vocal was a misstep, certainly compared to Arm's shattered intimation of oncoming doom: "What's easy for you, comes so hard/What you got, never got me far/There's no stopping, the end from coming." If much of *Mudhoney* was indeed "one note-ish," then here they were playing a new type of song altogether.

Had the abortive split single come to pass, one neat conceptual link between the compositions would have become apparent: "Revolution" begins with an invocation of The Stooges' "Loose," while "When Tomorrow Hits" lifts its bridge directly from "I Wanna Be Your Dog." The Mudhoney song's other act of homage, Arm insisted, was purely accidental: "It's sort of a Spacemen 3/Wire/Stooges song. You see, that bridge was the only thing in writing the song that was intentional, had to be someone else's. Then, as the song progressed and the ending came in where we just hit the chords really hard, it was like, 'Oh man, it's 'Lowdown' by Wire!'"

That Mudhoney could possibly have believed their treatment of "Revolution" would be sanctioned by its composer was a revealing glimpse into their capacity to compartmentalize emotion and humor. They thought their affectionate parody would be seen for what it was, and were genuinely surprised at Kember's reaction. "You can like their music and still think they're chumps!" said Turner. "But a lot of what they do is really great, and way beyond a lot of other bands," added Arm. "Sometimes their lyrics are really beautiful too. On a poetic level."*

One other intriguing aspect of the affair did not become generally known until much later. Proving that he could at least laugh at himself, by mid-1989 Mark Arm had been using heroin for two years. He began dabbling while he was in Green River, and believes it hastened his estrangement from the other members during the band's final few months. As to why such an obviously intelligent man began sliding toward a well-signposted dead end, he provides no new insights:

* "Mud, Sweat & Beers" by Keith Cameron, *Sounds*, November 18, 1989.

"I thought I could handle doing it at weekends. No one starts doing heroin thinking they'll become a junkie. It certainly wasn't a case of trying to emulate my heroes. It had probably more to do with curiosity and the people I was hanging around with. It wasn't like some jazz musicians would claim, 'If I do heroin, I'll play like Charlie Parker!' I didn't think that for a moment."

Initially, Arm was able to treat heroin just as he would MDA or LSD—avenues he'd take for a weekend blowout. A line was crossed, however, when he returned home from Mudhoney's nine-week European tour and his live-in girlfriend told him she'd been doing heroin every day. "I was just like, '*Holy shit*.' I knew what that meant."*

What kept his "hobby" manageable, at least at first, was the fact that no one else in the band shared it and that they were kept almost constantly busy. "In fact, I'm lucky they totally looked down upon it and wouldn't stand for me doing it on the road. So every time we went on tour I would have to stop doing it. The first couple of days of a tour, or the first week, I would not feel so great. I'm sure it was a major source of tension with the other guys."

Of the other members of Mudhoney, only Dan had experience of drug use in his family and he was the only one who would try to talk to Mark about it. Steve, his closest friend in the band, didn't feel qualified, reasoning that Mark was old enough and smart enough to make his own decisions—indeed, that it was his right to fuck himself up if that's what he wanted to do.

"We did not talk about Mark's drugs," says Turner. "I know he would dabble occasionally on tour—he had drug buddies in New York, I know he got into trouble there—but for the most part he wouldn't. I mean, I was with him all the time. We'd room together or we'd be in the van. Usually we'd start off a U.S. tour and we'd throw him in the back of the van and drive off. He'd sleep all the way to Minneapolis and then he'd get better."

"The first couple of days he'd be a little, uh, *irritable*," says Lukin. "But after that he'd be great, hanging out and drinking beer with us.

* *Grunge Is Dead*, 403.

I always wondered how he pulled that off. 'Cos a lot of other junkies can't do that."

Arm's ability to keep a grip on the physical depredations of heroin meant his drug use wasn't an issue—for now. Nonetheless, it's possible that his caustic refit of "Revolution" was part of an internal conversation that had yet to be resolved.

"The Spacemen 3 cover was Mark's sense of humor," says Ed Fotheringham. "But I think that's how he felt about drug addiction: it wasn't a badge of honor—it's stupid."

Viewed in this context, the mood of self-loathing that hangs over much of Mudhoney's early material, with its recurring images of dogs, sickness, and death, has extra resonance. Throw in the archetypal male agonies of love—be it unrequited, or ill-starred—then stand well back.

Arm once admitted: "I made some really stupid choices concerning women in my twenties. I romanticized fragile, unstable, and even downright insane personalities. I blame the song 'Hospital' by The Modern Lovers."* An appropriately clinical account of an obsessive relationship, Jonathan Richman's "Hospital" is narrated from the perspective of a man whose life is so lacking in sweetness he spends his days in bakeries, and who is fatally in love with a woman whose destructive tendencies have landed her in hospital. He says he can't stand what she does, but is doomed to always wait for her.

Little wonder then that Arm's screams were unleashed with such conviction, or that his rendering of, say, "No One Has" felt dragged from a desperate place, his voice caught between an indictment and a wounded howl of hurt. Lyrics such as "I've been so close to no way out/I don't lock the door no more," or, "Must've lost my mind at least a million times/Still ain't sure what I'm looking for," were part of that same, doubtless conflicted, internal conversation.

"Well, that's the mystery, right?" chuckles Arm. "You don't know what it is. There's maybe a certain emptiness, and you don't know

* "Interview with Thrasher Online" by Greg Smith, February 2001; quoted in *Mudhoney Articles & Interviews*, www.ocf.berkeley.edu/~ptn/mudhoney/articles/index.html

anyone who's been able to fill it . . . It's certainly not a Jesus-sized hole in your heart! No one you know has successfully managed to figure it out."

This feral undertow to Mudhoney's lecherous punk-rock splat offensive lent it deeper impact. It's also one reason for the band's enduring appeal. A song like "Here Comes Sickness" is played for maximum shlock value—Arm growling, "All the neighborhood dogs sniffin' at her crotch," while Turner's Big Muff slobbers in response—but the sheer relish of the delivery lends it transcendent qualities, or at least up to a point. Alternatively, it may be a dare to see how much continuous noise the lead guitarist can make.

"That song is not based in any kind of reality, in terms of anything," says Arm. "In the Seventies, listening to rock radio, there's all these shitty songs about . . . girls! And cars! So punk rock was a breath of fresh air. But after a while, it's like, Y'know, this is the essence of it: rock'n'roll *is* girls and cars. So I guess 'Here Comes Sickness' was just another attempt at getting back to songs about girls and cars! Also, hardcore wasn't all smart older people like The Dead Kennedys or Really Red or Crass—a lot of times it was 17-year-old kids with no experience of the world just parroting stupid political things that they picked up from *Maximum Rock'n'Roll.* So you'd go and listen to a Sonics record instead."

One week into a U.S. tour to promote the self-titled album was an interesting time to meet Mudhoney. Despite flu (Mark), tummy troubles (Matt), and fatigue (everyone), the intensity of their performances over three nights in Hoboken, Washington, D.C., and New York was remarkable. Only an elemental urge to rock could have sustained them through the discomfort that touring on a shoestring entailed, driving for 10 hours between gigs in a cramped van and then afterwards having to ask favors from fellow bands or fans in order to get a place to sleep for the night. In D.C., they crashed at the communal house of Positive Force, a group of radical activists with links to the city's hardcore punk scene. In observance of Positive Force's strict straight-edge policy, a disgruntled Lukin had to finish his beer on the pavement outside.

It was noted that Soundgarden—who only six months earlier had been Mudhoney's support band—now had a tour bus with proper beds and all mod cons. Though everyone professed themselves happy enough, there was a sense that this "mellow . . . short-term project" was turning into something no one could have foreseen. In the basement of the Rapp Arts Center, the venue for that night's Halloween gig in New York, Mark was ruminating a while on the whys and wherefores of motivation, and no doubt mindful of a tour schedule that stretched out for the next five months, when he suddenly snapped: "Aw, we'll probably get stuck in this rut and have no way out. Sign to a major label, put out bad music, but what the hell?! We don't have anything else to fall back on except Matt's carpentry. And that's not gonna feed all of us."*

Little did he know how prescient a statement that would prove to be.

⋆ ⋆ ⋆

On December 3, 1989, Mudhoney played to their biggest audience thus far—1,500 people at The Astoria in London, as Sub Pop staged a UK version of Lame Fest featuring the same three bands that had rocked the Moore Theatre six months earlier. The running order was the same too—Nirvana and TAD tossed a coin to see who would open, and Nirvana lost—much to Kurt Cobain's disgruntlement. Again, there was no question which band would headline. Mudhoney packed the same venue again the next day, this time without their Sub Pop brethren, as the culmination of another wildly successful UK tour.

Of the Sub Pop bands, however, it was Nirvana whose performance at Lame Fest UK turned heads, inasmuch as it highlighted just how potent a proposition they had become—in contrast to the stiff, nervous out-of-towners who had so singularly unimpressed Bruce Pavitt at The Central Tavern 18 months previously. "Nirvana stole the show [at Lame Fest UK] simply because, up until that point, they were the perennial opening act," said Pavitt. "They were Mudhoney's little brother."**

⋆ "Mud, Sweat & Beers" by Keith Cameron, *Sounds*, November 18, 1989.

⋆⋆"Nirvana vs. Mudhoney" by Alex Scordelis, www.*Papermag.com*, November 2012.

Cobain studied his labelmates avidly, Mark Arm in particular: the litany of Mudhoney's influence, conscious or otherwise, on Nirvana most obviously includes the proximity of the "Negative Creep" lyric ("Daddy's little girl ain't a girl no more") to "Sweet Young Thing Ain't Sweet No More," as well as the subsequent adoption of the Fang cover "The Money Will Roll Right In."

Not that Cobain was ever especially bashful about it. At the Moore Theatre Lame Fest, Kurt Danielson was next to Cobain during Mudhoney's set and watched him pogoing along. "It was the first time I heard him say, 'I wish more bands played music you could pogo to. I'm sick of this slow, heavy shit. I like energetic music, music you can slam dance to.' It was clear to me that Kurt looked up to Mark," says Danielson.

Certainly, on the night of Lame Fest UK, Cobain was eager to give Mudhoney their due. When asked after the gig to offer some *fin de siècle* perspective on the eighties by nominating his single of the decade, he didn't even blink before answering, "Definitely 'Touch Me I'm Sick,' by Mudhoney."

The new decade began with Mudhoney paying some respects of their own. In January 1990 they went to Reciprocal to record the backing track for "You Make Me Die," a Thee Mighty Caesars song to which Billy Childish would later add his vocals. The collaboration had been conceived during the previous month's UK tour, when Childish's latest band, Thee Headcoats, opened for Mudhoney in Portsmouth.

Soon after the session with Jack Endino, they made their first visit to Australia, something of a spiritual home given its myriad key musical antecedents like feedtime and The Scientists. As well as a post—Birthday Party seam of psychedelic weirdness, the island continent's underground rock scene had a pronounced Detroit accent, embodied by Deniz Tek, a native of Ann Arbor who relocated to Sydney in the early Seventies and formed the legendary Australian punk band Radio Birdman (named after a misheard Stooges lyric). Tek subsequently played in New Race, featuring Birdman's Rob Younger and Warwick Gilbert alongside The Stooges' Ron Asheton and MC5 drummer Dennis Thompson. Tek later returned to America where he became a surgeon in the U.S.

Marines, but the Michigan influence endured in the Oz rock scene via a string of Ig-noble bands like The Celibate Rifles, Eastern Dark, Seminal Rats, et. al.

So Mudhoney were always likely to be welcomed Down Under. The prohibitive distances between cities dictated a different touring regimen with the band based in one of the large metropolitan hubs for multiple days at a time, a far more sociable routine than the norm.

"We played several shows in Sydney and several shows in Melbourne," says Mark, "and we played one-off shows in Geelong and Canberra and Wollongong and Newcastle, and went up to Brisbane and down to Adelaide. But we hung out in Melbourne and Sydney for a week at a time. It's not like being on tour; it's like being on vacation and playing shows here and there. And you actually get to know people and hang out with them. By this time feedtime had broken up, but we met Tom, the drummer from feedtime, and we met Boris and James Baker who were in The Scientists at different times, and also in The Beasts of Bourbon. We met Spencer Jones [Beasts of Bourbon] then. It was very cool. It was a mutual exchange."

The leisurely schedule even permitted a recording session, at Sydney's Electric Avenue studio in early March, where Celibate Rifles guitarist Kent Steedman produced two new songs, "You're Gone" and "Thorn." Along with "You Make Me Die," they would comprise a new Mudhoney 12-inch single.

With the tail end of Australia's summer providing clement weather, as well as the hospitality of their appreciative hosts, Mudhoney's Antipodean debut couldn't have been better. "Australians like to drink a lot of beer," says Steve. "It worked out pretty good for us down there!"

In just two years of existence, Mudhoney had released one full album and one mini-LP, plus a clutch of singles, touring across the U.S., Europe, and Australia to huge acclaim. In the UK, they were music press cover stars. To some of their old friends in Seattle, this was hard to comprehend.

Since the end of Green River, Mark Arm hadn't seen much of Jeff Ament or Stone Gossard. Mudhoney's fourth ever gig had taken place at The Alamo, a Mexican eaterie in Pioneer Square where bands set up on a tiny stage between the entrance and the wall, with their backs to a window that faced onto the street.

"I remember turning around and seeing Stone watching us through the window," says Arm. "And he was actually complimentary and excited about what we were doing, which was nice."

But although Ament and Gossard's new band got under way around the same time, the similarities ended right there. With Andrew Wood on vocals, Bruce Fairweather on guitar, and Greg Gilmore on drums, Mother Love Bone immediately capitalized on the major record label contacts Ament had made during Green River's last days and became the subject of a bidding war. They also became a paradigm for the stereotype of corporate inertia versus independent action. Although Sub Pop were perpetually skirting bankruptcy, they made stuff happen fast, as if each record might be their last. Mother Love Bone spent a year making demos. Once they finally signed to PolyGram, things moved even slower.

"In some ways it was happening as quickly for us as it was for Mudhoney—we were writing tons of songs and playing shows," says Ament. "The only difference was that their first recording they made a record out of. The major label world was super-weird—we do two songs with this producer and spend $25,000 for three days in LA. Crazy shit. I remember seeing Mudhoney at the Motorsports Garage and going, 'Oh my god, there's 2,000 fuckin' people in this place. It's amazing!' And being jealous."

By the time of that Mudhoney gig, on July 14, 1990, their biggest Seattle show thus far, the Mother Love Bone album was finally poised to come out—posthumously. Andrew Wood died on March 19, from a heroin overdose. Ament and the others were devastated, but Mother Love Bone had long since become a textbook case for how not to do business with a major record label. "Even before Andy died, the band was kinda dead," says Ament. "We spent two years making a record. We got a quarter of a million dollars, but it all went into the recording, or lawyers. The classic horrible deal. I was still working my $5 an hour job at the coffee shop. Great!"

Mudhoney, by contrast, were moving so nimbly it had begun to freak Steve Turner out. In June 1990 they played a three-night residency at The Hibernian Club, a large Irish dancehall in west London. The "You're Gone"/"Thorn"/"You Make Me Die" 12-inch single was out, and in August they were booked to play the Reading Festival, the UK's traditional end-of-summer mud-fest. For someone who had never aspired to professional musicianship, this felt very much akin to being one.

Having assured his parents more than two-and-a-half years ago that he would be taking just 12 months out from his studies to play in this new band, Steve felt obliged to belatedly make good on his promise and return to the academic life. "I always knew I was going to go back. So I started making plans to go back. It was that simple. I was never in any doubt about that. When I moved home from Bellingham, I pretty much told my parents I'm gonna take a year off school, just let me do this thing—and they were very cool about it."

But it wasn't just about pleasing his parents. The notion of being a professional musician for life didn't fit with the pure aesthetic that had shaped Turner's original vision for Mudhoney: make one single, then get out and let history discover this oddball artifact 25 years later. His cultural rebellion began in the same way that he'd indicated dissent from Green River: with a haircut. In fact, Mark and Dan would follow him to the barber's chair to break away from the now established grunge cliché, but there was also a more mundane imperative at work.

"I had to get glasses," says Turner. "On the U.S. tour for the self-titled record I remember sitting in the front seat with Dan in the van, and he could see shit I could not see *at all*. So I got horn-rimmed glasses and I just couldn't make them work with the long hair. So the hair went. Then everybody else was pretty quick to follow. Part of it must have been some kind of gang mentality. But we were sick of having so much of the press talking about long hair."

There was less harmony concerning Turner's resolve to return to school, however. Interviews around the release of the new single suggested it was an awkward subject, one that the band hadn't properly discussed or thought through. If they had, they might have realized it was best kept in private, as opposed to airing in the press—which, given Mudhoney's high profile at the time, was naturally curious. Was the band breaking up?

"Maybe. Maybe not," said Turner. "I don't know. I'm not too worried about it. That's in the future. We'll get together and do reunion shows."* They might not have said so at the time, but the others found his action at best inconvenient, or at worst selfish.

"It happened at a really weird time, when the band was probably doing its best and we were building up a lot of momentum," says Peters. "And Turner decides he wants to go back to school. We're all just like, What?? Right *now*?! I think that's Steve's way of going into self-preservation mode; he had always that fear: 'I don't wanna be in a touring band and make this my career choice.' I don't know if it was to keep at bay his feelings of not wanting to, for lack of a better term, sell out or be in a legitimate rock'n'roll band. But I don't think he realized at the time what everybody else had invested in it. I put all my eggs in my drum basket, as it were. So when it happened, I searched high and low to find another band that I could hop in with."

If anything, Lukin was even less impressed. "I felt, 'That's kinda fucked up—I don't need this guy dictating what's going to happen with my future with his little whims of going back to school.' That took some wind out of my sails."

Arm's perspective, meanwhile, was increasingly focused elsewhere. "How did I feel at the time? I was probably kinda disappointed and maybe even a little pissed off, but y'know, I don't really remember at this point. I might have thought: 'This is going pretty good, why would you do that?' I do remember Steve saying—and being pretty adamant—that a band only has three good years in it before they start to suck. Obviously, I don't think you need to follow that template. But I don't remember how it went down—I might have read it in an interview, for all I know! At this point I was starting to get pretty heavily into heroin—and this might have been a driver of why Steve felt like he might need a break. Like, 'Ahhh, this can't last!' I'm not sure how aware he was of it at the time."

"I don't think that had much to do with it, honestly," says Turner. "It was uncomfortable, of course. It certainly wasn't my scene. But I

* "Dirty Deeds Done Cheap" by Damon Wise, *Sounds*, June 30, 1990.

don't think that had anything to do with it. It was really just set in my head that I needed to go back to school."

With Lukin and Peters affronted, and Arm disgruntled but somewhat oblivious, Turner's decision to return to college would be one of the very few moments where the existence of a class divide in Mudhoney's ranks—blue-collar engine-room on one side, university-educated aesthetes on the other—was even apparent, let alone an issue. It certainly didn't impact upon their performances in the summer of 1990, which had a luminous, almost carefree quality that may or may not have been attributable to a collective realization between band and audience that the mudride might be entering the final go-round. Prior to the trip to Europe for Reading and some other festivals, the band did a run of U.S. West Coast dates with Thee Headcoats, of which the July 14 Motorsports International Garage gig was the second.

The first was at the Chambers Prairie Grange Hall, just outside Olympia, where the band set up on a tiny stage with doors off either side and with a large painting stretched across the back wall. It looked like they were playing in someone's living room, an illusion heightened whenever Bob Whittaker opened one of the doors to assess the scene—which he did after the power cut out midway through "This Gift." Of course, the technically uninterested Whittaker wasn't rushing to fix the problem, but rather to fist-pump as the crowd picked up singing duties and the band carried on regardless. Some incredible amateur video footage from this gig gives a taste of the happy mayhem that was the essence of Mudhoney during this period.*

The band's set at the Reading Festival, meanwhile, was a surreal source of joy from the moment Steve walked on stage and performed a perfect handstand as Mark declared, "Hello Glasgow!" The festival was by far the biggest audience the band had played to.

"My recollection is being onstage and seeing people to the horizon," says Arm. "It was overwhelming."

Mudhoney had a mid-afternoon slot on the opening day, below headliners The Cramps, Faith No More, and Nick Cave & The Bad

* Posted by www.*krecs.com*, see www.youtube.com/watch?y=agLbEoEQj58

Seeds, and due to appear above Jane's Addiction. There was sweet irony in this billing, given how the disastrous final Green River gig had been as openers for the cult LA band. Now, three years later, Mark Arm's new group would be looking down on Jane's Addiction.

Alas, it never came to pass. Amid rumors that their management were furious with the band's place on the schedule, Jane's Addiction didn't play, claiming that singer Perry Farrell had lost his voice. There was no chance of Mark letting this pass without comment. "Stick around for Jane's Addiction!" he quipped to the 40,000 crowd as Mudhoney took their triumphant bows after a tonsil-torturing finale of "Hate the Police."

Amid the unresolved questions over their future, Mudhoney's performance at Reading was the perfect response. If this did indeed prove to be their farewell to the UK, they couldn't have done it better.

After completing the European festival tour, the band returned home in early September. For some members, however, the future was less uncertain than others. Dan Peters was refusing to let Steve's lifestyle change dictate his chosen career path. In a few weeks time, he would be back onstage at the Motorsports International Garage—as the new drummer for Nirvana.

6

Penetrate and Pull the Strings

There is something of the eagle about Mark Arm. It's not just the famously prominent nose, though it's hard enough to get past, as Arm himself once hilariously noted: "My whole world is framed by my enormous nasal passage. I just look around and see this lump sticking out between my eyes . . . Would you live a happy life if all you saw was this?"*

But with an upright, imperious bearing and a chilly gaze, he can project an intimidating air, especially when that stern look is potentially allied to a lash from an acid tongue. It's quite possible to imagine him as the very finest Eagle Scout: a future leader of men, or at the very least, a first-class cutter of crap.

One of the most stressful moments of Megan Jasper's initial period working at Sub Pop came when Mark Arm needed money. In itself, this was not an unusual situation. "If a musician came in and said 'I need money to pay my rent,' we would somehow often find funds to distribute in that moment," says Bruce Pavitt—although by Arm's own admission, his cash-flow problems were more invariably drug-related.

What made this particular instance problematic, however, was that neither Pavitt not Jonathan Poneman were in town. So they asked

* "Shrink Rap," *Melody Maker*, July 15,1989.

Jasper to write Arm a check and to forge their signatures—which she did.

"It was two or three hundred bucks, not a ton of money," she says. "But I didn't know his real last name wasn't Arm. I thought he had legally changed his name. So I wrote the check out to 'Mark Arm' and then he couldn't cash it. I remember putting my head in my hands and thinking, 'This is the biggest fuck-up I could ever have made.' The reason why I felt that was because it was *Mark Arm*. With some of the other artists I could say, 'Y'know what? I fucked that up—let me turn it around.' With Mark and Mudhoney, you just didn't fuck up. Fucking up was not an option."

It has to be said that this forbidding aura doesn't linger for any length of time in his good-natured company. But on the night of September 22, 1990, Mark seemed far from his usual cool self. Indeed, he was positively enthused—and understandably so. From his vantage point, pressed against the stage of the Motorsports International Garage with a frenzied 1,500 people behind him, Mark Arm was enjoying what (for him) was a relatively novel experience: watching Dan Peters play the drums—specifically, playing the drums with Nirvana. He felt very pleased for Dan, and excited too: "Maybe because Dan was drumming. Or . . . it seemed like something was about to happen."

Indeed, something was. This was Nirvana's biggest Seattle show to date. Twelve months later, they would release the epochal *Nevermind*. In the more immediate future, Dan Peters was about to be at the center of a curious little episode, where he would suffer grievously at the hands of people he considered friends, and from which the only positive aspect that remained was confirmation of what he already knew: Mudhoney was his band for life.

Not long after Nirvana had parted company with Chad Channing, their drummer of two years, Peters ran into Kurt Cobain's girlfriend, Tracy Marander, and Shelli Novoselic, wife of Krist, at The Vogue. He told them of Mudhoney's impending state of abeyance, and that he'd be interested in filling Nirvana's vacancy. It wasn't long before he got a called from Cobain, who, in a measure of his enduring love for

Mudhoney, was flabbergasted that Peters would consider playing with Nirvana in the first place.

"They were like 'Wow, you wanna play with *us*?'" says Peters. "I was like, 'Hell yeah, let's hook it up and have some fun.'"

The new trio soon got down to rehearsal, following a meeting at Peters' house, where Cobain and Novoselic played him a tape of new songs Nirvana had recorded in April with Butch Vig at Smart Studios in Madison, Wisconsin—ostensibly for their second Sub Pop album, though in fact the band soon made multiple cassette copies and treated the session as a demo to attract potential new record labels.

Loading Nirvana's gear into his room at the Dutchman, where Mudhoney also rehearsed, Peters immediately realized there might be issues.

"I've got this little drum set—a 20-inch kick drum, 13-inch rack tom—and they're into Bigger Is Better. Kurt doesn't really say much, a man of few words. He comes in and puts up the biggest guitar rig that's ever been in my practice space. Turns it on and starts playing. And it's just loud as shit. Kurt's like, 'Stop. I can't hear your drums.' No shit, neither can I. I'm fucking playing them and I can't hear 'em! Krist has got his foot next to my bass drum so he can feel it. Mudhoney used small amps, but Kurt has a stack and a weird pre-amp, which he turns to 10. I was totally drowned out."

For the second rehearsal, Cobain and Novoselic drove up from Tacoma to collect Peters from his house and then headed to The Dutchman in South Seattle. Dan couldn't help but notice a drum kit in the back of the van. Would he mind playing it, they eventually asked? Peters was aghast.

"It's like something they dragged out of the garbage. It's a huge drum set—a 24-inch kick, 14-inch rack tom, totally deep. I didn't think it was necessary—I'm like, 'Well I'll use the tom, I'll use bits and pieces.' So the problem remained: they couldn't hear me. And I'm not a basher. From that time on I became known as 'Tippy-Tap' by the members of Mudhoney. But we did work on a brand new song, which I got to put my own stamp on."

That song was "Sliver," a watershed moment for Nirvana, explicitly laying bare Cobain's intention for his pure pop instincts to dictate the band's future direction. The fact that Nirvana never wrote another song quite like it is testimony to the character of Peters' contribution.

Certainly, after the initial practice, Cobain and Novoselic assured Dan that he was their man. As if to seal the deal, the new model Nirvana showed up at Reciprocal on July 11, 1990. Sub Pop wanted to release a new Nirvana single and already had one side covered with "Dive," recorded with Chad Channing at the Smart session. "Sliver" would make up the other side. One slight problem was that TAD were already in situ at the studio, recording demos for their forthcoming album *8-Way Santa*, but Jack Endino assured them he could get Nirvana in and out during the lunch break. As an added inducement, Krist Novoselic brought a herbadaceous peace gift.

"When the van arrived, Krist offered us a big bud to smoke as compensation," says Kurt Danielson, "and we accepted, lighting up while Dan adjusted Steve's drum kit and Krist plugged into my bass rig. Kurt I believe used Tad's guitar rig." Nirvana duly blitzed through the song, using TAD's equipment, then left.

"'Sliver''s a great song," says Peters. "A great song will play itself, you know exactly what to do. It was written in a day and it came together in an hour, one take. Good to go."

The problem was that Nirvana really did need a basher. Specifically, Kurt Cobain wanted Dale Crover and always had, ever since Crover helped out his friends by playing on the January 1988 demo that first alerted Jonathan Poneman to the band's promise; three songs from this session were used on *Bleach* when attempts to rerecord them with Chad Channing were deemed inadequate.

In August 1990, Crover once again sat in for Nirvana on a short West Coast tour supporting Sonic Youth—Peters couldn't play these gigs as they overlapped with Mudhoney's European festival tour. Once Peters returned from Europe, he hunkered down with Cobain and Novoselic to prepare for the Motorsports gig. But on the night of September 22, as his hallmark snare roll propelled Nirvana at roadrunner pace into "Pay to Play," the countdown to his exit was already well under way.

Indeed, Dan's chosen successor was actually in the crowd, checking out his new band. Later on, he would help Dan load his drums into Nirvana's van and waved as Peters hopped away into the night with friends to celebrate a good job well done. ("It was no Mudhoney gig," says Peters, "but it was a good gig!") And he was at Krist Novoselic's house in Tacoma the next day when Dan arrived to take part in a Nirvana interview and a photo-shoot for a forthcoming cover of *Sounds*.

Squeezed awkwardly in between the amps and guitar cases on the hour's drive south to Tacoma, the guy was introduced to *Sounds* photographer Ian Tilton and myself as simply "Dave"; he drove Nirvana's van on the day of the Motorsports gig, was a friend of The Melvins, and was staying with Krist awhile until he worked out what to do next following the recent breakup of his band, Washington, D.C. hardcore outfit Scream.

Dave hung out amiably at a Sunday afternoon barbecue hosted by the Novoselics, just a fellow member of the drummers' union chatting to Dan about Mudhoney's recent European tour. Later on, he met the members of TAD, who dropped in on their way home from a photo-shoot with Charles Peterson at the Puyallup County Fair. The atmosphere was a little awkward, but there was nothing to suggest the deception being perpetrated upon Dan Peters: while he took part in the *Sounds* interview and photo-shoot, for an article due to coincide with Nirvana's November UK tour, Dave knew all along that he would actually be playing drums for Nirvana on the tour.

Dave Grohl was publicly announced as Nirvana's new drummer—albeit to a fairly select audience—two days later, when Cobain broke the news as the guest of Beat Happening's Calvin Johnson on the Evergreen College radio station, KAOS FM. Not until Cobain, Grohl, and Novoselic had returned from meeting prospective new record labels in Los Angeles, several days later, was Dan Peters officially told.

The Fluid's Garrett Shavlik happened to be staying at Peters' house at the time: "It's 10:30 in the morning, Dan and I are at the dining room table having a cup of coffee and he gets a phone call. It's Kurt on the line. Dan's like, 'Oh hey, what's going on man?' They were supposed to go to England in a little bit, so Dan's talking about visas. Then . . .

'Oh. Oh really? Oh *really*?' I'm looking at Dan, I just see his face drop. 'OK. Thanks.' He hangs up. 'I just got fired from Nirvana. Fuck!'"

Once he'd processed the shock, Peters was actually relieved. Playing in Nirvana had felt like a clock-in clock-out job—in contrast to Mudhoney.

"I never really bonded with those guys," he says. "On practice days, they'd pick me up, Kurt would be asleep in the back of the van, we'd get to the practice space, Kurt would turn the amp up to 10, and we'd practice. Then we'd leave and they'd drop me off at home. Rehearsals were always a sullen time, they were never fun, it wasn't like we were gonna hang out and go partying together. It was really the only time I'd ever played music with people that were just acquaintances, not full-on buddies. But it wasn't until the article in *Sounds* came out that I totally got bent out of shape and pissed, because I thought I was totally made a fool of."

Garbled news of Peters' replacement by Grohl emerged prior to the publication of the *Sounds* cover story on October 27, 1990, though even then the situation remained vague; reports maintained that it had been too late to change Nirvana's UK work permits and so Peters would play with them after all. Amid such confusion, the magazine's editor elected to run with the original story and front cover, with the only reference to Dan's status being a regrettable quip about him being told to "bugger off."

Peters was understandably hurt. "I just felt like an idiot. I'm on the cover, with Nirvana, blissfully ignorant. Matt from Mudhoney told me that Krist had come up to him at the actual show and told him I wasn't going to be in the band anymore. And Matt's like, 'Have you told Dan?' 'No, we haven't told Dan.' 'You gotta fucking tell him, that's bullshit.' My take on it is, if they were honest with me and upfront with me, I would have totally accepted it, but the way they went about it bummed me out. Because Dave was at the show, Dave had been practicing with them in Tacoma for probably a good week and a half, he was in the band—but they did the show with me anyhow, because they didn't have the balls to tell me."

Whatever communication issues Mudhoney might have had at the time, Nirvana dealt in more intrigue and subterfuge than a KGB cell.

Greetings from Seattle: Mudhoney, late 1991. IDOLS/PHOTOSHOT

Four Go Mad in Amsterdam. Mudhoney enjoy a pedalo ride during the spring 1989 European tour. MARK ARM PRIVATE COLLECTIO

Various Mudhoney and Thee Headcoats members, plus friends and associates, gather outside Millie's Coffee House, Silver Lake, Los Angeles, July 1990: (from left) Steve Turner, Tim Hayes (Thee Headcoats' tour manager), Billy Childish, Dan Peters, Emily Rieman, Bob Whittaker, Bruce Brand (Thee Headcoats' drummer), Matt Lukin, Terry Pearson (Mudhoney's sound engineer) and Johnny Johnson (Thee Headcoats' bassist). MARK ARM PRIVATE COLLECTION

Built for speed and not to last? Mudhoney in London, August 1991: (clockwise from bottom left) Mark Arm, Dan Peters, Matt Lukin, Steve Turner. Reflected in the windscreen of his own Lada is photographer Steve Gullick. STEVE GULLICK

Time to "Fudge" it up, London, August 1991. STEVE DOUBLE

he name of the band is . . . Mudhoney in rehearsal, 1992. From the *Piece of Cake* inside cover shoot. CHARLES PETERSON

"Here comes sickness." Mudhoney and their fans enjoy an onstage communion. CHARLES PETERSON

Kurt Cobain joins Mudhoney for "The Money Will Roll Right In," Castaic Lake Natural Amphitheater, California, September 26 1992. LINDSAY BRICE/MICHAEL OCHS ARCHIVES/GETTY IMAGES

Mark Arm meets Iggy Pop for the first time, Roseland Ballroom, New York, October 29, 1992. David Katznelson, Mudhoney's A&R man at Warner Bros. is on Arm's left. MARK ARM PRIVATE COLLECTION

Hawaii, 1993. Mudhoney manager Bob Whittaker and Mark Arm give it the big aloha. MARK ARM PRIVATE COLLECTION

Matt Lukin gets the better of Nick Cave on the Big Day Out tour, Australia, 1993. "I must say, Nick Cave's not a very good wrestler," says Lukin. "I thought Australians were a little tougher than that!" MARK ARM PRIVATE COLLECTION

He's SuperFuzz, I'm Big Muff. Mark and Steve compare weaponry, Seattle, 1992. CHARLES PETERSON

Peters would later find himself pondering a conversation he had with Cobain and Novoselic on the day they came to his house, before the first rehearsal. After listening to the Butch Vig demo tape, they went for drinks at a nearby bar and Peters told Cobain how much he hated heroin and the people who used it.

"Kurt sits there, nodding," says Peters. "I didn't know Kurt was a fucking junkie! He was a nonperson in terms of hanging out with in Seattle. Talk about foot in mouth. But Dave was the proper drummer for them. They made the right choice. The way they went about making that choice was . . . irritating."

⋆ ⋆ ⋆

In the same issue of *Sounds* featuring Dan on the cover with Nirvana, a short news story suggested that reports of Mudhoney's death had been greatly exaggerated. The band was, apparently, "back in the studio, with Dan on drums, recording a double LP which will be half new material and half cover versions."* The same story also mentioned that Mark Arm would be releasing a version of Bob Dylan's "Masters of War" as a solo single. The latter part, at least, was perfectly true. Recorded with Jack Endino on September 19 and released under the name The Freewheelin' Mark Arm, with a sleeve pastiching *The Freewheelin' Bob Dylan*'s cover image of Bobby Zimmerman and Suze Rotolo walking in Greenwich Village, Arm's spartan, scalding take on the definitive antiwar song was very apt for apocalyptic times: the Middle East was simmering inexorably to a full-on U.S.-led military campaign against Iraq in January 1991.

As regards Mudhoney, the story was not complete hoo-hah either—though the double LP concept never came to pass. But beneath the band's careless façade, a change of direction was being plotted and the driving force behind it was the same man who had ostensibly derailed their momentum earlier in the year.

At Steve Turner's insistence, for the first time Mudhoney were about to record somewhere other than Reciprocal and with someone other

* "Nirvana Drummer Saga Continues," *Sounds*, October 27, 1990, 2.

than Jack Endino. Turner had identified a potential new producer, Conrad Uno, whose studio was named Egg after the cartons he stuck on the walls in an optimistic attempt to protect his U-District neighbors (as well as his long-suffering wife upstairs, Emily) from the noise of bands recording in the basement. Uno had earned local renown for recording The Young Fresh Fellows, a group of pop-smart wiseacres led by Scott McCaughey—who would later become REM's auxiliary guitarist—and releasing them on his own Popllama label. He had also produced and released a Fastbacks album. What qualified Uno most, in Turner's mind, was that he had nothing to do with Sub Pop or the sights and sounds of what had already become codified as an identifiable scene. He had never even heard Mudhoney.

"I would have been fine—and I think everybody else would—with recording with Jack Endino again," says Mark Arm. "But Steve really wanted to shake things up."

At the beginning of December the band checked into Egg and blasted through some punk rock covers to see if the new surroundings were going to work. The material was nasty, brutish, and short: The Damned's "Stab Yor Back," The Adolescents' "Who Is Who," Void's "Dehumanized," Black Flag's "Fix Me." Essentially, Steve Turner was done with the G-word.

"The grunge clichés were already pretty hot and heavy," he says. "Hence the cutting of the hair—I wanted to be a punk rocker again! I've always loved punk rock, but getting to go to England, I bought hundreds of old '77–'79 English punk rock singles on Mudhoney's first couple of trips over there. I was bringing home boxes of them. I was totally enamoured of the B-through-Z-grade punk rock. I was really, *really* loving Sham 69. Anthems, but stupid anthems."

Just as he had been the principal architect of Mudhoney's musical DNA, Turner now sensed before anyone else that what was exciting two years ago had, by 1990, become diluted with repetition, its purity debased by substandard copies—including those by Mudhoney themselves. Things were soon to become much worse, of course, when the industrial processes of the pop mainstream took over following the success of Nirvana and Pearl Jam. For now, though, Turner sought to revitalize his band through rebooting Mudhoney's sound in a manner closest to his own instincts. To which end, Conrad Uno's basement would suffice as the next best thing to a garage.

"We got on with Conrad immediately," says Turner. "I knew it was going to be good when I phoned him up to say we wanted to book some time to come and record [the covers] at the end of 1990, and he just laughed and said: 'Why?!' Which I thought was an awesome response. It was a really good fit."

The punk covers session was a successful experiment. Egg was go! Mudhoney duly recorded their next album with Uno during the spring of 1991.

Although touring was off the agenda, Turner had resumed his anthropology studies in Seattle and so the band was able to work at weekends, and during the gap between semesters. The guitarist's emergence as instigator-in-chief correlated with Mark Arm's increasing immersion in heroin. Unless there was Mudhoney business to attend to, Arm now rarely socialized with the other three members.

"I'm sure I just wasn't as present as I had been before," he says. "At that point Dan and Steve lived in a house together, with Ed Fotheringham and Jason Finn [drummer with Love Battery and later Presidents of the United States of America], and I think a couple of other people rotated out of there. So they were always hanging out and doing stuff. I don't think I was around very much at all."

The house, at 2359 Franklin Avenue in the Eastlake neighborhood, was the venue for some staunch partying. One weekend, Turner returned from a trip to New York accompanied by his mother. They were greeted at the front door by Matt Lukin—who had been drinking since the previous day with Cosmic Psychos, a heroically primitive Australian trio signed to Sub Pop—dressed only in his underpants and with penises inked on his legs and stomach. Patricia Turner never even blinked. A little later, Kurt Danielson and his wife, Roni, were walking towards the front door when Lukin emerged, beer in hand.

"In honor of Roni—I think—he whipped off his underwear and commenced to prance around the yard totally naked," says Danielson. "It was still early, the sun was still out, and Matt was totally unembarrassed, acting as if it was a natural thing for him to meet people while he himself was completely naked."

As the evening progressed, so did Lukin's body art. Someone took a photograph of him with a newly inked third eye on his forehead, wearing a quizzical look and little else besides, beyond the five penile members, the four bars of the Black Flag logo, and the inscription "I Fuck Arses" on his chest. The picture subsequently appeared as the sleeve of a Mudhoney covers EP released in Australia—aptly enough, given that Cosmic Psychos were the perpetrators.

But Mark Arm missed out on the fun. "If I hadn't been concentrating on doing drugs, I would have been there hanging out with everyone, drinking beer, and drawing on Matt."

Nor was Arm in Vancouver on March 8, 1991, to participate in one of the greater by-products of Mudhoney's hiatus. After his brief, action-packed sojourn with Nirvana, Dan Peters took solace in his own band's semi-active state—a few gigs in November, the promise of a new album to record—but the prospect of no regular touring work meant he was open to offers. One duly came from Ellensburg, a small town 100 miles east of Seattle on the other side of the Cascade Mountains, noted for its farms, its rodeo, and various annual festivals; every summer, lovers of low-rise canine pugnacity flock to Ellensburg for Dachshunds on Parade.

A singular place, Ellensburg's most famous band fittingly broke the mold. Screaming Trees were fronted by Mark Lanegan, a shy, moody, physically imposing man with a tarpit baritone voice and a criminal record, engaged in a forever triangulating war of attrition with the even more physically imposing Conner brothers, guitarist Gary Lee and bassist Van, who formed the band in 1985 along with drummer Mark Pickerel.

"We didn't have a damn thing in common except insanity," says Lanegan. "So we fought a lot. And we had two brothers, who fought like brothers. Only they were huge and spent a lot of time in an Econoline van. We're driving along, stop at a gas station. Go inside. Come back out and Lee Conner would be sitting there with blood all over his face. Turns out, after we'd all got out of the van, they'd just had a quick little 30-second fight."

The band's music was a deep, psychedelic rock stew dominated by Lanegan's gloomy croon, but capturing their live power on record was a fraught process. By 1990, they had made five albums but liked only one: 1989's *Buzz Factory*, recorded with Jack Endino because of his work with Mudhoney. Indeed, the Trees' fourth album (a double) was scrapped as a result of *Superfuzz Bigmuff*.

"When we heard the first Mudhoney EP, we thought, 'We want to sound like this,'" says Lanegan. "We felt our record sounded weak."

With Endino at the desk, the Trees certainly beefed up nicely. After Sub Pop released the *Change Has Come* EP, the band was courted by major labels, eventually signing to Epic but losing Pickerel in the process. So in late 1990, with Mudhoney still vaguely on hold, Screaming Trees asked Dan if he'd join them for a U.S. tour beginning in February 1991. Peters accepted and immediately plunged into the band's peculiar emotional biosphere, a smoldering mix of oversensitivity, fisticuffs, and terrible diet.

"Those guys are hypochondriacs," says Peters. "On a daily basis it was like: 'Hey, what's the symptoms of a heart attack?' 'What's it feel like when something's gonna burst?' Well, that coulda been the six-pack of cheeseburgers you got from the mini-mart—what's gonna burst is your fucking colon . . . "

One of Screaming Trees' inviolable rules was that no member strayed into another's onstage space. "Because if you touched somebody else, there had to be a fight, on the spot," says Lanegan. Another was that Mark Lanegan never did encores—indeed, he developed a routine of walking off the stage before the band had finished the final song. One night, as he got to the wings following his exit, he heard sounds of an onstage commotion and turned back to find Van Conner beating up his brother. Lee had trashed his guitar and then started on the spare, only to forget that it actually belonged to Van.

"It was like prison," sighs Lanegan. "Without the sex."

In Vancouver's Commodore Ballroom on March 8, 1991, despite the especially feverish response to the Trees from a crowd already hyped by that night's support band, Nirvana—two months prior to recording *Nevermind*—Lanegan would not budge on his no-encores hard line. But

Van Conner didn't want to stop playing. The presence of some friends from Seattle meant that three quarters of his favorite band were in the hall and he would be damned if he wasn't going to get them on stage.

"Hey folks," he announced, "this is Matt and Steve. They're in a band called Mudhoney!"* Whereupon Lukin and Turner joined Screaming Trees—and therefore Dan—to play "In'n'out of Grace," with Van taking Mark's role and hollering from the drum riser.

When it came to the recording session, however, Mark Arm was very much present. Everyone loved working with the genially eccentric Uno and enthusiastically pitched in with Turner's blueprint for spring-cleaning Mudhoney's sound. Mark bought a Farfisa organ to add a garage garnish to the new material—and finding at last a practical application for the piano lessons he so hated as a child. Sharing a house with Steve had enlightened Dan to the way of the garage and his beats became simpler, lighter, and even niftier. Turner's growing infatuation with sixties folk music icons like Phil Ochs had influenced his melodic sensibilities, while he also learned to play guitar and harmonica at the same time.

The short-haired rock revolution kicked in most graphically with two songs, "Good Enough" and "Who You Drivin' Now?," the latter of which had originally been written as an archaeological experiment. Estrus Records, a Bellingham-based label specializing in garage and surf punk, approached Mudhoney to appear on *Half Rack*, a compilation of "The 12 Drunkest Bands in Showbiz"; mindful of the label's house style, the band tasked themselves with recording a fake Sonics song. Almost comically raw and crunchy, with some of Arm's greatest howled vocals and self-mocking lyrics ("You're drivin my T-bird/But the gauge is on empty"), the result was, with all due respect to Estrus, too good to be buried on a limited edition seven-inch single box set. So Mudhoney kept "Who You Drivin' Now?" for their album and instead Estrus got "March to Fuzz," an instrumental spin on Phil Ochs' "I Ain't Marching Any More" in the style of biker movie soundtrack doyen Davie Allan. "Good Enough," meanwhile, was pure "Psychotic Reaction"-era West

* "Tree Fellers" by Nils Bernstein, *Sounds*, April 6, 1991.

Coast R&B—hustling brushed drums, a repetitive snaking guitar riff and a vocal dripping with catatonic resignation: "I've made mistakes/ That I'm sure I'll make again . . . "

Another key influence on the new album was Neil Young—"I was listening to him a lot," says Turner, "his guitar solos are more drawn out and maybe a bit more melodic than Blue Cheer"—though, as Arm points out, early Neil Young & Crazy Horse essentially qualifies as garage rock too. "It might be slower and more hippyish but, y'know, he did one-note guitar solos! You have to be really confident in what you're doing to pull that off. He puts a lot of guitar pyrotechnics to shame, because there's so much feeling there."

The debt was overtly acknowledged on "Broken Hands," the album's astonishing centerpiece, which opens by quoting the addendum riffage from Young's "Cinnamon Girl" and then imagines what might have come next: a six-minute epic guitar parabola with desolate lyrics intimating a relationship's imminent doom. ("Sometimes it's so hard to know/When you can't change what's gonna come . . . I loved your fragile fingers/Oh, how they used to soothe me.") The end comes amid writhing sound effects, which both Arm and Peters thought reminiscent of "Out of the Blue" by Roxy Music.

Sequenced perfectly, at the album's midpoint, offsetting the clipped trash-punk workouts on either side, "Broken Hands" was a startling statement of serious artistic intent, from a band that would have instinctively bridled at such a notion.

"I think it might be our best fake Neil Young song," says Arm. "We tried one on the previous album, "Come to Mind," which didn't work so well, but "Broken Hands" was a rousing success. I'm not really sure at this point what it's about, but it's got some good imagery. Some great guitar playing on Steve's part. It's one of my favorite songs we've ever put down."

So vehement were the performances, especially on the splintering frenzy of "Let It Slide" and a new version of "Thorn," that the earthiness of eight-track recording enhanced the sense of a band reconnecting with their purest impulses. Part of the motivation behind making the album with Uno was Egg's eight-track facility: "Touch Me I'm Sick" and "Sweet Young Thing" had been recorded on eight-track and subsequent 16-track recordings had failed to capture their unrefined pungency, so perhaps a return to the more basic setup would yield that same magic?

Of course, seeking to replicate the unique circumstances that dictated that debut single's primitive chops was a futile quest—but the new record would prove Mudhoney's strongest for years to come.

Both the album title, *Every Good Boy Deserves Fudge* (a mnemonic for the notes on the treble clef), and its sleeve design suggested Mudhoney were placing distance between themselves and their record label's brand signifiers, in particular the bold, block-heavy typography that, along with Charles Peterson's black and white photography, had helped create Sub Pop's generic visual style. The cover artwork was a colorful Ed Fotheringham illustration with happy stick people enjoying a boat party. The reverse side offered a clue to the source of the record's *joie de vivre*: a house with the number "2359," the Rock Mecca abode of Fotheringham, Peters, and Turner.

Intentionally or not, by sticking a spoke in the Mudhoney funwagon's wheels, Steve Turner had prompted all concerned to raise their game and make a brilliant album. Now all Sub Pop had to do was stay in business long enough to release it.

★ ★ ★

Midway through his second quarter at college, Steve realized that the anthropology/rock'n'roll band cohabitation thing wasn't going to work. It wasn't just Mudhoney: during his educational retreat he played guitar in The Sad and Lonely(s), also featuring Joe Culver and Ed Fotheringham, and bass in The Fall-Outs and The Monkeywrench, the latter a blues-flavored all-star affair with Mark Arm on vocals, Poison 13's Tim Kerr and the U-Men's Tom Price on guitar, and Lubricated Goat's Martin Bland on drums. All three bands recorded 1991 albums with Conrad Uno, in addition to Mudhoney.

"The music took over again, definitely," says Turner. "I wasn't giving enough time to my studies in the second quarter, knowing that I was in the studio with Mudhoney—I couldn't do both. So I laid school to rest for a little while, thinking I would come back in another year or something."

He also decided that, with a completed record in the can, it made sense for Mudhoney to go out on tour. This meant Dan Peters had a choice to make. The Screaming Trees tour had ended in disarray after Mark Lanegan fell disastrously off the wagon, but now they were regrouping and preparing to record their next album. Lanegan wanted to record with a drummer who could also tour.

"The choice was an easy one," says Peters. "Mudhoney is my band. Always. I was desperate to record with the Trees, but there was nothing like the power of playing a Mudhoney show—the sheer chaos and good vibes and the good time we had. I called the Trees and told them. Mark was expecting it and Van took it all right, but Gary Lee Conner got totally pissed off and started throwing shit around his apartment."

By now, Bob Whittaker was performing tasks that a bonafide band manager might recognize as part of the job spec. He liaised with Mudhoney's various booking agents in territories across the world and kept an eye on what was happening at Sub Pop. What he saw there troubled him.

"Sub Pop was faltering on payments and the band was always bitching about it," he says. "The tapes for *Every Good Boy Deserves Fudge* were in the can and Mark just turned them in. I was like, 'Oh shit . . . ' I was worried, because now they were committed and Sub Pop felt so shaky."

At the sharp end of Sub Pop's haphazard business practices sat Megan Jasper. The receptionist was the first point of contact at the label for angry creditors, be they record pressing plants, distributors, or bands. "I hated how many lights were lit on the telephones because I knew it was that many people waiting to yell at me," she says. "So I'd be like, 'Sub Pop—can you please hold?' 'Nooooo! I need money!' 'I'm so sorry, please hold, I promise I'll be right back . . . ' It was one after the next, after the next . . . There was no money to do anything, it was constant juggling. The Mudhoney record *had* to come out: the band needed it out, Sub Pop needed it out—but to be able to afford the things around such an anticipated record, like advertisements, was not easy. That summer was so rough. "

Sub Pop's Pavitt and Poneman were out of their depth, their schemes overextended, a mom-and-pop organization now competing with corporations—and losing. Aware that Nirvana were shopping around their 1990 Smart demo, Sub Pop decided to use the tape themselves as bait to land a distribution deal with Columbia Records and, thereby, to hopefully persuade Nirvana to stay with the label. The plan failed on both counts: Sub Pop wound up with a five-figure bill for legal fees and, at the end of April 1991, Nirvana signed with Geffen Records—a deal that would eventually confer solvency upon Sub Pop, but not before Pavitt and Poneman were forced to lay off most of the company's staff, including Megan, during the summer.

In May, an audit of the accounts revealed that Sub Pop owed $250,000 and had just $5,000 in the bank. A couple of months later, Seattle's music weekly, *The Rocket*, ran a front cover picture of Bruce Pavitt, beneath the headline: "Sub Plop: Is the Price of World Domination Too High?" Signing bands from beyond the Pacific Northwest, such as L7 from Los Angeles or The Afghan Whigs from Ohio, though doubtless a logical step for building a long-term dynamic business, had diluted the label's localized ethos. This became a particularly sore point when expansion was perceived as occurring at the expense of Sub Pop's only established artists of real commercial viability.

With a European tour booked, Mudhoney needed to know when their album was going to come out and when they might see the money the label owed them. Sub Pop couldn't deliver any answers. But, so it seemed to Mudhoney, they could afford to fly The Afghan Whigs from Cincinnati to Seattle, stick them in a hotel, and pay for them to record at Bear Creek, a far-from-shabby residential studio out in the country beyond the Eastside suburb of Bothel.

"Basically, they were borrowing money from us and doing things with it that we didn't agree with," says Turner. "We were like: 'We already earned that money, if you're blowing it on The Afghan Whigs what happens if you guys go out of business—we'll never see it? That's gonna really suck.'"

A tipping point came when Steve Turner came to the Sub Pop office, looked at Bruce Pavitt, and said: "Jonathan told me I could pick up $5,000 today. I'd like to pick up that $5,000."

Pavitt burst out laughing. He knew there was barely $100 in the Sub Pop account: "Steve took offense that I would laugh in his face when he asked for money that I knew was not there. But I wasn't being disrespectful, more like, 'I think I might be losing my mind at this moment because I cannot deal with the reality.' Steve was like, 'Fuck these guys, let's leave, they're broke and we're getting jacked around.' Understandable."

In a desperate attempt to persuade Mudhoney that their long-term future lay with Sub Pop, Pavitt and Poneman had offered the band stock in the company. Turner assumed they were joking. "It seemed nonsensical. Stock? In what?!"

Poneman had a similar conversation with Dan Peters, who was his usual gentlemanly self before cutting to the chase: "Is this really worth anything?"

Poneman was forced to admit that it was not. "Had I been in their place," he says, "I wouldn't have gone with it either."

Throughout this tense period, Mark Arm's financial concerns were informed by the very specific demands of heroin. On occasions, if he needed drug money, he would ask Pavitt, who would do his best to oblige. Consequently, Arm was less exercised by the Sub Pop situation than other members of the band.

"I wasn't really focused on, or aware of, anything—except what my little world consisted of at that time. Steve and Dan were saying, 'We should really look elsewhere because Sub Pop are having a hard time.' And I was like, 'OK...' Except it really bummed me out, because I'd known Jonathan and Bruce a long time and was good friends with both, particularly at that time with Bruce."

Trying to involve Arm in business discussions became unintentionally comedic. "Phone calls with him were just ridiculous," says Turner. "Because he'd be watching TV *and* high, so it could be literally two minutes between words. It got to be a joke."

The other band members received a rare insight to the reality of Arm's everyday life when they shot a video for the *Every Good Boy . . .*

track "Into the Drink," by an outdoor swimming pool at the apartment block where he lived with his girlfriend.

"It was the most depressing scenario," says Peters. "We had to hang out there for the day and it was just a bummer. Icky!"

In the video, the band mime the song in a deliberately cack-handed fashion, tossing household appliances into the pool as Arm barks the lyric's litany of complaints down a telephone: "I don't feel your lousy love . . . You're a useless piece of weaponry . . . " Eventually he follows a toaster, hairdryer, and the phone by hurling himself "into the drink."

The video location was apt, inasmuch as the song's lyric was inspired by Arm's disenchantment at his domestic situation: "I saw some footage of all this expensive military hardware—helicopters, tanks, etc.—getting tossed off of an aircraft carrier," he said. "It fit my feelings concerning the relationship I was mixed up in at the time. I should've hedged my bets and applied it to the next one before it got started."*

In the last week of July, Sub Pop finally got *Every Good Boy Deserves Fudge* into the shops. No sooner had it arrived than it tended to leave—fast. Topping the UK independent charts was no surprise, but the album even entered the mainstream UK Top 40 and went on to sell 75,000 copies worldwide. Heady stuff for a punk rock band on an indie label.

Mudhoney kept the lights on at Sub Pop, immediately easing the label's cash-flow problems. But Turner's traumatic encounter with Bruce Pavitt had convinced the band to seek alternative arrangements.

"Everyone was friends with Jon and Bruce," says Bob Whittaker. "But the friendships are stressful, and the business is stressful to the friendships and vice versa. And it was starting to head towards, 'Let's see what it's like out there. Maybe we can actually be on a label that's a little more stable.'"

Loath to sign with a major, they initially had a meeting with Keith Wood of Caroline, the large New York–based independent that already distributed Sub Pop releases. Wood said Mudhoney would have to be prepared to tour for nine months in the year—because that was what worked for Smashing Pumpkins—as well as to "sweeten up" their guitar

* *March to Fuzz* liner notes (Sub Pop, 2000).

sounds, and forego side projects. Given that this was a band who practically drove themselves mad touring for nine weeks, let alone nine months, who had recorded their new hit album on eight-track after deeming a 16-track set-up too ritzy, and whose guitarist and singer had just recorded an album with The Monkeywrench, their new side project, it's difficult to imagine how the meeting could have gone any worse.

Whittaker was tasked with putting the word out to major labels that Mudhoney were open to offers. "Everyone agreed that no one likes creepy band managers," he says, "so the idea was, how about I be the conduit or the spokesperson for the band? It's a collective, the five of us making decisions: I bring labels to the band and we digest them, cook them down, and then I go back to the labels. And Mudhoney agreed: 'OK, let's have Bob be our creepy manager.'"

On Halloween, Mudhoney played Seattle's prestigious concert hall, the 3,000-capacity Paramount Theatre. It was to be their last live performance for a couple of months, the climax of a lengthy tour stint in support of the new album that began in the UK and Europe, then took them round the U.S. in six weeks. Also completing their U.S. tour schedule at the Paramount that night were Nirvana. This show was planned as the last of a trio of joint headlining gigs, along with Vancouver the night before and Portland on the 29th, with proceeds split evenly between the two bands, who would take turns to play last: Nirvana in Portland and Mudhoney in Seattle.

But the idea had been cooked up before the September 24, 1991 release of *Nevermind*. At every club on their U.S. tour, Mudhoney would hear "Smells Like Teen Spirit," the album's calling card, over the PA before they went on. Once Nirvana's album was released, the omnipresence of the song on the radio and MTV intensified. By the time they met up in Portland, in terms of public consciousness Nirvana were no longer Mudhoney's baby brother band. That very day, *Nevermind* was certified gold—it had sold 500,000 copies in a month. Nirvana inevitably headlined all three shows.

"Within two weeks of the tour starting, it was obvious that's what would happen," says Arm. "And it wasn't like we were, 'Oh fuck them.' It was amazing."

In Seattle, Dan Peters saw his brother. "Fuck, Dan," said Jim Peters, "Dave Grohl just won the lottery!"

As the Paramount shook to Nirvana at the peak of their game and the audience vented its collective hysteria, a six-camera film crew got to work. The jaws of the machine were already gripped around the band's throat.

"You couldn't get near to the stage to see Nirvana," says Dan. "I remember leaving and looking back at this theatre full of people going apeshit and thinking, 'Well, we get 50 percent of this.' Their record went gold—I mean at that time, whose records go *gold*? Aerosmith goes gold. Suddenly we became this little shunted-to-the-side band. One time [later], I'm looking at Anton [Brookes, UK publicist for Mudhoney and Nirvana] and he's got a fucking Nirvana *watch* on. I'm like, 'Whoa, where'd you get that?' He's like, 'When you go gold, you can have one of these too.' Oh, is that the way it is? I guess I'll never get one of *those* watches."

Also in the audience at the Paramount were Anita and Calvin McLaughlin. As soon as the band had been able to go to Europe and play shows in Germany, Mark's mother was finally able to acknowledge her son's music as an achievement. "Even though she didn't understand or like what we did, she kinda got secretly proud," he says. "In fact, not even secretly—openly! Any time there was some article on us in the local paper she would clip it out, highlight it, send me a copy, and buy a copy for herself and show it around to people in the church."

That night, as Mudhoney blazed through their set, Anita turned to a young woman sitting next to her: "That's my son up there," she said. From the stage, Anita's son announced: "My mom is in the audience tonight and this is her favorite song." And then the band played "Touch Me I'm Sick."

* * *

David Katznelson felt apprehensive. A 22-year-old from Berkeley, California, he had been working full-time in the A&R department at Warner Bros for only a year and was now on his way to Seattle to try to sign one of his favorite bands. Through his boss, the legendary Warners A&R Roberta Petersen—who signed Devo and Jane's Addiction, among many others—Katznelson had been talking to Jeff Saltzman, manager of Bay Area thrash metal band Testament and also the lawyer who Bob Whittaker had hired to help land a deal for Mudhoney. When Saltzman told him Mudhoney might be interested in a record deal, Katznelson just laughed.

"I assumed they would forever be on Sub Pop," he says. "I was one of the original members of the Sub Pop Singles Club, and I loved the label. I had no desire to poach bands from them. I had met Mark very briefly when they played Berkeley Square in 1989, but that was as a fan. These were people whose career I had been following for a long time. Their attitude to major labels and corporate culture was very defined. So I was very nervous."

Given that he was both a longtime fan and a representative of a filthy rich multinational corporation, David Katznelson's initial meeting with Mudhoney, the day after the Paramount show, went as well as he could have expected: "It was a little prickly. I wouldn't say that they were receptive. Steve Turner definitely had the most defiant, punk-rock attitude towards me. He wasn't trying to punch me or anything but he was definitely cynical and sarcastic whenever he could be. I was walking on eggshells. And I was young, so I couldn't necessarily take it as easily as I could now. They were asking a lot of questions. They were truly considering their options. And I think there were some members of the band who saw what Nirvana had just gone through—with *Nevermind*, their rough edges were gone, there were sequencers on there, the live feeling was gone—and Mudhoney, being one of the great independently minded bands, were with good reason worried about what could happen if they joined a major label."

Whittaker and Mudhoney liked Katznelson immediately—he was young, obviously a fan of the band, and an enthusiast about music in general. They liked him even more once they'd talked to some other A&R people. With a formidable collective nose for bullshit, it became quickly obvious that Warner Bros' Burbank HQ would be the only record company building where Mudhoney actually felt comfortable.

Katznelson was clearly adored by the label's top brass, Mo Ostin and Lenny Waronker. Ostin was an old-school record executive—he had been hired by Frank Sinatra to run his record label, Reprise, and remained in the position when Warners bought Reprise in 1963—and Waronker was a legendary producer, who both in turn impressed the band with their evident conviction that music was best made by musicians. This was, after all, the label that Neil Young came back to after his nightmare experience in the mid-eighties when David Geffen sued him for making records "unrepresentative of Neil Young."

Mudhoney were treated as equals, as just another bunch of music fanatics. In the unlikely event that Ostin and Waronker ran out of war stories, they could call in Ted Templeman, the man who'd produced both Captain Beefheart and Sammy Hagar's band Montrose, thereby delighting the deepest fanboy instincts of Mark Arm and Matt Lukin, respectively.

Mudhoney made it clear that they weren't looking for a ton of money; indeed, had it not been for Sub Pop's financial instability they wouldn't be having the conversation. Warners said the band could do whatever they wanted—side projects included—and agreed that some of the best records ever made had been recorded on eight-track (in fact Lenny Waronker had probably produced them). This was a far cry from Caroline, a pumped-up indie demanding they sound more like Smashing Pumpkins.

"There didn't seem to be a whole lot of bullshit," says Arm. "There weren't a whole lot of promises made. We didn't go chasing after a big advance, 'cos we knew that would be something that would trap us. We wanted to be in a situation similar to Sub Pop: we get to make the records we want, work with who we want . . . and luckily for us, Nirvana and Pearl Jam busting down the doors, probably throwing a lot of establishment major label people back onto their heels, worked to our advantage. I'm sure there were people saying, 'We gotta get another one of *them*!' We just happened to be another band from Seattle at the same time. So it was probably an easy sell to some of the executives who might not have totally understood what we were doing."

It took a couple of months for the contract to be thrashed out, as the band was very specific on copper-plating guarantees of artistic control and a low advance/high royalty ratio. Before the deal was signed, Mudhoney visited Egg once more to record a song for the soundtrack of a film shot in Seattle during the spring of 1991. Directed by erstwhile *Rolling Stone* journalist Cameron Crowe, in crude terms *Singles* was *Friends*-goes-grunge: a rom-com with the city's rock scene as its backdrop, starring Bridget Fonda as a coffee-shop waitress in love with Matt Dillon as the dopey, deluded Cliff Poncier, lead singer of the band Citizen Dick, whose crowd-pleasing "Touch Me I'm Dick" bore more than a passing resemblance to a similarly titled Mudhoney song. Dillon's bandmates were Jeff Ament and Stone Gossard, plus drummer Eddie Vedder—in reality, the singer for Ament and Gossard's new band, Pearl Jam, whose manager, Kelly Curtis, was the film's associate producer.

Unsurprisingly, *Singles*' music content was dominated by artists represented either by Curtis or his associate, Susan Silver, who managed Soundgarden and Alice in Chains. That Sub Pop managed some product placement—a T-shirt here and there, plus a speaking role for Tad Doyle—was thanks to Mark Arm and Steve Turner accompanying Bruce Pavitt to knock on the door of Crowe's office and remind him that "the other guys" from Green River deserved a piece of the action too. Crowe was thrilled to have them on board.

Ironically, however, until the seismic impact of Nirvana's *Nevermind* reaching number one in January 1992 kicked grunge into the mainstream, Crowe's movie was mired in post-production, with wrangles over key scenes, the ending, and even its title, which Warners marketing executives wanted to change to *Come as You Are* after the Nirvana song. The one thing Crowe could rely upon was the potency of the film's soundtrack, which Epic was desperate to hurry into the shops to surf the grunge wave. The Hollywood studio was forced to acquiesce to the director's wishes. "The hometown music that helped inspire the script is now our best ally in getting the movie released," wrote Crowe in his diary.*

Thanks to their bold piece of doorstepping, Mudhoney were included on the soundtrack, cashing in on the confluence of movie

* "Making the Scene" by Cameron Crowe, *Rolling Stone*, October 1, 1992.

and music business corporate troughs. Given a budget of $20,000 to record a new song, instead of expanding their typical modus operandi to fit the major label ethos and spending two weeks at a pricey studio with a name producer, they returned to Egg, paid Conrad Uno $164 for a day's work, and trousered the rest. Their contribution to an album that ended up selling a million copies was "Overblown": a sour plum in the grunge sweetie jar, satirizing the self-important tendencies of any successful cultural movement, but possibly also applying it to certain members of the Seattle rock scene. One line clearly evoked Chris Cornell's inability to play a gig fully clothed—"You're up there shirtless and flexing/A display of a macho freak"—but verse three's scope was somehow both wider and more acute, nailing the crass imperatives of a gold-rush mentality and the woeful impact it wreaked upon art: "You got a sack full of candy/All I got was a rock," sneered Arm. "They got you by your big business boy/Nice to know you're packing extra socks."

A month after pulling off their miniature version of the Great Rock'n'Roll Swindle, Mudhoney signed with Warner Bros. The deal was modest, especially by the ludicrously inflated—indeed, overblown—standards that applied in the post-*Nevermind* era. Their records would be released on the illustrious Reprise imprint, with a modest advance in exchange for a superior royalty rate.

"We didn't want to be in debt to the record label," says Turner. "We were not babes in the woods; we were not hoping for Nirvana's success. Nirvana might have been, but we were all pretty much realists when it came to that stuff."

While Mudhoney put pen to paper with a no-frills ceremony at Bob Whittaker's house in West Seattle, the mood at Sub Pop felt somber, curiously so for a company that six months earlier had been on the brink of extinction but that was now viable, thanks to the nuts and bolts of the deal Nirvana signed with Geffen. Sub Pop received $75,000 as a buyout fee for the remainder of the contract that Nirvana had, perhaps ironically, demanded Sub Pop draw up for them, plus a 2 percent royalty on every sale of the band's next two albums. Given that the first of those two albums was currently selling around 300,000 copies a week in the

U.S. alone, for the first time in its existence Sub Pop was not about to go out of business anytime soon.

Mark Arm would later wryly comment: "Guess we should have taken them up on that stock offer after all!"

But for Bruce Pavitt and Jonathan Poneman, Mudhoney's departure was only the last of many—Soundgarden, Nirvana, TAD, and The Fluid had all signed to majors—and it hurt the most, because the bonds of friendship had been stronger.

Pavitt's public pronouncements at the time were bullish: "Mudhoney going to Warner Brothers? Great! If Warner Brothers wants to spend hundreds of thousands of dollars promoting our act, and we sell the back catalog, I have no problems with that at all."* Yet behind his spin doctor's smile, he was hurting.

"When all those people we had established relationships with left, it changed the whole situation," he says now. The loss of Mudhoney instigated Pavitt's slow disengagement from the music business. He left Sub Pop in 1995.

"It was particularly heartbreaking for Bruce," says Poneman. "Mark and I knew each other, but those guys used to really hang out. What was heartbreaking for me was that Mudhoney had so much trust and idealism, they held out for us. And our disorganization, our entropy, caught up with us."

A different kind of entropy was to impact upon Mudhoney as the year progressed. But everyone seemed happy on March 6, 1992, as the band played The Palace in Hollywood with the Warner Bros. top brass out in force to check their new signings.

Midway through Mudhoney's set, David Katznelson caught a look from Michael Ostin, Mo Ostin's son and the head of A&R at Warners. Ostin gave Katznelson a huge grin and mouthed the words: "Good job!" Katznelson shrugged modestly, as if to say: "Piece of cake!" Not that it had been, of course—and what followed would be anything but.

* *Our Band Could Be Your Life*, 452.

7

All I Got Was a Rock

Staged amid pancake-flat farmland next to the River Thames, on the outskirts of a light industrial town, it's inevitable that Reading fulfills the underdog role in any chronicle of the British rock festival. Its consistently stolid image lacks Glastonbury's romantic allure—no association with English mythology, no ley lines, no druids—and favors honest toil over New Age pretense. Yet thanks to its origins as the National Jazz Festival, Reading does possess a radical pedigree that played its part in the evolution of British rock music. In 1963, when still staged in the grounds of Richmond Athletic Association, the festival offered its patrons a future vision: while Acker Bilk's Paramount Jazz Band tootled merrily on the main stage, a little-known rhythm and blues outfit called The Rolling Stones attracted an uncomfortably packed crowd to the adjacent rugby clubhouse. The Stones would headline the following year's event, now renamed the National Jazz & Blues Festival, and nothing was ever the same again.

By the early nineties, Reading had been revived from the moribund hard-rock lineups and dwindling crowds of the previous decade by the brainwave of simply booking whoever clocked up a healthy presence in the independent charts that year. Mudhoney made their debut in 1990, and, although not booked to play in 1991, the band had finished a 12-date UK tour the day before and took the opportunity to enjoy the sights, sounds, and smells of a Reading Friday, the same day that Nirvana played the festival for the first time. Inviting herself onto the van for the short journey along the M4 from London was Courtney Love of Hole—who had been the support band on Mudhoney's tour.

Twelve months on, Nirvana headlined the festival and the notion that they could possibly have occupied an early afternoon slot just a year earlier felt like a defective memory. But in 1992, post-*Nevermind*, the entire last day on the festival's main stage had been booked at Kurt Cobain's discretion. Mudhoney were third top of the bill, beneath Nick Cave and Nirvana. Also playing were Screaming Trees and The Melvins, with Buzz Osborne less than happy that Cobain, his former roadie, had approved a running order that landed his band with the dreaded "hangover" slot, opening Sunday's proceedings at noon beneath Björn Again, an ABBA tribute band. Nonetheless, the atmosphere among the Seattle groups was understandably feverish. It wasn't so long ago that they had all been happy pulling a hundred people to The Vogue or Central Tavern; now one of their own had booked them to play on another continent, with an audience of 40,000.

One aspect that never changed at Reading over the years was the weather. Since 1973, the festival had found a permanent calendar berth on the August Bank Holiday weekend, traditionally marking the end of the British summer: wet, muddy conditions were accepted as a prerequisite, as was the duty of the crowd to hurl mud at the bands. Especially if one of the bands was called Mudhoney . . .

Conditions on Sunday August 30, 1992, were bad even by Reading's standards. High winds compounded the heavy rain; the roof blew off the tented secondary stage, causing it to be closed down midway through the afternoon. There was mud aplenty and it was being lobbed around, albeit none too accurately. Still, perhaps it wasn't the smartest idea to criticize the crowd's throwing capabilities, as Mark Arm did shortly before playing "This Gift."

"Well," he reasons, "they were already throwing mud before we came on. They were throwing mud at L7—not because they hated L7, it seemed like they were trying to interact with the band somehow.

And how do you do that in a venue that's got 40,000 people and a giant barrier between you and the stage? I guess you throw a projectile. It wasn't really too bad, except when you would get a mudball that had rocks in it. So of course, I decided to make a very foolish move by saying something like: 'In America we have this game called baseball and everyone really knows how to aim when they throw. But I guess you guys play soccer . . . ' As soon as I say that, a big chunk of mud hits me in the face. I was asking for it."

Reading had been the UK's first chance to see if major-label largesse might change Mudhoney. Aside from Mark's shiny new white guitar—which finished the set decidedly off-white—the answer had to be an unequivocal "no."

The point was rammed home a little over a month later with the release of the band's third full-length album, *Piece of Cake*. This was assuredly not their *Nevermind*. Recorded in the same basement studio and with the same producer as the previous album, Mudhoney's major label debut was the work of a band consciously overcompensating for what they considered to be the corruption of U.S. underground bands who lost their edge upon entering the corporate realm. Although arguably coming from a paranoid perspective, Mudhoney were smart enough to realize there was no way their unvarnished qualities could sustain the overbearing upgrade given to Nirvana and still make an impact.

No one would have quibbled with their rationale if the material had been of a similar caliber to *Every Good Boy Deserves Fudge*. But although a credible case can be made for *Piece of Cake* containing Mudhoney's greatest song—released as a single, "Suck You Dry" is as definitive and undeniable a knock-down as "Touch Me I'm Sick"—the nonchalant attitude implied by the title was evident in too many by-rote compositions and performances.

"I think by that time we'd actually taken things for granted," says Arm. "The early career path of the band was so enormously without challenge: our friends were starting up a record label, we wanted to record a couple of songs, and from there everything spun out of control. Next thing you know we're in Europe. That's unlike anything that's happened to any band except maybe Led Zeppelin—not that we achieved anything like Led Zeppelin! But the chances of a band that's been around a year, going to Europe and having people give a shit, that was pretty strange. The title, *Piece of Cake*, was just like this whole rock thing is super-easy! And we were maybe a little cavalier about it. Instead of getting in there and really focusing upon the task in hand. But what the hell? We were in our twenties and having a good time."

In actual fact, Mark Arm was 30 and not in such great shape. He looked rake-thin and sickly pale when interviewed on the Warner Bros sofa in London two days after playing Reading, chuckling when reminded of his 1989 prediction that they would eventually get stuck in a rut, sign to a major label, and put out bad music. But *Piece of Cake* wasn't so much bad as careless.

"It's the album that suffered the most due to my inattention to detail and lack of focus," he says now. "Before I went to the studio, I had to go and get my daily dose of drugs, and then I had to leave early to get more. If we were supposed to be there at 11 a.m. I probably didn't show up until 12:30 or 1 p.m., consistently, for the three weeks or however long it took to record. Unless I got the drugs, I would have been mentally incapable—it would have been all I would have been thinking about."

While Turner had picked up the slack on the previous record, this time no one's hand seemed to be gripping the tiller. "Mark was really fucked up," says Steve. "There's no way that wasn't a big part of it. But I was really naïve about drug use, so I certainly wouldn't have told people back then that Mark was getting deeper into drugs. To me he was just showing up late because he was late. We were blasé to a fault, I'm sure, but at the time it seemed like the winning strategy."

Nor was the new record company standing over their shoulder, demanding to hear hits. Signing the band for a small advance meant Warner Bros. had less invested up front and was less inclined to intervene than might otherwise have been the case. But a bigger factor was that the company's upper echelons had been so confused by the sudden inversion of the established order that they felt it best to let the "grungers" do their thing.

David Katznelson, meanwhile, was young, awed, and even a little intimidated by his heroes. He left them well alone. "When I got *Piece of*

Cake, I liked it, but I wasn't in love with it like I was with some of the other Mudhoney records," he admits. "At that point I became a yes-man. I tried to keep true to what I said to them about letting them steer the ship. In retrospect I wish I had cracked the whip. They might have told me to go fuck myself, even though by then I was on better terms with Steve, who would literally go into my wallet and grab my credit card, and say, 'Let's go and get a really expensive dinner'—now that he was on a major label he became into how much could he suck out of [it]. But on an artistic level I was very hands-off."

In the midst of the session, which stretched over most of July 1992, Dan Peters took off to Las Vegas for five days to get married to Donna, his girlfriend of three years. It was a joint ceremony with their friends Kevin Whitworth, from the band Love Battery, and his fiancée, Kim; the idea to tie the knot was drunkenly hatched at six in the morning, when the quartet were the last people standing at a party in Peters' apartment. It was only when on the plane to Las Vegas, four hours later, that Dan remembered he was supposed to be in the studio the next day. In a panic he grabbed the in-seat phone, swiped his credit card, and called Steve Turner to break the news that they would have to make it through the next week without him. Most of his drum parts were already recorded, but Peters' absence was symptomatic of the prevailing mindset.

"We definitely felt we could just whip a record out and not overthink it and take things too seriously," says Dan. "As a band, we collectively feel it's one of our weakest records. Which is unfortunate."

Typifying the air of drift were four short, untitled pieces interspersed throughout the album, the result of each band member giving themselves 45 minutes to write, record, and produce a solo track, like a grunge version of Pink Floyd's *Ummagumma*. Thus Mark delivered a parody of German techno (his brayed exclamation "Sprockets!" sounded like a tribute to Mike Myers' *Saturday Night Live* character, Dieter); Steve's was a peg-legged country hoedown; Dan offered a piece of neolithic speed metal, while Matt made fart noises with his hands. Plausibly funny as it may have been, Arm's mad-for-it Teutonic rooster was perhaps not the best way to unveil the band amid the new world order—as David Katznelson discovered when he played his Warners bosses the keenly anticipated album by their very own Seattle stars, the band who Nirvana had aspired to be. At one meeting he couldn't move fast enough to skip the CD onto track two, "No End in Sight," which, although hardly "In'n'out of Grace," was at least more representative of the Mudhoney *oeuvre*.

"The opening track did not help me when it came to some of the big meetings," says Katznelson. "For some of these people it was the first time they'd heard the band, and they're looking at me like: 'What the fuck is this?!' And I'm the guy who signed The Flaming Lips, the band who sold 12,000 copies of *Hit to Death in the Future Head*, a record that cost a quarter of a million dollars to make, and then I'm coming up with... *this*! Luckily, I don't think they ever got to the farts track."

As far as Warner Bros were concerned, however, the big difference between Mudhoney and The Flaming Lips was that Mudhoney hadn't spent a quarter of a million dollars recording an album. Even after almost a month in the studio—an unprecedented amount of time for them—the bill came to a mere $30,000 by virtue of being recorded in Conrad Uno's basement. It was certainly a substantial sum, but loose change from a total recording budget of $120,000, which was itself modest by major label standards of the time. Meanwhile, the nature of Mudhoney's deal meant the band was allowed to keep anything left over from the recording budget. Ker-ching!

The figures on the other side of the sheet looked respectable too. Whipped along by grunge's El Niño effect, *Piece of Cake* sold 150,000 copies in swift order.

"Warners were hoping for Nirvana numbers, but still, it was nothing to sneeze at," says Katznelson. "For a couple of weeks there I had one of the top-selling bands on the label. It was definitely looked on as a success."

No wonder that, during 1992, Mark Arm could lead the life of an "ethical junkie,"* able to support his own habit as well as that of his girlfriend without ever having to steal from friends or family. But an indication that he was on a downward trajectory came when abiding

* *Everybody Loves Our Town*, 395.

friend Bruce Pavitt and Steve Turner felt they had no option but to visit Mark in person and tell him to go into detox; otherwise, the band wouldn't be able to tour.

"We just had to confront it: 'Look, we can't go on the road with you like this,'" says Turner. "It was obviously a real uncomfortable thing. Because, as I told him then, it's not really my place to tell him not to do something. My only point was: 'We have these things that are planned, and if we're going to do it, *you* have to do *this*.' He agreed to it immediately—I think he was probably thankful for it."

Arm and his girlfriend decided they would try and get clean together. Having signed up to the waiting list, they spent nine days at a King County detoxification center.

"It's brutal," says Mark. "They put you in there for however long it takes you to dry out from whatever you're on, but then there's nothing after that. It's up to you, I guess, to go to some 12-step program. So essentially, after completing the nine days I think we were calling the dealer within four hours of getting released. It's a tough thing to get sober when you're in a relationship with someone who's also fucked up. It doesn't take much to make the dominoes fall over."

David Katznelson had no idea initially of quite how bad Arm's situation had become. As well as an ethical junkie, Mark was a functioning one too—at least when it came to the business of the band, and Mudhoney were a busy band. Like Turner and the others, Katznelson had to endure some excruciatingly protracted phone calls and one or two interviews got missed, but otherwise commitments were fulfilled.

"Mark, in all of his damage, was still somewhat of a responsible individual," he testifies. "A couple of times when he would be down in LA—there was one Castaic Lake show [on September 26, 1992] specifically: Kurt and Courtney showed up, and that always brought a black cloud on everything, and he left with them. Mark and Kurt and Courtney were this damaged trio running around. You knew what was going on. It made me *sad*."

Ten days after Castaic Lake, a festival northeast of Los Angeles where Kurt Cobain had joined the band for an encore of "The Money Will Roll Right In," Mudhoney began a UK tour in Sheffield. It was during this two-week trip that Arm called his girlfriend and told her the party was over. "I said, 'Look, I want you out of the house by the time I get home.'"

None of which impacted upon the band's public profile whatsoever. No gigs got canceled. Anyone attending a Mudhoney live show during this period saw them as fierce and funny as ever, occasionally flirting with collapse but always finding a way out, trading banter and arcane song references with audiences.

The gig at Sheffield Octagon was a case in point: after complaining about individual audience members' unintelligible between-song remarks, Mark declared: "You sound like a bunch of British walruses!"

To which the Yorkshire crowd swiftly got its act together for that timeless classic: "You fat bastards! You fat bastards!"

Mark smiled. "OK, we understand that one . . . but we don't understand why you're calling us fat." To which the crowd responded by pointing en masse at Lukin.

Later, Turner announced "Blinding Sun" as "Hash Cake '77," a Hawkwind song to sort out the real Hawkwind fans from the part-timers. Business as usual then, except for one small detail: this was the one short period when "Touch Me I'm Sick" was consistently omitted from set lists. During the last quarter of 1992 it was more an exception than the rule for audiences to hear it. This was Mark Arm's call.

"Mark didn't like playing it for a little while in there," says Steve. "Just his contrary nature. He didn't like that we were expected to play it. I always thought we should play it. But, I understand getting sick of certain songs. And he was always the guy who was in charge of the set lists."

Viewed with the benefit of 20 years' hindsight, *Piece of Cake* feels more like a wasted opportunity than an outright failure. There's a bright 10-track album lurking within its lackadaisical cloud of 17 tracks (including the untitled snippets). As David Katznelson could attest, the sequencing is questionable, but more bewildering decisions were taken over the final track listing. Recorded during the same July sessions at Egg, both "Deception Pass" and "Underide" are far superior to at least two songs on the album yet never made the cut (they appeared as B-sides on the 12-inch version of "Suck You Dry"). Named after the strait separating Fidalgo and Whidbey Islands in the farthest northwesterly point of Washington state and spanned by a 180-foot bridge that's a frequent suicide location, "Deception Pass" is a rollicking tale of a lost soul in turmoil ("Tried to sell my way out/But the devil wasn't there") who eventually discovers, "It's not so bad/When you're on top of Deception Pass." "Underide," meanwhile, is a terrific curio; named after a drivers' education film that Dan remembered seeing as a teenager, over terse skeletal guitar chops Mark narrates a tale of a fatally botched bank heist. It's like The Fall covering The Velvet Underground's "The Gift."

Twenty years on, Arm has completely forgotten "Underide" and needs it played to him to be reminded. "That was from the *Piece of Cake* era?" he asks. "I wonder why that song didn't make it on the record, because it's probably better than some of the songs that are on there."

Such inconsistency seems another facet of the distracted mood. Yet one of the album's later compositions, "Suck You Dry," is a peak Mudhoney experience; the brusque guitar separation possesses an alien quality that never dates and it's also possibly Dan Peters' finest performance—which is saying a lot. Towards the end of the album, "Ritzville" emerges from a torpid sequence with one of the band's great unfettered performances and an opening couplet—"With my heart on my sleeve and my head on the curb/Got a sign on my cell that reads 'Do Not Disturb'"—that's archetypal Arm noir. "As good a place as any to go and die," according to the chorus, Ritzville is a small town of very little in eastern Washington, where traffic police sit in wait for drivers hurrying through on Interstate 90 en route to somewhere worth going.

"It's just a little municipality seeking to increase its coffers by pulling over speeders," says Arm. "There's nothing ritzy about Ritzville."

The album closes pointedly with "Acetone," a country blues account of a couple in the grip of addiction: "Look at me and answer truthful now/Did you drink that last spoonful down? . . . Oh Lord, what have we become?/We're not fooling anyone." It's as transparent a broadcast as Arm ever gave of his circumstances; nonetheless, without intimate knowledge of the singer's personal life, it could simply be a deftly delivered homage to Townes Van Zandt, with Charley Patton's "A Spoonful Blues" as its root source.

Not everyone appreciated this step away from the grunge mainframe: Mark remembers receiving a letter from a disgruntled "ex-fan" demanding to know what exactly Mudhoney had become, citing "Acetone" as Exhibit A for the prosecution. "And it was a girl too—girls are meant to like that sappy shit!" he laughs. "Man, I haven't listened to that song in a very long time."

That the details of his heroin use didn't emerge until many years later must be at least partly due to his refusal to become defined by the drug. He was certainly aided by his bandmates' disavowal of the junkie lifestyle, but also by fear of being revealed as what he later termed, "a total cliché—[I was] a rock guy, strung out on heroin and actually for a while was going out with a stripper."* Then there were the residual ties of family. For all the generational angst of his upbringing, Mark loved his parents and was terrified at the prospect of them finding out.

"He was very good at hiding it—he didn't need his drug problem to become public knowledge," says Charles Peterson. "And it wouldn't have served the band at all, it wouldn't have served him as a musician. Unlike some others, I'd say Layne Staley or Kurt Cobain—heroin almost served to fuel their myth, their personality."

It all caught up with Mark Arm on New Year's Eve 1992. With his girlfriend no longer part of the picture, he'd managed to stay clear of drugs since returning from the UK tour, but that night he overdosed in Kurt Cobain and Courtney Love's room at The Inn at the Market, an expensive hotel in downtown Seattle.

"I think one of the reasons I OD'd that night was because I hadn't been doing heroin," he says. "I didn't have any tolerance. Also, I was drinking. It was New Year's Eve. I was pretty drunk. And then someone says, 'Hey, d'you wanna come over and do some drugs?' 'Sure!' That was not a series of good decisions. It was a series of poor decisions. And I did a shot of heroin and I was like, 'I'd like to get

* *I'm Now: The Story of Mudhoney*, directed by Ryan Short and Adam Pease (King of Hearts Productions, 2012).

higher.' And so I went and got more. I wasn't satisfied. I guess I wanted *complete* obliteration."

In the account of Ron Heathman, the guitarist with The Supersuckers who had accompanied Mark to the Cobains' room, Arm began turning blue.* On previous occasions when he had overdosed, there had always been someone present and sufficiently compos mentis to call the emergency services. This time, while Cobain and Heathman attempted to resuscitate him, Love's first instinct was apparently not to call 911.

"I don't know why," says Arm. "Because she didn't want the publicity?"

Accounts vary as to who she did call—Heathman and Courtney herself suggest Jonathan Poneman; "Absolutely not true," says Poneman—but eventually the paramedics arrived and Arm was taken to Harborview Hospital.

To be revived from an overdose for possibly the fourth or fifth (but definitely the last) time.

"It was after that, I thought, 'I don't think I can hang around Kurt and Courtney anymore,'" says Mark.

* * *

Following a worrisome start to 1993, it was a relief to escape to a happier place. Australia was Mudhoney's spiritual home. Ever since Mark Arm discovered The Birthday Party at university, and Steve Turner subsequently plugged The Scientists and feedtime into the band's molecular structure, something about the place and its people made them a perfect fit. If Seattle was a frontier town at the edge of a nation, Australia was a frontier continent at the edge of the world—with all the appropriately careless appetites. Australians have little time for pretense and like to make noise. Mudhoney's reputation thus far had been stoked by their live shows' playful bacchanalia. What could go wrong?

"It felt like everyone knew what we were about before we got there, and were ready for it," says Mark.

* *Everybody Loves Our Town*, 397.

Their first Australian tour, early in 1990, had been a roaring success. Playing multiple nights in each of eastern Australia's major cities over three weeks, Mudhoney hung out with new friends like Lubricated Goat—who they had first met in Seattle the previous year—and were generally considered "blokes you can trust," as the no-nonsense vernacular of Cosmic Psychos would have it.

The visit began auspiciously. Upon landing in Melbourne during the middle of the Australian summer, they dropped their bags off at the hotel in the seaside suburb of St. Kilda and decided to enjoy what was, for Seattleites, the uncommon sight of sunshine in February.

Strolling along a boardwalk above the beach, Arm and Turner couldn't help but notice some of the female sunbathers were topless. Motioning to the others, they suddenly realized the others were already aware of this fact. Arm stared open mouthed as Matt Lukin and Dan Peters yomped down the middle of the sandy beach, still in their wet-weather boots, like dogs on heat. "They're ogling at these ladies. I'm like, 'Oh man, I'm trying to play it cool here!'"

When they returned for a second trip at the end of the year, the notion of summer in December still took some getting used to. Dan spent the first day of the tour on Bondi Beach, without wearing any UV block. Not one of nature's sun-worshippers, Peters rationalized that his fair skin was going to burn anyway, so what was the point of bothering with sunscreen? He returned from Bondi with his face contorted by blisters.

"He looked like Alligator Man," says Turner. "He was feverish and fucked up. So at the show he had a headband on and his blisters were oozing out of the headband."

Once again, Australia and Mudhoney proved they had a certain understanding. The last gig of the tour was an open-air set at Sydney's Bondi Pavilion, which the police curtailed due to excessive noise levels. Permitted one more song, Mudhoney inevitably played "Hate the Police," before band and audience gently wound proceedings down by throwing beer cans at each other.

The year 1993 promised even higher levels of mania. The Big Day Out was Australia's newest rock festival, founded by promoter Ken

West in the name of "urban mayhem . . . controlled chaos."* After Nirvana had played its inaugural staging in 1992 to 10,000 people at the Sydney Showgrounds, Mudhoney was invited to be part of Big Day Out's debut as an itinerant circus, where a core of bands toured the major cities across the country, playing to crowds of 40,000.

This would have been exciting enough, but the lineup was a stellar array of Mudhoney heroes and friends, old and new. The friends contingent included Cosmic Psychos and Beasts of Bourbon, featuring ex-Scientist Kim Salmon, whom they had met on previous tours. Australian beach-punks The Hard-Ons were playing with Jerry A, the singer from Portland, Oregon, hardcore legends Poison Idea. By this point, having shared so many insalubrious dressing rooms around the world, Sonic Youth were virtually family. Then, in the hero category—at least as far as Mark was concerned—stood Nick Cave & The Bad Seeds; but above them all, both in his headline billing and godhead status, there was Iggy Pop.

Their one previous meeting had been just three months earlier in New York, where Arm was so nervous he hid in the bathroom backstage at the Roseland Ballroom in order to compose himself. This time, Mark promised, would be much cooler. And so it was. Having known both Iggy and Mudhoney for many years, Sonic Youth were a social intersection for both parties, while Beasts of Bourbon were friends with The Bad Seeds and could thus bring Cave into the circle. Any initial awkwardness soon passed.

"It was all very entertaining," says Thurston Moore. There was an occasional veneer of starry *hauteur* with Iggy, whose manager would cordon off the side of the stage so the other bands couldn't climb up there to watch. Moore also noticed that Iggy tended to gravitate towards Cave, having assessed the situation and decided that "he seems to be the big cheese here." But there were no hierarchies onstage. For Sonic Youth's encore in Sydney, Mark and Matt joined Iggy Pop and Nick Cave for an ensemble romp through The Stooges' "I Wanna Be Your Dog," which ended in a mass pileup as Lukin tackled Iggy to

* *Peace, Love + Brown Rice* (www.peaceloveandbrownrice.com) by Sophie Howarth.

the ground. On another night, Mudhoney joined Iggy, Sonic Youth, and Beasts of Bourbon during The Bad Seeds' set for a version of The Stooges' "Little Doll."

All was sweetness and light—at least until the tour took a day off, and Mark found himself in a restaurant sitting down to dinner next to Iggy.

"It was unfortunate," says Arm. "Iggy always seemed really pleasant and happy to see me, up until this one dinner. I got really, really drunk, and finally I figured that now was the time to ask all my questions about Ron Asheton. Like, 'Why the fuck did you fuck off and fuck over Ron?!'"

Across the table, Thurston Moore watched, aghast, as Arm unraveled in front of his idol. "Mark's next to Iggy, it's like he's sitting next to Jesus Christ. Initially I thought he was nervous about this, but as it turned out he was completely drunk. He could hardly talk he was so drunk. He was so drunk he was looking at Iggy like he was looking at a painting. I could see Iggy looking round, as if to see if there was a security guy anywhere. Y'know, 'Umm . . . ?'"

Moore tried to steer the conversation into safer territory by saying that James Williamson, whose usurpation of Ron Asheton in The Stooges had so outraged Mark, was a great guitarist in his own right. Mark agreed—but wouldn't be derailed. "Why'd you do that to Ron?" he kept saying, before adding, for good measure, "How did you get that sound on *Fun House*?" Iggy humored him until the end of the meal, then got up and left.

"For the rest of the tour," says Arm, "I would see Iggy see me approaching, walking down a hallway—and he'd suddenly duck into a room! Like, 'Oh, *this* guy . . . '" He sighs. "I can only imagine how horrible that was."

Matt Lukin's approach to breaking the ice with the loftier members of the Big Day Out entourage was typically more blunt. He wrestled them. One day, Arm looked round to see Lukin and Nick Cave grappling with each other through a cloud of grass and dirt. Aware that Matt wasn't the world's biggest Cave fan, Mark assumed that Lukin was the aggressor. But in fact, it was the other way round. It's possible that, in Cave's mind, with his Marlboro-branded shorts and ever-present bottle of beer, Lukin represented a beacon of authenticity amid the showbiz posturing that afflicts even supposedly countercultural events such as the rock festival. Not quite yet the urbane social chameleon he's become, Cave may have doubted whether his reputation permitted giving Lukin a kiss and a cuddle, so a wrestle was a more acceptably masculine—more *Australian*—alternative. Mudhoney manager Bob Whittaker had noticed this phenomenon before, when Lukin took to goading Henry Rollins with cigarettes at a European festival, thereby breaking the ice with the legendarily clean-living iron man of hardcore. "Lukin always shines when you least expect it," says Whittaker. "He could draw these stoic rock stars out of character—they would come out of their shell for Lukin, this warm, jovial man. It was fun to see Lukin bring these guys up to his level."

Cave always instigated the wrestling bouts, in which Lukin found himself at a disadvantage, having fallen off the stage while watching the Bad Seeds' set on the opening show of the tour. But even with a cracked rib and a beer in one hand, there was, Lukin claims, only ever one winner: "I must say, Nick Cave's not a very good wrestler. I thought Australians were a little tougher than that! I could get on top of him and hold him down. In fact, I got pulled off him one time by his band members because I kept rubbing his face in the grass. They were like, 'That's enough, Matt!' Well, he asked for it! We barely talked—it would just be these wrestling matches that would break out when he tackled me. But heck, he seemed like a cool guy. I liked him a lot after that."

The last night of the tour saw an impromptu party around the pool of the swish Perth hotel where most of the Big Day Out's 70-strong retinue of artists and staff were staying. The mood was delirious. Nick Cave and Thurston Moore sprawled on sun loungers, smoking cigarettes and looking on indulgently as the younger generation raised hell. A team of skateboarders who had been giving displays during the tour were now climbing up to the balconies of rooms that overlooked the pool and jumping in. The higher they climbed, the closer one would come to splatting on the concrete, or injuring the people actually in the pool. A hotel manager came out and told the skaters to stop. Though he was roundly booed, eventually the skaters complied as their behavior was irritating everyone else. Emboldened by his success, however, the hotel official then attempted to clear the entire pool area by declaring the party over. As he stood by the pool, his yells and gesticulations were drowned out by catcalls from some and ignored by the rest. Suddenly, Mark Arm ran forward and summoned up the best approximation of a strongside linebacker his skinny frame would allow. Both Mark and the hotel manager fell into the pool. By now insensible with rage, the manager thrashed around the water screaming at the injustice of it all. Hurrying away to change his clothes, lest he be fingered as the culprit, Mark was grabbed into a manly embrace by Nick Cave, who hailed his debunking of authority as an act of anarchic genius. "You," Cave declared, "are my hero for all time."

Far away from the turbulence of Seattle, Mudhoney had found succor in the more ordinary madness offered Down Under. Their performances, in front of massive and enthusiastic crowds, were riotously powerful. The bonhomie and mutual respect among the musicians was genuine. Even today, Steve Turner's face brightens at the mere mention of Australia—"our first love!"—and in particular the Big Day Out. "I still consider that to be the greatest tour we ever got to do. Just because of the other bands—Nick Cave, Sonic Youth, Beasts of Bourbon, Iggy. Lotta good music there. And lots of fun hanging out. It was a high watermark for me."

The Big Day Out came at an important moment for the band. Not least because its reservoir of happy memories would provide valuable sustenance amid 1993's ongoing grunge folderol.

* * *

Ten days after returning from Australia, Mudhoney played a gig in Seattle, an all-ages event at the Oddfellows Hall on Capitol Hill. (It was shut down early by the police, citing the ever-preposterous Teen Dance Ordinance; the point at which City Hall would sense the benefits of a thriving local music industry was still some way off.)

Three weeks later they were in Hawaii supporting Sonic Youth, and a month after that a U.S. tour began. Indeed, there would only be one month in the whole of 1993 when the band weren't on the road somewhere in the world.

Amid this busy schedule, the band members were slowly recalibrating their lives. All four began the process of investing their grunge windfall by putting down payments on houses. Steve was first, purchasing a $189,000 property on Capitol Hill with an incredible view of the Olympic mountains. They were buying at just the right time: in a couple of years Seattle real estate prices would be among the highest in the U.S., as the city surfed the high-tech industry boom. Dan and his wife bought a place in Ballard, while the newly married Matt Lukin settled down in West Seattle. As for Mark, in August he and Emily Rieman started going out once more. It was a crossroads moment in his life.

"She goes, 'So, are you ever gonna do heroin again?' And I gave this wishy-washy answer: '*Weeeell...* you never know what the future holds.' I wasn't totally prepared, I guess, to say: I will never do this again. Because up until that point I had still been doing it, actually, on occasion. Emily just looked at me and goes: 'If you ever do it again, I am out of here.' That was enough of a push that I needed to go, 'OK.' That made up my mind."

There was no recourse to a rehab facility, or Narcotics Anonymous, or a 12-step program. Mark knew what he had to do and he did it privately, without fuss. For old friends like Ed Fotheringham, who hadn't been able to stay close to him during the lowest depths of his addiction, it was remarkable to witness.

"He was quiet about his quitting—mainly because I didn't see much of him—but there were never any post-addiction heroics," confirms Ed. "There was never any martyrdom, or wanting to be seen as a special person because he'd overcome it. Unlike myself, Mark is an incredibly controlled individual. He's not uptight, but he is a bit of a perfectionist, so I don't know if he was doing drugs to loosen up or lose control, but it was just weird, considering his past behavior. I recall living with Mark in a house called The White House, near UW—I had almost graduated from college, so it would have been '86. I remember watching him put peanut butter on toast. And it took forever. He had to hit the margins perfectly . . . And then he started shooting heroin—I don't get it! He was in a bad way, a very bad way for a couple of years, but he turned himself around quick-smart. And for those of us that know and love him, it's great."

Amid this period of flux and reorganization, David Katznelson thought that the Mudhoney tour wagon needed a new record to fuel its journey. There were a only handful of new songs written, not enough for an album, so Katznelson suggested an EP. Immediately after returning from a week in Japan, the band did a day's recording with The Fastbacks' Kurt Bloch, in Seattle, yielding four new songs and a wildly superior rerecording of "Make It Now" from *Piece of Cake*.

Stylistically, the new recordings were all over the map: the ripping "No Song III" had some Hawkwind-compatible ring modulator action; "Between Me & You Kid" served up fire and brimstone R&B; "Six Two One" took a dive back to the Billy Childish manual; while opener "In the Blood," with pellucid guitar and spooky organ, was a striking departure into country-soul territory, reminiscent of Alex Chilton.

There was much to admire, but the material's sheer diversity, allied to the EP format, suggested a band scrambling to muster enough songs for a release, an impression that the gambit of including "Deception Pass" and "Underide" along with the restyled "Make It Now Again" did nothing to dispel.

Titled *Five Dollar Bob's Mock Cooter Stew*, it struggled for attention either from the public or the Warner Bros. promotional machine. Following an undercooked album with a record that was neither one thing nor another had merely stalled the band's momentum.

"I like it a lot," says Turner. "I thought it was a really diverse blend of songs, and Kurt Bloch produced great sounds. But I think we should have held off and done another LP—of that material and some other stuff. It took the wind out of our sails a little bit."

Five Dollar Bob's Mock Cooter Stew was released in the last week of October, just as Mudhoney completed their first arena tour. Not that they were headlining; having hitherto turned down invitations to play large venues opening up for other bands, they finally accepted an offer to join Nirvana on the opening Midwest leg of the *In Utero* tour. For good measure, they were then booked to do likewise for Pearl Jam a month later.

These engagements with the twin commercial spearheads of the grunge phenomenon seemed an acceptable compromise, inasmuch as Mudhoney had shared history with both bands. Of the two it was the Nirvana tour they were looking forward to, and not just because of the likelihood that Nirvana's audience would be more receptive to Mudhoney's sensibilities. Mark Arm had barely seen Jeff Ament and Stone Gossard since the breakup of Green River and they certainly hadn't spoken at any length. Doubtless mindful of Mudhoney's iron-clad integrity, Kurt Cobain had maintained visible links with his erstwhile Sub Pop labelmates—Nirvana were the unannounced support band for two Mudhoney shows in October 1992—while going out of his way to badmouth Pearl Jam in the press for vague crimes against alternative rock. So the prospect of lingering awkwardness was very real.

"You didn't really know what the other one thought," says Arm. "You could make up all sorts of stuff in your head that might or might not be true. The perception at the time was that Pearl Jam was a sell-out major label band and Nirvana was the band that came up through punk rock—which was a crazy myth, but that's the way things were. Jeff was in a hardcore band, he had a fanzine, he was more involved in the punk rock and hardcore scene than Kurt Cobain ever was. And Stone and Jeff were in Green River, which was on Sub Pop. The roots are just as deep."

In fact it was the Nirvana tour that turned out to be a nightmare. Uneasy personal interaction had been a part of Nirvana's DNA from the very beginning, but now the band was a million-dollar industry dependent on a vulnerable, depressed drug addict. Craig Montgomery, who had been mixing Nirvana's live sound since 1989, was dismissed on the eve of the tour after Cobain heard adverse reports of the band's recent *Saturday Night Live* appearance. Paranoia stalked the corridors backstage at the tour's various convention centers and sports halls, as Nirvana employees feared for their jobs. Mudhoney were completely unprepared for what lay in store.

"It was dark and depressing," says Lukin. "Jeez, you guys do this every day?! No wonder you don't like it. Nirvana were the opposite of nirvana. They were quite dull. In fact, I felt we were just annoying them by being there and having a good time. They'd become the opposite of what I thought they'd started out to be."

The dysfunctional culture of the Nirvana organization was exemplified by a decision to keep the backstage areas alcohol-free—as if Cobain's problem at this point was booze. No sane person's first choice as the ideal support band on a dry tour, after much haggling between Bob Whittaker and Nirvana's management, Mudhoney were permitted beer in their dressing room.

"So Nirvana would come into our room and drink our beer," says Mark. "Even their fucking manager asked us for a beer! It was absurd."

In Chicago, where both bands had lots of friends on the guest list, Mudhoney's dressing room was the place to be. Soon the beer ran out and Phillip Hertz, a former drummer with The Scientists, went to the catering area and took a case of 12 bottles. The reaction was as if Fort Knox had been ram-raided. It took Whittaker three conference calls involving Nirvana's tour manager and manager to prevent Mudhoney being kicked off the tour.

Having endured seven shows with their "cool" friends, thoughts now turned to the prospect of six shows with their "uncool" counterparts—how uncool was the uncool tour going to be? The auguries weren't good. If pressure was a numbers game, then Pearl Jam at the end of November 1993 knew its exact coordinates. Propelled by the frenzied mainstream crossover of their debut album, *Ten*, their new album, *Vs*, had sold over 950,000 copies during its first week of release in the U.S. alone. But while Nirvana dutifully submitted to the industrial strictures of the music business—the expensive videos, the *Rolling Stone* front cover—Pearl Jam got militant. They would make no videos, they would give no interviews. And they would take Mudhoney on tour and have fun.

The notion of reuniting the estranged Green River camps came from Eddie Vedder, who brought an outsider's perspective to the situation. "Ed asked Stone and I, 'Hey, what do you think about Mudhoney for the tour?'" says Jeff Ament. "It seemed like the right time to reach across the aisle and say, 'Let's bury the hatchet.' Because there was still a bit of tension in the air. I think it started to subside a little bit, and then Kurt Cobain started saying shit again. Basically he was just saying what Mark had said a few years previous. I mean, Kurt didn't know us. He didn't really have any real basis for what he said other than the fact that he hated our music. Well, that's one thing. But it was more of a personal attack, and I think a lot of that was just Kurt mimicking Mark—which I think he did a lot. You listen to early Nirvana and there's a lot of Mudhoney in that. So those wounds stayed open longer than they should have. Once we were on tour it was like, 'Fuck I can't believe that we didn't do this sooner.' It made me remember how much I liked those guys."

For Mudhoney, touring with Pearl Jam was the flipside of their Nirvana experience. Crowds were indifferent to them, but the congenial atmosphere behind the scenes more than compensated.

"Our shows suck," says Dan. "We have a good time, but the audience don't wanna see anybody except for Eddie. Fair enough. They didn't boo us by any means, but they just sit there and politely wait for their Eddie to come out. But that tour was a gas. Pearl Jam's a band you could look at as a model of how to do things properly in the rock world. They treat people with respect, they surround themselves with straight-up, honest people."

So successful were the backstage bonding sessions—group meals, ping-pong, skateboarding—that by the third date, in Las Vegas, Pearl Jam's set ended with a Green River reunion—or as close as was possible, given that Alex Shumway now lived in Japan. Arm and Turner joined Ament and Gossard, plus Chuck Treece from openers Urge Overkill on drums, to play "Swallow My Pride" and "Ain't Nothing to Do." There was a similar finale to the tour closer in Reno, this time with Dan Peters and Pearl Jam drummer Dave Abbruzzese joining the fun.

For Mudhoney, touring with Pearl Jam illustrated that commercial success needn't be incompatible with civility. That the Nirvana tour should have suggested the opposite was a timely reminder that espousing the egalitarian values of punk meant nothing unless values were underpinned by deeds. In this regard, reuniting their old band had special resonance: on June 26, 1986, Green River opened for Public Image Ltd. at the Paramount Theatre and were shabbily treated in the old-school rock tradition that the punk movement had supposedly renounced (though Green River did return the favor, trashing PiL's dressing room while the band played). And while Mother Love Bone had acquiesced to the excesses of corporate rock culture, when Ament and Gossard put Pearl Jam together they took a different approach.

"By the time Mudhoney came on tour with us, every single person on our crew was a friend," says Ament. "Pearl Jam was an opportunity to do things the way that Mudhoney do it."

The links between the two bands would only strengthen in the years ahead. They were on tour together again four months later, playing 10,000-capacity arenas on the East Coast, when the news broke on April 8, 1994, that Kurt Cobain was dead. In the Washington, D.C. hotel room he was sharing with Matt Lukin, Dan Peters woke to the sound of the telephone. It was his wife:

"She said, 'Have you seen the news? You should turn it on.' So I did. Matt was in the shower when I saw it: 'Aw, Jeez.' So I waited for Matt to come out of the shower and told him what had happened. Everybody was in a daze."

That evening's show at the Fairfax Patriot Center went ahead, but in an atmosphere of collective shock. Backstage, Eddie Vedder was talking to the Fugazi and former Minor Threat singer Ian MacKaye. Ordinarily, Steve Turner would have been there too, chatting to the man who was both a peer and a childhood musical hero, but this was not the time.

"It was a rough night," he says. "Everybody was so bummed, the crowd was bummed . . . Kurt's death didn't surprise us, really. It was just numbing. God, what a waste."

Things got weirder the next day. Pearl Jam were due at the White House for a meeting with President Clinton's special policy adviser, George Stephanopoulos, about the possibility of playing gigs in communities affected by military base closures; now they also invited Mudhoney to come along.

Before getting in the shuttle bus that would take them to 1600 Pennsylvania Avenue, Lukin shared a joint with Arm and Peters. He had another in his pocket but thought it best not to smoke it in front of an official White House driver, especially as that driver was telling them about the stringent Secret Service checkpoint they would soon be going through.

"Next thing I know we're pulling into the White House compound," says Lukin. "Fuck, I've got this joint on me, what do I do with it?! I ended up eating it! I don't think you can really get that high from eating it; I just didn't want it to go to waste. I'm sitting there eating this dry joint. Already stoned from the one I'd smoked. So I'm walking around all baked and I remember this guy being introduced to us as "the strongest drug-free policeman"—he'd won some weightlifting competition amongst all the policemen in the country. Of course, when they said "drug-free" they meant "steroid-free" . . . but what I was thinking they meant was that he was the strongest DEA agent—like he's hot stuff and he's going to arrest me for being stoned! Fuck!"

Soon after arriving at the White House, the two bands got separated by officials. Pearl Jam were ushered into the Oval Office to meet Bill Clinton, which hadn't been part of the original plan—apparently, the president wanted to seek advice on whether he should address the nation in the wake of Cobain's suicide.

Mudhoney, meanwhile, were assigned a Secret Service agent who gave them a behind-the-scenes tour of the White House. As they were ushered past the velvet ropes, tourists waiting in line for a regular tour ran up and asked for autographs.

"Obviously word had got around that Pearl Jam was in the House, but these old ladies didn't know what Pearl Jam looked like," says Peters. "We're saying, 'Yeah, we're not Pearl Jam.' And they were like, 'Ha ha! Just give us your autograph.' Still, it was a nice diversion from the whole Kurt-blowing-his-head-off thing."

The two bands' paths eventually crossed in the White House Press Room, where Arm and Vedder had their picture taken shaking hands over the presidential seal on the podium.

"It was a great private tour," says Turner. "The Secret Service guy was telling us about the different people that have been killed on the White House lawn. There was one guy dressed in full ninja gear who thought he was invisible, coming across the lawn. They finally just shot him. I don't recall hearing about that on the news! It was a surreal day. I remember being almost troubled that the President of the United States of America is taking the time to meet Eddie Vedder. Like, that's top of today's agenda? Really?!"

As the world reeled in shock at Cobain's death, Mudhoney were thankful to be far away from the soap opera of its aftermath in Seattle: public vigil, memorial service, rival wakes, etc. The tour ran until April 17. The final show, at the Paramount Theatre in New York's Madison Square Garden, ended with Mark Arm joining Pearl Jam for a livid version of The Dead Boys' "Sonic Reducer." The contrast between this smarting underdog anthem, a declaration of self-worth against an indifferent world—with its suddenly pointed refrain "ain't no loser"—and the media-churned beatification of a punk-rock casualty was very apt.

One night, during their brief, miserable tour with Nirvana the previous autumn, Mudhoney had given their crew the run of the van and hitched a ride on Nirvana's luxurious tour bus. As they drove between Davenport, Iowa, and Chicago, Kurt Cobain asked Mark Arm how he'd been able to stop doing heroin.

"I said I just wanted to stop bad enough," says Mark. "It wasn't any fun anymore, I wasn't having a good time . . . I wanted to stop bad enough and I stopped. And the one thing that I held back from saying—which I really wish I had said—was that I'd stopped hanging around with my friends who were junkies and I fucking broke up with my junkie girlfriend."

For the remainder of 1994, Mudhoney kept a low public profile. But this was not a band in retreat. With a new practice room in the basement of Mark and Emily's house in West Seattle, they wrote and rehearsed, completing the long, slow process of regrouping after the *Piece of Cake* misfire.

Additionally, Mark was enjoying playing guitar in Bloodloss, a band of ex-pat Australians featuring former members of Lubricated Goat: drummer Martin Bland, bassist Guy Maddison, and saxophone-toting frontman Eric Reynolds, a.k.a. Renestair E. J., a.k.a. Ren. Thanks to the rich contributions from all concerned, Bloodloss's deep-broiled Beefheart skronk had immense character.

Come October, Mudhoney were ready and loaded their gear downstairs at The Storeroom Tavern in Eastlake, which had a very basic basement space known as The Ranch. They also brought Jack Endino with them and a rented 24-track recording machine. With delicious contrariness, just as the media were declaring grunge dead in the wake of Kurt Cobain's suicide, the band that originally synthesized its component parts were reuniting with the form's sonic architect. It was the first time they had worked with Endino since 1989.

"Right from the get-go it was clear some things had changed," he says. "The band's whole vibe had improved, for specific reasons that are best explained by Mark himself. The band wanted to experiment a bit with sounds and instrumentation. And of course, by then I had six more years of experience under my belt."

The recording session was happy and productive, in spite (or because) of taking place beneath a pub. A typical day's work would end upstairs at the bar, plying dollars into the Store Room's legendary jukebox—where Western swing king Bob Wills shared needle-time with Fear, Nick Cave, and The Crucifucks. With the tavern a mere half-mile down Capitol Hill from his house, Steve Turner could simply ride his bike there each morning and wobble home at night.

"We were having a good time," he testifies. "Mark was cleaned up and doing great. I think being in Bloodloss was a big influence on his guitar playing. We were all just more together."

The team spirit was sufficiently robust to withstand both guest musicians and guest instruments. Dan Peters dragged his newly purchased marimba into the studio and wielded the mallets in tribute to The Flesh Eaters' DJ Bonebrake. John Wahl from Clawhammer, a California band that Bob Whittaker was also managing, blew some harmonica, while Ren added tenor sax to "1995," an apocalyptic rumination upon The Stooges' "1969." With the band fully engaged with each other and their music, the creative climate was a marked contrast to the inertia that clouded *Piece of Cake*.

"I was definitely more involved and trying to make a good record," says Arm. "I was more confident in what the band was doing."

When David Katznelson heard the rough mixes of the album, he was stunned not just by how sharp the material sounded, but the specific content of the songs. Although telephone conversations had proved to him how Mark Arm was refocused ("he was like a different person, someone you could have a normal conversation with"), what took the Warners A&R man's breath away was the pointed clarity of these new lyrics.

"What happened?" he reflects. "Well, Kurt died. And Mudhoney, being a fabulously reactive punk band, wrote a rock opera—although if they ever heard me say that I'd probably lose my testicles—about the impact Nirvana's fame had on both Kurt and the Seattle movement in general. They sent me the demo and I was just floored. Truly amazed."

One song in particular, a vituperative spasm of rage at the madness that had befallen Seattle, proved to be Mudhoney's very own "Sonic Reducer." The song was called "Into Yer Shtik," and even before it was released it would land Mudhoney in trouble.

8

Everybody's Got a Price

The shtik hit the fan on February 21, 1995: Mark Arm's 33rd birthday. Mudhoney was at Warner Bros. HQ in Burbank for a meeting with David Katznelson, to discuss plans for what was shaping up to be a busy year. The new album, *My Brother the Cow*, had a release date scheduled for the end of March; tours and a promotional campaign were being organized.

Then, just as the candles were being lit on the cake, the telephone rang in David Katznelson's office. It was Danny Goldberg, the new Chairman and CEO of Warner Bros. Records. There was, he informed Katznelson, a problem. Goldberg had just spoken with Courtney Love about a song on the forthcoming Mudhoney album: "Into Yer Shtik" had a lyric—"Why don't you blow your brains out too?"—which she assumed was about her. She was unhappy, and when Courtney was unhappy, Danny Goldberg took notice. Prior to landing the top job at Warner Bros., he had been head of Atlantic Records and, before that, Gold Mountain, the management company that looked after both Nirvana and Love's band, Hole. For good measure, his wife, Rosemary Carroll, was Courtney Love's lawyer. Goldberg repeated to David Katznelson what Love had told him.

"Danny was very tight with Courtney," says Katznelson. "That's the relationship they had, and I respect them for it. So Courtney—

obviously very sensitive about her public image—listens to the record, and when it got to 'Into Yer Shtik' and the 'blow your brains out too' line, it was a very, very big problem for her. So she called Danny and complained about it. And that didn't go down well with Danny, because her complaints were not your normal complaints."

Love declared that, because of "Into Yer Shtik," she was going to have to go back into therapy—that it was going to cause her to have a breakdown. She found it especially upsetting that someone she'd considered a personal friend could have done this.

"This was when I found out the details of what happened with Mark's OD on New Year's Eve 1992," says Katznelson,"because Courtney's claiming, 'I'm the one who took him to the hospital and if it wasn't for me he'd be dead, and the fact that he's coming out and saying this is so repugnant!' Actually she didn't say 'repugnant,' that's much too big a word; it was a synonym of that. So, a very surreal moment. Mark's sitting there with a birthday cake. Danny didn't even know Mudhoney was in the building. I was worried—and I was befuddled at what was going on here. Danny is a big proponent of ACLU [the American Civil Liberties Union] and his politics are truly wonderful—and yet this is a band using free speech."

Katznelson agreed to meet with Goldberg that evening. By lunchtime the following day, they had smoothed everything out. In the meantime, however, the Warner Bros. CEO did not come and sing "Happy Birthday" to Mark Arm.

"Into Yer Shtik" certainly caused a kerfuffle. But as Arm later said: "It was meant to be heard."*

With his mind now sharply in focus, Mark had taken a long hard look at the city he lived in and the music business where he—for want of a better term—worked. It did not make for pleasant viewing. The death of Kurt Cobain was simply the most horrific manifestation of an industry that takes people as its raw material and grinds away at them. Cobain was a conflicted character: part of him wanted to be rich and

* *Piece of Cake/My Brother the Cow* reissue review by Keith Cameron, *MOJO*, September 2003.

famous, and he enjoyed aspects of what money could bring him, but he was ill equipped to deal with the stresses of becoming a marketable item. As far as Arm could see, none of the industry figures who worked closely with Cobain had been either sufficiently willing or able to help him because they had too much at stake in the process of him being a rock star.

"Kurt never found a way out," he said. "He was just surrounded by sycophants."*

On a banal level, the same industrial processes debased everyday life. Seattle's magnetic appeal for grunge rubberneckers—as Steve puts it, "all these bozos suddenly walking round looking like Chris Cornell"—took on more sinister aspects. Eddie Vedder became an increasingly reclusive figure, living with 24-hour security. He had issues with stalkers. One day, a woman drove a car at 50 miles per hour into the wall of his house (she survived). Vedder wrote a song about his situation, wherein he loses his house keys, walks to the supermarket, but finds people staring at him; having found his keys, he returns home to find his door open and inside there's a woman who claims he raped her and fathered her son. The song was called "Lukin"; in order to escape the madness, Vedder would go to Matt Lukin's house, sit on a stool in the kitchen, and drink beer. Lukin's was his safe haven.

"He was too afraid to go home because that girl might be there," says Matt. "We'd get drunk in the kitchen and goof off. And I don't know if he likes me because I flip him shit once in a while—y'know, he's a big rock star and I'll give him shit about him and his band or whatever. Maybe he appreciates the honesty. You never quite know where everyone stands when you're in a position like him—are they being nice to me because I'm famous? Or are they genuinely being nice to me? He realizes I'm somewhat genuine, because I don't kiss his ass."

There was a lot of ass-kissing at the time, however, and "Into Yer Shtik" confronted the issue head on. The song divides into three distinct sections. In the first, over a repetitive hanging guitar figure,

* "In 'n' out of Grace" by Keith Cameron, *Q Classic Ultimate Edition: Nirvana & the Story of Grunge*, December 2003.

guided gently but insistently by some of Peters' deftest loose snare snaps, Arm addresses a nameless figure of unspecified gender: "You're so tormented," he begins, "Demented . . . "

A slight maniacal quaver in his voice dispels any notion that there's going to be much sympathy for this person: "Indebted," he continues, "to all the assholes—just like you." The "just like you" almost collides with the end of the first half of the line and is placed in the left channel, conveying the impression of someone else standing behind Arm's shoulder, chipping in for good measure. The trick is repeated in the next line, this time in the right channel: "Who've come and gone—before you." The next line is simply one word, "Predictable," but drawn out, with the last syllable tossed to the floor in a show of contempt to ensure it rhymes with the following, "Just plain dull." Having identified the person's malaise, the singer has a suggestion for how it can be remedied: "Why don't you/Blow your brains out too?" The drums start to churn and slide guitars join in at this point, as if to reinforce the notion that it really is the best possible solution for all concerned, because, as the next line avers, "You're so, into your . . . shtik." There's a pause before the last word, held back and delivered with a *sotto voce* relish.

Then after a few beats, Peters' snare taps take us to the second verse, which reprises the pattern of the first. "You're so hounded/Surrounded . . . " As in verse one, there's a faint possibility of sympathy in these words, but the third line stomps on the notion: [you're] "Surrounded—by scum-sucking leeches who will shovel your shit." The line's a mouthful, but Arm enunciates with such precision that there can be no mistaking his feelings. We're told these leeches sweep up the person's dirt, perhaps as a nurse would tend to an incontinent patient, then they "Feed your ego/They never tell you 'no.'" As we near the end of section one, verse two, the attack is two-fold: against the person and also these others, be they acolytes or employees. Then Arm's voice starts to open and the distressed slide guitars kick up a few notches: "All of you/Make—me—SICK!" Why? Well of course, "You're so into your shtik"—but it's more than that. Suddenly, as Peters reprises the pause from the end of verse one, just as we might be expecting a third verse, or even a chorus—because there hasn't been a chorus, thus far, the only lyric repeated is, "You're so into your shtik"—the drums and guitar move into a bridge of sorts, or more of a holding pattern, while Arm stalks around the line, "And they're alllll, into your shtik." Then Peters accelerates, the guitars are with him, and Arm is off into the song's second section.

What follows, at this newly urgent 4/4 pace, are three character sketches: first up is Mitchell, whose "new girl," a "Hollywood model" is "Up here to support the scene/It's all part of his rock and roll fantasy." The slide guitars are mewling. Sketch two concerns Stan, who's at a bar, his hands bandaged: "They tried to dry him out/And he got mad." Apparently Stan put his fist through glass at the hospital: "Made his myth/Now he's trapped." The guitars are squealing. Now for sketch three, about Susie, a girl in New York, "Working with the management to the stars," where, "Kissing ass is part of her job." Arm's voice is now rising, as if he's listened to that last line on simultaneous playback and realized he's getting to the heart of the matter. The slide guitars chime in. "It's part of her job," he repeats, and repeats again. Then his voice is lowered: "Oh, she loves her job," before rearing up again: "What the hell, she does it so well!" Now we slip into the last section of the song, a coda with the same beats as the vignettes, but now the sniping, griping guitars accompany Arm throughout this moment of reckoning: "I'm not perfect," he says, "I've lived a life of mistakes . . . " But? "But there's one thing I can't take." And that is? "YOU!/Are into your shtik! You're SO!/Into your shtik!/And THEY'RE so into your shtik!" Arm is virtually retching with disgust now, as he summons up one final spluttering scream: "FUCK YOU! YOU MAKE ME SICK!" And there it ends, the final chord decaying as the tub of hatred is snapped shut by Peters' muted drumbeat.

Inevitably, given the manner of Kurt Cobain's suicide, attention zoomed in on one particular line from the song's first verse. Arm responded by cautioning that the lyric's scope was much broader than the obvious: "That song was never intended to point at one specific person. There's loads of people who are so fully into their shtiks, entertainers all across the board. But since my world is the alternative rock'n'roll world, and that's what I know best, I'm singing about my work. It's in the punk rock tradition, singing about the job you hate, or aspects of it you hate. There's just no reason for anyone to go out of their way to be an asshole to anyone."*

Subsequently, he elaborated: "The thing that's really missed about that song is that it definitely applies to who you think it applies to, but it applies to so many more people than that. It probably applies to Puff Daddy, but I just don't know him! The one thing I regret is at the end, where there's these three little vignettes, and I didn't specifically name the people. Nothing else about that song was particularly subtle."**

Mitchell, Stan, and Susie were indeed aliases: by the time "Into Yer Shtik" was released to the public on *My Brother the Cow*, it had already been toned down by its composer. The original demo version that Katznelson heard during the summer of 1994 featured the real names of the people cited in the vignettes: Eric Erlandson, guitarist in Hole, whose girlfriend at the time was actress Drew Barrymore; Alice in Chains singer Layne Staley, already trapped by the rock-star junkie persona that would shroud him until his death in 2002; and Janet Billig, whose clients at Gold Mountain management included Hole. In later years, when performing the song live, Arm would reinstate the original names. Today, the song has long since dropped off the band's set list.

"That was something I had to get out of my system and put out there," says Arm. "At this point, I like 'Into Yer Shtik,' but I don't really have the anger about all that anymore. It's dead and gone to me. I would feel weird playing that song now."

Incredibly, Katznelson says that once Danny Goldberg's worries about the song had been assuaged, he persuaded both Goldberg and the Warners radio department that "Into Yer Shtik" should be released as a single. But Arm vetoed the idea.

"What a great single that would have been!" says Katznelson. "To me, 'Into Yer Shtik' was immediately the gem on the record. In the middle, where it goes into the second part of the song, it's very reminiscent of

* "Udderly Brudderly" by Keith Cameron, *New Musical Express*, May 27, 1995.

** *Piece of Cake/My Brother the Cow* reissue review by Keith Cameron, *MOJO*, September 2003.

'A Quick One' by The Who—I get the same goosebumps with both. I was completely blown away by it. What a damning, pointed piece of vomit on all the crap that was going on at the time."

"Into Yer Shtik" would be released as a single (albeit a limited edition seven-inch) on Steve Turner's Super Electro label. Instead, for the album's calling card, Warner Bros. went with "Generation Spokesmodel," a lighter jab at delusional rock-star behavior and the music industry's exploitative tendencies: "Thanks to the kids for making me who I am/Twenty percent of the gross goes straight to the man."

Not every song on the album fitted Katznelson's "rock-opera" classification, but clarity and candor were consistent traits no matter what the subject matter. Featuring a two-note guitar-solo homage to Buzzcocks' "Boredom," "F.D.K. (Fearless Doctor Killers)" aimed a brilliant, punked-out salvo at the hypocrisy of the Christian fundamentalist anti-abortion lobby. "In My Finest Suit," meanwhile, was a ragged slow burn, like Alice Cooper's "The Ballad of Dwight Fry" morphing into "This Gift," featuring a poignant lyric wherein a troubled soul pays tribute to the person who "came along and somehow made it right." The refrain's dedication, "I got you/That's a lot to lose . . . I'd give up anything for you," suggests a heartfelt ode to Arm's wife, Emily.

"Autobiographical? Possibly," he says. "I don't want to get into that."

Released almost a year after Kurt Cobain's death, *My Brother the Cow* didn't sell nearly as well as *Piece of Cake*, despite being a far stronger album. But then the factors that made the 1992 album sell by default were now in retrograde. The grunge backlash was evident on any number of levels in 1995. That year saw Coca-Cola discontinue OK, a soft drink launched in 1993, after utterly failing to convince its target Generation X demographic that they should ignore their disdain for commercial chicanery and buy a product specifically conceived to be unappealing. Some of the faces on the can designs were drawn by cartoonists Charles Burns and Daniel Clowes, both of whom had produced sleeves for Sub Pop; Clowes said he based his can character's eyes on those of Charles Manson.

More specifically, if being lampooned by mainstream television is indicative of a scene on the slide, then Mudhoney knew the gig was up when they went to Hollywood in the early summer to film a pilot for a Fox TV sitcom called *Daisy & Chess*. Their performance of "Generation Spokesmodel" to an inauthentically healthy-looking rock club crowd provided the backdrop to the trauma of bartender Daisy (played by Rosanna Arquette), a former groupie who can't remember which bass player has fathered her son, Chess. The show was so dire it never got commissioned, but at least Matt Lukin got a speaking role, growling, "We're done!" and slamming his bass into a wall.

There were further auguries of change when Mudhoney arrived in the UK at the end of August, for their third Reading Festival appearance. The official program notes weren't exactly effusive about the band appearing fourth from the top of Sunday's bill. After misquoting a lyric from "Generation Spokesmodel"—apparently the 20 percent goes to "the band" not "the man"—it was suggested that:

> Mudhoney are bitter at being just about the only group out of their contemporaries who have yet to achieve massive worldwide acclaim, and that all that's left for them to do is mock the truly successful and languish in their own obscurity.*

The program was written by a group of *Melody Maker* journalists; with the hedonistic Britpop surge underway, the mainstream UK music press's attention was elsewhere.

"We were like, 'Wow, that's amazing—even the people who booked the festival didn't like us,'" says Steve. "It was because Nirvana was dead. Like, 'We wanted to get Nirvana but they're dead, so we're stuck with these bastards!'"

It didn't help that Mudhoney were already weary after the best part of four months on the road, or that their Reading visit was one stop on a European festival tour they undertook as part of a package of bands—"probably the six most horrible bands in the world at that time," according to Mark. The tour's headliners were Soundgarden, whose daily temper tantrums eventually ground down even the normally irrepressible Dan Peters.

* *Mean Fiddler Presents Reading '95 Official Programme* by Paul Lester

"Soundgarden were just petulant and none of them were talking to each other," says Turner. "That depressed Dan more than anything. Dan's a really good barometer of where things are at. If he's bummed about something, it sucks."

It would be seven years before Mudhoney toured Europe again. Things might have been getting a little tough—but they were going to get much worse.

★ ★ ★

Bob Whittaker knew there was something odd about Mudhoney's tax affairs when he discovered he was paying more to the Internal Revenue Service than the band. In terms of income, Whittaker was an equal partner. Mudhoney had no truck with the traditional music industry practice whereby the manager took a commission—typically 20 percent, as referenced in "Generation Spokesmodel"—and thereby had a vested interest in hiking budgets for videos, tours, and recording, all factors in placing the artist in debt to the record label. So with everything split five ways, there shouldn't have been such huge discrepancies between Whittaker's tax liability as an individual and Mudhoney's, which was organized as a corporation. After looking through some paperwork, Whittaker had two questions: 1) Were the band paying enough taxes? 2) Should he get inside the corporation?

It was a delicate issue, because the band's taxes were handled by Mark's father. After retiring from Boeing, Calvin McLaughlin did some work for H&R Block, a franchise-operated tax preparation service with offices in malls and main streets all across the U.S. Eventually he set up his own budget tax business, which he ran from home.

"I think it was fine for just regular people who needed help with their taxes," says Mark, "but for something more complex I don't think he maybe understood all the ins and outs of it, and also I don't think we really provided him with all the necessary details because we didn't know what they were. Bob just couldn't get over how much more tax he owed than we did."

Whittaker took the band's completed tax returns to Voldal Wartelle, an accounting firm based in Kirkland that specialized in clients from the entertainment industries; the company originally made its name representing Heart, the first Seattle rock band to impact on an international scale.

"When I showed them the tax returns that Mark's father had done," says Whittaker, "the blood drained out of their faces and they said, 'Oh no.' Then it drained out of my face and then the band's faces."

Voldal Wartelle confirmed that Mudhoney had indeed been underpaying taxes for several years. The next decision was whether to keep quiet and hope the IRS wouldn't find out—but that risked greater penalties if they did. So the accountants proceeded to amend the band's tax returns, in the hope that the authorities would show them clemency for having come forward. But there was none.

"We got fucked," says Mark. "Interest and penalties were accrued from day one. It wasn't like, 'OK, you can just pay the money that you owe without the four years of interest and penalties.' It was insane. So that was a really, really big amount. Which I don't remember, because I put that shit out of my head." He laughs. "But Dan probably remembers!"

"The IRS gave us each 30 days to come up with $50,000, or else they would start seizing property," says Dan. "Of course, I had invested money and we all had purchased houses at that time, but I didn't have $50,000. So I ended up having to liquidate all the investments that I'd made and I had to take a second mortgage out on the house."

Matt was in a slightly better place. He didn't have to remortgage, but he'd been in the process of rewiring his basement so he could convert it into a workshop for carpentry—and had planned to use his blue-chip stock funds to pay for the conversion and all the tools he would require. They paid his tax bill instead. "So that pretty much left me flat broke," he says. "It taught me it's not good to fool with the IRS—they don't play around. But I'm also wondering, 'Jesus Christ, how much of a percentage of fucking taxes do they take?! I owe you *this* much?! I don't even remember making it!'"

Steve was able to pay his $50,000 out of savings he had earmarked to remodel his house. Mark, meanwhile, is still traumatized at being reminded just how much money he had to pay: "Fifty thousand? Oh God. I don't even know how that was done."

Mudhoney's tax misfortunes were a symptom of the Seattle scene's "mad dash to legitimacy," a phrase coined by Jonathan Poneman to describe the process by which Sub Pop engaged with more established components of the music business, but equally applicable here. Here was a punk-rock cottage industry attempting to duck and dive its way through the corporate jungle, but clunking its head on a low-hanging branch.

The timing was especially bad, as the crisis unfolded just as *My Brother the Cow* was released. David Katznelson would be calling Bob Whittaker to thrash out a marketing strategy, and Whittaker would have to break off to take a call from either Voldal Wartelle or the IRS.

But for all the strife it caused, little changed when it came to the coalface realities of being Mudhoney. Their 1995 shows were intensely enjoyable for audiences and band alike. In London, for instance, as pre-gig entertainment in the dressing room, Lukin and Ross Knight from the supporting Cosmic Psychos performed a puppet show with their testicles and an artfully arranged velvet curtain. As Thurston Moore observes: "Matt Lukin is a fascinating person."

Nor did the tax issues impact upon the band's work ethic. "Yes, they were pissed, they were bummed, it was destroying," says Katznelson. "But when you talked to them, they were still themselves. It wasn't as if they retreated into a dark cave of emotion. Those guys are some of the nicest guys you could ever meet. They're honest guys. They had to deal with that stuff, but that doesn't mean they changed the way they are as human beings. I mean, they understood—if anything, they wanted to work; they needed to make money."

So it was further unfortunate timing when Steve Turner chose this moment to declare, at a band meeting, that he wouldn't be going on tour for the foreseeable future. "I was burnt out, all the touring in '95 dragged me down," he says. "I'd always had an inner conflict about doing this thing full-time anyway. And my girlfriend and I were starting to have some trouble, basically because I was gone so much. The way I brought it to the band was, 'Either I quit or we take some time out.' They weren't real happy about it. They wanted to tour, to pay off some of the IRS stuff. But my personal relationship was what I thought I had to focus on."

To say the others were not happy is an understatement. Their meeting, on the deck outside Bob Whittaker's house in West Seattle, had been called specifically to discuss a U.S. tour to help pay the IRS.

"Maybe Steve was a little more frugal with his own money," says Mark Arm. "He didn't feel that *he* needed to do it, but didn't really seem to have much empathy for the rest of us who did. That pissed the rest of us off. A great deal."

On hearing Turner's statement, Lukin got to his feet and threw up his hands. "You might as well quit!" he said, then stormed off. The others looked at each other in shock. They weren't quite sure if Matt had said he was quitting, or that Steve should quit.

"I went straight home," says Lukin, "and told my wife: 'We can get a dog now, because I'm gonna be home for a while.'"

"It was so demoralizing," says Whittaker. "The timing was a head-scratcher—but everyone has their reasons. That was an incredibly unfortunate chain of events. You're in this band, this extended family, and you have all this camaraderie, and then when the situation gets a little hot; it's too bad we couldn't bond together a little better."

Thrown into stasis yet again by one of Turner's edicts, the rest of the band were examining their options when Australia came a-calling once more. Kim Salmon was due in Seattle to play a gig with his latest band, The Surrealists. Over the phone, Mark explained Mudhoney's situation and asked if he'd be interested in jamming with himself, Dan, and Matt. Thus, over five days in October 1995, Salmon plus the three guys from Mudhoney worked out eight songs and recorded them.

"I had a good time with it," says Lukin. "It might have been an effort on our part to go, 'Well Jeez, if Steve's not going to tour, we'll get another guitar player—and maybe that'll light a fire under Steve . . . '"

Any possibility that this session could evolve into a new configuration of Mudhoney was soon scotched when Arm found himself unhappy with the finished results: "I thought, 'This is a little poppier than I imagined it was going to be,' and it just fell by the wayside. It was forgotten about over time. It was cool to work with Kim, but it definitely didn't have the same feeling of working with Steve. Listening to it now, I think it sounds great, but at the time I didn't want people thinking this is the next incarnation of Mudhoney."

For the remainder of 1995 and the first half of 1996, Arm busied himself with Bloodloss. In a measure of how much credit David Katznelson had accrued with his bosses—thanks to success with The Flaming Lips and, to a lesser degree, Mudhoney—Ren's skronking minstrels were signed to Warner Bros. and made an album, *Live My Way*. They also undertook a grueling month-long circuit of the U.S., which proved an eye-opening experience.

"Bloodloss wasn't well-known or popular; it was more challenging music," says Mark. "And then to have one member of the band almost out of commission . . . " Bloodloss gave Arm his own taste of touring with a junkie. "We were carrying the carcass of Ren around the country, trying to prop him up to play shows. Leaving Seattle he would take several days to withdraw in the van. We were playing really tiny clubs to not a whole lot of people, but especially as Ren got a little healthier we were having really good shows and a lot of fun."

But when the tour reached New York in early May, Ren disappeared on a drug hunt and didn't return in time for the band's set. They struggled home and did a West Coast tour before recording another album, during which Ren had a nervous breakdown and went into a recovery program in California.

"The thought was, this record will be finished once he gets cleaned up and comes back here . . . We eventually finished it without him ever properly getting cleaned up, 12, 13, 15 years later, whatever it was." Mark sighs. "Compared to Mudhoney, it was all kinda brutal."

Dan Peters, meanwhile, had been recording and touring with Love Battery, who had lost their drummer Jason Finn to Presidents of the United States of America. He then toured backing Mike Johnson, with whom he'd also played in a band Mark Lanegan put together in the summer of 1995 to support Johnny Cash for two dates in Seattle and Portland. But none of this activity compensated for Mudhoney's absence. Eventually, during the summer of 1996, Dan called up Steve and suggested they go for a few beers. Within a couple of hours, Peters had persuaded Turner that enough was enough: it was time to get back in the mud.

"Dan could usually get me back around," says Steve. "He's a very wise man."

Mudhoney played the annual Seattle Bumbershoot festival on September 2, their first gig in 12 months. But as they fell back into the old routines of rehearsing in Mark's basement and started making plans for the next record, it became clear that fundamental shifts had occurred during the year's hiatus. Most critically, Matt Lukin seemed somewhat removed, as if part of him never returned from that day he walked out on the band meeting.

"He would be begrudgingly there at practice," says Arm. "Somewhere along the line it seems he also lost interest in drinking beer. Which is fair enough—it runs its course. You know what's going to happen every time you do it! So I noticed that he wouldn't be drinking at practice anymore, and if we went out on the road he would suddenly start drinking—so he could be 'Matt Lukin'! He's actually a really shy, understated person—well, maybe not understated . . . He told me he'd actually stopped *listening* to music."

The year off made Lukin realize there was very little he liked about being in a band. He certainly didn't miss "being Matt Lukin," whose designated role in the Mudhoney machine was reduced to babbling incoherently between songs and occasionally dropping his trousers. He wasn't into that shtik anymore. Matt had made his own myth—and now felt trapped. An increasing estrangement from Turner compounded his dissatisfaction.

"There was always that little inkling in the back of my head that said: 'When is Steve going to get tired of it again and put the band on hold?'" says Matt. "It was always, 'What does Steve think? Does he wanna do it? How much can I rely on this guy?' That took the wind out of my sails. I think a lot of it had to do with getting a little bit of success and being on a major label and having to be a salesman. Selling yourself. It's a gross business when it gets down to it. And I just didn't really find it that worthy. This really isn't as important as a lot of people make it out to be. When you step outside of it, you see there's a whole world beyond music. I needed to explore that for a little while. I just got fed up with the whole music business: sleazy people."

Over at Warner Bros., the latest personnel upheaval didn't help Lukin's sense of alienation. The artist-friendly golden age of Mo Ostin and Lenny Waronker was long gone; Ostin had left at the start of 1995, after refusing to implement staff cuts demanded by the Time Warner parent company; rather than inherit a poisoned chalice, Waronker chose to follow his mentor out of the door, thus prompting the hasty promotion of Danny Goldberg. But Goldberg too was now gone. In his stead, Mudhoney had a new corporate nemesis: David Kahne, Warners' new vice-president of A&R.

Kahne was a producer with a gold-plated reputation for delivering mega-hit records that rotated heavily on Top 40 radio. Warners gave him the A&R VP job after he gave them the double-platinum album *Floored* by funk-metal band Sugar Ray. In the brutal new world where artistic license was a luxury and the short-term bottom line ruled, Kahne was king. (He would later earn unwanted notoriety by dropping Wilco from Reprise, after rejecting their album *Yankee Hotel Foxtrot*, only for the band to re-sign to a different Warners label.)

By now, David Katznelson was the lone surviving member of the Ostin/Waronker-era A&R team. He hated his new boss and suspected the feeling was mutual. But although unhappy in the changing corporate climate, his position was secure: he had a contract and, in The Flaming Lips, a relatively successful band. Yet it was by no means guaranteed that Kahne would keep Mudhoney on the label, as their "firm" deal had been for two albums, after which the label had the option of whether or not to retain them. With the band's commercial stock diminished since the crazy days of 1992, Katznelson was keeping his expectations low.

"David Kahne assumed that he wasn't going to like Mudhoney," says Katznelson. "There was a chance they were gonna get dropped on the spot. He was going through the roster and slashing. He's the guy who famously dropped Wilco without asking permission. This is the guy who made The Bangles cry. While he is talented as a producer, he is not everyone's cup of tea. He came to my office and was basically like: 'The last Mudhoney record sold like crap and grunge is dead; what's the point?' Yet at the same time, we did have this investment—so he wanted to hear demos."

It was the first time Mudhoney had been told to submit demo recordings for approval before being permitted to make an album, and it stuck in the craw. Steve Turner, in particular, was all for walking away there and then. But another function of Mudhoney's deal meant that, with this album being "optional," the band would not be allowed to keep the back end of the recording budget; what they didn't spend from the pot containing $150,000 reverted to the record label. Therefore, with no benefit in recording cheaply, the band realized this would be their first—and, given the prevailing musical and corporate climate, probably their last—opportunity to make a record with a large budget. Arm and Peters, in particular, were keen to give it a go. Turner, very conscious that he owed the others after refusing to tour during the band's hour of need, assented to the majority's wishes.

"My point of view was that Warners didn't want us there," says Steve. "They really didn't know what to do with us. They'd given up. They'd realized, finally, that we weren't going to be the next Nirvana. And to me it seemed like our time had come and gone there. But the other guys had totally valid points—no one else was ever going to give us a budget to record! So we might as well use this last one and step it up, actually hire a producer and all that stuff. I stated my case and they stated theirs. I tried to be as agreeable as possible."

Much to everyone's surprise, David Kahne loved one of the many demos Mudhoney recorded during 1997. "Oblivion" was a slow-burning swamp blues based around two character studies that Arm detailed with crisp, evocative lyrics. In the first verse, a woman in a wheelchair took her glass of Kahlua and cream from the bar to a karaoke machine, where "she sang the shit out of 'Dancing Queen'"; the second concerned a heroin addict who fled town to a commune in New Mexico and gained weight, after he "dropped the spoon and picked up the fork." A beautifully framed snapshot of lives in imbalance, with people striving to make the best of the hand they'd been dealt, the inspiration for "Oblivion" was real: the first verse described the exact scene witnessed by Bloodloss bassist Guy Maddison one evening in a bar on California Avenue, West Seattle; the second verse's ex-junkie-turned-New-Ager was a conflation of two people Arm knew. The singer's performance was wry but sympathetic, and ultimately impassioned as he declaimed: "Everybody wants everything to be all right."

This was Mudhoney venturing into a broader emotional spectrum. Nonetheless, David Katznelson was taken aback by the intensity of Kahne's response to the song: "All of a sudden, I found myself for the first time being asked to come into his office. Usually I was kept out, pretty much, unless he wanted to yell at me about something. He would play me 'Oblivion' and then he'd start telling me the epic saga of what 'Oblivion' could be. He was talking about the movie rights and getting Brad Pitt to play the main character, and we'd hire Terrence Malick to make this epic . . . The song was going to tell the tale of universal love and laughter and loss within three minutes. It was this really weird situation. David Kahne didn't want to talk about any other song except 'Oblivion.'"

So Warners picked up the option and Mudhoney would make another album for Reprise. But it was going to be on the label's terms, which meant the band would be working with a capital "P" producer, someone with an executive influence over the sound of the record. Although Jack Endino had been credited as coproducing *My Brother the Cow*, in reality his role was much closer to that of an engineer, facilitating the technical process of recording the music as opposed to directing its creation. Producers come in many guises; some insist on getting actively involved, not just with the recording but with actual composition; others have a more elusive presence and assume a role closer to that of a therapist or guru. Luckily for Mudhoney, Warners was smart enough to realize that a band with such deeply ingrained anti-authoritarian instincts were not going to respond well to having a Phil Spector or Rick Rubin imposed upon them. Instead, the label invited the band to choose someone.

"So we had to find a producer who we could live with," says Mark. "There's all these guys out there that have 'a sound', and they conform the band to 'their sound.' And we didn't want that. But the only other band that Bob managed was Clawhammer, and they had worked with Jim Dickinson, and had liked the experience."

Dickinson was a legendary Memphis songwriter and session musician, a pianist and guitarist who had played on records by an eclectic range of artists from Aretha Franklin and The Rolling Stones to Spiritualized. As a producer, he'd earned outsider kudos from his work with Big Star, The Replacements, and The Cramps. As luck would have it, Dickinson had also produced Tex-Mex fusion band The Texas Tornados, who David Katznelson had signed to Reprise.

So Katznelson suggested that he approach Dickinson. The one sticky point concerned Dickinson's modus operandi, which was to record bands at Ardent Studios in Memphis with his regular engineer, John Hampton. But Dickinson could at least be tempted away from home by the prospect of a very substantial fee. In contrast, there was no way the band could get Matt Lukin to leave Seattle.

"Writing the album with Matt was . . . I guess the cliché would be 'pulling teeth,'" says Arm. "Usually he had a couple of riffs, at least, but he was not contributing at all. He just showed up at practice and sat there reluctantly the whole time. It was a draining, soul-killing experience for everyone."

Building wooden model airplanes was Lukin's new passion and he would bring his kits into rehearsal, picking up his bass only when absolutely necessary. "I started having an attitude about things," he says. "I was kind of a dick."

So with one reluctant producer and a barely present band member, sessions began at Stone Gossard's Studio Litho on January 7, 1998. Against the odds, however, Jim Dickinson and Matt Lukin formed a mutual appreciation society. In withdrawing from the creative process, Lukin's bass playing became so understated and minimal that he was now solidly in-the-pocket with the drums—the place where bassists belong, to Jim Dickinson's mind, but which the assertive primacy of heavy rock styles from the seventies onwards had rendered unfashionable.

"He said I was a throwback!" says Lukin. "Apparently, ever since punk rock, bass players have always been in front of the beat—I don't even understand what any of that means really, but for some reason I was always behind the beat. Just a little bit slow! It was funny, because it was probably the record where I tried the least and it ended up being one of my better performances. Like all of sudden, now that I don't care, I seem to know what I'm doing!"

After 10 days, Dickinson declared the session finished. The wintry weather hadn't exactly raised his spirits, and he'd felt a chilly atmosphere in the control room also. Recording the session was Adam Kasper, a local engineer whose work with Pearl Jam and Soundgarden had led to him being offered his first producer credits. He seemed less than impressed by Dickinson's methods.

"I think he was a little miffed that he wasn't producing," says Mark Arm.

Then again, the producer's techniques were certainly opaque, as Turner acknowledges: "I think Adam just saw Dickinson, who is not a hands-on producer, and was like: 'What's this guy doing here?! He's just sitting in the corner, smoking pot! That's the producer?!' But the weather was so horrible [that] Dickinson just gave up and went back to Memphis."

With all the parts tracked, it was agreed that mixing would begin at Ardent in two weeks' time. Lukin didn't bother making the trip to Tennessee; he'd recorded his parts and couldn't see how his presence during mixing would make any difference. Once the three others were in situ at Ardent, however, it became clear that Dickinson had his own agenda.

"I thought I had done all my vocals in Seattle," says Arm, "and Steve and I thought we'd done our guitar parts. But we get down to Memphis and Jim is like: 'OK, I want you to take another stab at these vocals.' Which I'm really glad he did, because it was a marked improvement. With a producer like Jim, it's hard to tell what he does, 'cos he's not working the knobs, he's just standing there. He would say: 'If you want to get someone to stop thinking about the zebra, you can't just tell them to stop thinking about the zebra, because then they'll just be thinking about trying not to think about the zebra.' For him, there was a weird psychology he had to use. It was cool. I think he had a big hand in the record—a bigger hand than maybe some of the other guys in the band might even see or understand."

Mudhoney had never made a record outside Seattle before. For their weeklong Memphis session, Mark, Dan, and Steve were squirreled together in an old four-bedroom house attached to Ardent, where they enjoyed the intensely relaxed and civil atmosphere for which the studio is renowned. The sense of history was tangible, not least in the person of Jody Stephens, Ardent's studio manager and the drummer in Big Star. Back on home turf and with John Hampton behind the desk, Dickinson started working his Memphis magic on the band. He decorated the studio with voodoo roots and lit candles. He even persuaded Steve to come with him to Sun Studios, to see if the room where the first rock'n'roll records were made could permeate the skeptical heart of the man *Rolling Stone* once memorably dubbed "the Eric Clapton of grunge."*

Turner can't actually remember what he recorded there: "We just knocked out one lead guitar track or something. Jim really made a point of dragging me to Sun Studios. Maybe he wanted the slap-back reverb. But Memphis was great, a really awesome experience for us."

"Jim felt that if he took the band out of Seattle he might be able to get something different out of them," says David Katznelson. "There were a lot of things Jim really loved about Mudhoney. He loved Mark's voice and attitude. He loved Dan's drumming. He loved Matt's take on music. He saw Steve as this amazingly wonderful guitar player who he felt was fighting his own talent. Steve at that point was playing *anti*-solos—trying to be as punk rock as he could be when delivering guitar lines, and yet when he wasn't thinking about it he would deliver these beautiful things. Jim thought having him work with some of the tried—and—true Memphis legends would get something else out."

Having worked with Dickinson before, Katznelson was prepared for the mind games. But even before the Memphis session got under way, he felt that this unlikely marriage had already been vindicated.

"Jim Dickinson is a legendary producer and he works in very mysterious ways," he says. "One of the ways that worked on this record was his true generosity of spirit with Matt Lukin. I think we got as much out of Matt as we did because of Jim Dickinson. Jim had a passion for Matt's sensibilities as a musician. Matt would be putting together models

* "Grunge City" by Michael Azerrad, *Rolling Stone*, April 16, 1992.

of airplanes in the studio—and Jim loved that! Matt's performance on the record is great and I really think it was because of Jim."

Perhaps the greatest testimony to Dickinson's methods is that Lukin didn't notice he had any. "I probably would have done the exact same thing if he was there or not," he says. "He seemed pretty relaxed. He had his big bag of weed and was rolling joints and kicking back. I was like, 'Well fuck, I can do that!'"

Dan Peters came to Memphis excited at the prospect of working in a city with such a rich musical heritage. But having lobbied hard for Mudhoney to take advantage of their one and only opportunity to make a major label record with a major label budget, he became increasingly convinced that little of substance lurked beneath Jim Dickinson's cloud of sweet-smelling smoke.

"I didn't really jive with it," he says. "It almost seemed like people were being pitted against each other. I felt like my place was to sit there—I heard a lot of, 'Don't worry, son, we've got it all taken care of . . . ' I didn't enjoy it."

Of the trio in Memphis, Peters felt Lukin's absence most keenly. It was a foretaste of things to come.

★ ★ ★

Having brought Mudhoney to the other side of the country to mix the album, Dickinson proceeded to do no mixing whatsoever. His priority had been securing the enhanced performances from Arm and Turner. Once the band members returned to Seattle, he mixed a couple of songs as a test and sent them on. The band received them in Hawaii, where they were playing a couple of gigs with Pearl Jam; the second took place on Mark's 36th birthday, a happier affair than his 33rd—this time he got both a cake and a rendition of "Happy Birthday" from a backstage gathering including Neil Young, who happened to be at the show.

But the euphoria was short-lived. Dickinson's mixes felt very thin. David Katznelson had been in Memphis for a few days and couldn't equate what he heard now with what he remembered hearing on the Ardent speakers.

"We're like, 'Fuck! All this money and this record's fuckin' horrible!'" says Peters. "That's when we decided we'd have somebody else do the mix. Jim got pissed off about that—I guess rightly so."

Once again operating on the premise that they might as well spend-spend-spend, because this was money they weren't going to see again, Mudhoney hired one of the best—and priciest—mix specialists in Los Angeles. David Bianco was an amiable gentleman with a golden smile and platinum ears—he'd served his apprenticeship through the late seventies and early eighties on big LA records by the likes of Neil Diamond, Tom Petty, KISS, and Stevie Nicks. Off-duty, he regaled Mudhoney with tall tales of Hollywood excess. But when he got to work, they saw just how he earned his fee. Bianco took two weeks to mix the album, as long as the band had taken to record it. Arm, Peters, and Turner would come in, listen to a song, and assume it was finished. Then Bianco would send them away for a few hours.

"We're thinking, 'God, what could he be doing?!'" says Mark. "Then we'd listen to it again and it sounds even better."

"David Bianco is a seriously talented dude," says Steve. "He made that record. Jim Dickinson got the recordings out of us, but [Bianco] really made that record sound great. He worked hard. So much of what he was doing, I couldn't even be there for it, because it was so painstakingly slow and technical. But I couldn't believe how good it sounded. Big."

Aside from David Bianco's dedication, mixing took as long as it did because David Kahne made a slight return to his ongoing obsession with "Oblivion." It was up to David Katznelson to liaise between the sounds in Kahne's head and the man tasked with finishing Mudhoney's album:

"I'd be like, 'David [Bianco], David Kahne needs the snare to erupt right before the chorus breaks.' But David [Kahne] would never think what we had done that night in the mixing studio was perfect. To be really honest, I didn't hear this as being some major single—I'm just following his lead at this point in time, for the best of the record. I'm trying to keep the song as the band envisioned it. So we ended up going to the studio to mix this thing, seven, eight, nine times. It was all minor shit. Finally, he liked it. Whether he truly liked it or he had contributed to this process enough that he could claim victory, I don't know."

Mudhoney emerged from their taste of how big money records are made feeling strangely positive. Strangely, because the record they'd made was downcast in the extreme. The title said it all: *Tomorrow Hit Today*. Almost 10 years after intimating that the moment "when tomorrow hits" would not be a cue for dancing naked in the street, with their fifth full-length album Mudhoney served up the confirmation: *it* had indeed hit hard, resulting in what Mark Arm terms "a heavy bummer of a record." The sleeve photograph featured a decrepit motel complex in what looked like some godforsaken backwater of Middle America; in fact, it was Seattle, on the notorious Aurora Avenue strip, a world way from the grunge boomtown of legend.

The ominous organ drones of the opening track, "A Thousand Forms of Mind," set the mood: Mudhoney had evolved into a mournful, heavy, psychedelic blues band (or, as Jim Dickinson opined: "Black Sabbath meets Dr. John? Pure genius!").* The group's internal dynamic was faltering, with Lukin visibly fading away, while externally Mudhoney were besieged both by the fickle diktats of fashion and, rather more seriously, by the IRS—which, after tasting blood in 1995, had then subjected the band to an audit and was now chasing them for another $250,000, this time in unpaid payroll taxes. With Voldal Wartelle's attorney, Larry Johnson, fighting the IRS, the case would drag on for years.

The situation was ripe for Arm's darkest gallows humor, and he delivered with relish. The queasily yawing slide guitars of "I Have to Laugh" framed a litany of misfortune: "Woke up this morning/I had to laugh/Saw you lying there/I had to laugh . . . " Another key song was "Poisoned Water," debuted live as early as 1995 and performed in prototype form by the band in *Black Sheep*, a 1996 Penelope Spheeris film starring comedian Chris Farley. Its lyric posited the band as both physically embattled ("Like stacks and stacks of rats on rafts/Clutching anything we can") and spiritually diseased. "Real Low Vibe" used avian imagery to detail the direness of these straits: "I feel your stare, the eyes of a buzzard/Yeah, I've been there, behind the shrike." Meanwhile,

* Sleeve notes, *March to Fuzz* (Sub Pop, 2000).

on "This Is the Life," Arm scarily embodied the capitalist leviathan: "I make tiny starving fingers sew your comfy running shoes/And I make more money than any man could ever use." Amid the all-pervasive persecution complex, "Night of the Hunted," a spindly garage rocker and the only song on the album wholly recorded in Seattle, was a rallying cry of defiance: "They're all around/Trying to shoot us down/We'll stand our ground." The grinding finale, "Beneath the Valley of the Underdog," felt like a crushed man's dying soliloquy: "Even those who once called me friend/Were liars, thieves or fakers."

We were a long way from "Flat out Fucked." Right down to its hidden track—"Talkin' Randy Tate's Specter Blues," a folk-blues excoriation of a Christian conservative congressman from Seattle, with the songwriting credit "Trad/Arr: Mudhoney & Jim Dickinson"—*Tomorrow Hit Today* was a multilayered, powerful, often poetic piece of work. The band was justifiably proud.

"I don't think we actually ever made a great complete record until *Tomorrow Hit Today*," says Mark. "Except *Superfuzz Bigmuff*, but that was a six-song EP. I remember Bob Bert [former Sonic Youth drummer] getting a copy and writing to me: 'My God, who'd have thought you'd do your best record 10 years after you started . . . ' The downer feel was reflective of where the band was. Although I was actually pretty happy for the most part of my life at that point."

But even before the album's release, on September 22, 1998, the band sensed this was the end—of an era, at the very least. There would be no European tour; Mudhoney's booking agents said there simply wasn't enough interest to make it financially viable. As anticipated by Mark's goof-off intro to *Piece of Cake*, techno had killed rock. In the UK, they played just one gig at the 600-capacity Garage in north London, where an impassioned audience greeted the band as tribunes of a heroic lost cause.

In lieu of demand anywhere else, they toured the U.S. twice. But crowds were smaller than they had been, press interest was minimal, and Warner Bros. clearly had other priorities.

"I think it's fair to say that it did not get the attention that a Green Day record or a Neil Young record was gonna get," says David

Katznelson. "That was always disappointing to me. Look at their situation objectively for one second: their movement had passed. While it's a great record, there wasn't a song on it that felt like a hit on the radio. And unfortunately, Warners had turned into a business that was not about band development. As soon as it went out to radio and got some play but not enough to grab a hold of something, the label very quickly moved on."

As far as Steve Turner was concerned, Warners' attitude vindicated his belief that Mudhoney would be better served by an independent label—though of course, they would not have been able to make the same record for an indie. Warners licensed the vinyl edition of the album to Turner's Super Electro imprint and he sold 4,500 copies, at the lowest point of the format's slump in popularity. After eight months, CD sales numbered only around 10,000.

"I could have sold 20,000 CDs without even trying, on my shitty little label," says Turner. "To me it seemed hard to sell so few CDs if the vinyl was selling like that. I think it proved Warner Bros. did not give a shit about us."

The long U.S. tour was prefaced by a few shows opening for Pearl Jam in vast sports arenas. As well as the usual hardcore indifference of the audience, these gigs threw up a stark illustration of the bands' contrasting fortunes. After playing the 18,000-capacity Hardee's Walnut Creek Amphitheater in Raleigh, North Carolina, Mudhoney hitched a ride on Pearl Jam's private jet to Atlanta, Georgia, in readiness for playing the 19,000-capacity Lakewood Amphitheater the next day. In Atlanta, there were four cars waiting at the airport to deliver the bands to their respective hotels. In one car, the driver turned round to Matt and Dan:

"So, where are we all going?" she asked, cheerily.

"To the Days Inn over by the baseball field," replied Peters.

At the mention of Days Inn, a budget motel chain, the driver did a double take. "What the hell are y'all staying there for?!" she exclaimed. "You got off a private jet!"

Lukin leaned over and gave her a conspiratorial wink. "Yeah," he drawled, "we're trying to keep it low-key."

It wasn't all doom and gloom on the road, despite playing to some pretty sparse crowds—especially in the South. And everyone's spirits were raised as the year ended in Australia, where they toured with Rocket from the Crypt, the high-octane, horn-toting punk rock sextet from San Diego.

"Even Matt had a blast," says Mark. "But Matt has a pretty strong connection to Australia and was probably really super-happy to see the guys from Cosmic Psychos and stuff like that. Rocket from the Crypt were great guys to hang out with. And even in the U.S., where we're playing to maybe 100 or 150 people—there's a lot of bands out there that would be really happy to play to that many people. If that was Bloodloss, we'd have been stoked!"

The long run of touring in support of *Tomorrow Hit Today* came to an end on the night of April 14, 1999, in Tokyo. Six hours and many beers later, Dan Peters told Matt Lukin that if he was really as miserable as he seemed then he should quit the band.

"I feel bad," said Lukin, "because it's just me. What will you do?"

Peters shook his head. "Don't worry about me. If you're not having fun, it's not fun for anybody else."

The next day, on the plane back to Seattle, Mark Arm began discussing the next album—he wanted to get back into the studio right away. Matt didn't say anything, but inwardly he blanched at the prospect. "I need a fucking break," he thought. "I need to get away from this."

Shortly after the band returned home, it fell to David Katznelson to break the news that everyone had been expecting for months: Mudhoney were being released from their contract by Warner Bros. There was a collective sigh of relief.

"The deal they had, though not huge, was too big to sustain a lack of album sales," says Katznelson. "It only could have been different if Mo Ostin and Lenny Waronker were still at the helm and the music industry was not a multinational corporate entity. My power was diminished. The writing was on the wall." Within 12 months, Katznelson would quit Warners and return to San Francisco.

A month or so later, full of foreboding, Mark Arm went round to Matt Lukin's house. He knew what he should say: "This can't go on."

What he said thereafter would depend on Matt. He might even have to ask Matt to leave Mudhoney. In the end, thankfully, it wasn't necessary.

"I got there and Matt said, 'Y'know, Mark—I think I need to quit the band.' I'm really glad I didn't have to ask him!" He laughs. "I think we're both not very good at breaking up with people."

Lukin estimates that he had wanted to quit for at least two years. "I was kinda hoping somebody else would do it before me, 'cos I hate being the guy that quits something. But it just got to the point where I wasn't liking it at all and I had to step aside. I was just really tired. After a while I was like, 'I don't wanna be drunk every night and feel like shit every day. Something's gotta change here.' The first day after I quit the band I was working by myself doing some carpentry. I'm like, 'This is the tits, man—the only one making fuckin' decisions here is me.' It just felt nice that all of a sudden I could make some money doing this by myself."

Lukin's departure begged the question: What future did Mudhoney have without him? Dan Peters, for one, doubted whether the band could or should exist beyond the participation of the four founding members.

"I thought that might be it," says Dan. "I knew Mark was gunning to get another bass player and carry straight on. That to me was not an option. We definitely needed to step aside for a while. I didn't want to do it without Matt."

When Mark Arm had phoned him to break the news about Lukin quitting, Peters immediately flashed back to that drunken conversation in Tokyo and cursed himself: if he hadn't broached the subject, perhaps Matt wouldn't have made his fateful decision. But deep down he knew otherwise. Although the pair had bonded fast from that first New Year's Day practice session, 11 and a half years earlier, and grew close from rooming together on the road, in truth Matt had been withdrawing from Dan as well as the band for some time.

"Dan really had to work hard to get to see Lukin sometimes," says Steve. "He'd go over to his house and bang on the door: 'I know you're in there, your car's here!' Dan missed Matt."

With their drummer effectively in mourning, Arm and Turner knew better than to force the issue. "We dealt with it like guys would: we don't talk about it, we just ignore it," says Arm. "We dealt with it by not doing anything about it for a year."

In the ultimate manifestation of tomorrow hitting today, one by one the members of Mudhoney eased themselves back into civilian life. Lukin was actually ahead of this particular curve, having resumed carpentry while still in the band. Mark got a job in the warehouse of Fantagraphics, the renowned comic-book publisher. Dan went back to where he'd left off before the band's first ever European trip in 1988, becoming a legal messenger—delivering subpoenas and lawsuits to unwilling recipients. His wife, Donna, went to law school and they decided to start a family.

Steve, meanwhile, surprised everybody by not going back to school. Instead, he took some casual landscape gardening jobs and began spending time down at the new Sub Pop offices in Belltown. After a choppy voyage through the latter half of the Nineties—during which Warners bought a 49 percent stake in the company, Jonathan Poneman survived an attempted coup by key employees and the specter of bankruptcy loomed yet again—the label was now rationalizing its business practices along common-sense lines. As part of the process, Sub Pop wanted to release a double-CD Mudhoney *Best Of*, comprising both the Sub Pop and Warners eras. Turner threw himself into the job of curating the project and, in so doing, found himself becoming defiantly proud of the band's musical achievements.

"I was like, 'I don't give a shit if anyone else likes it or not—we like it,'" he says. "I was trying to figure out, 'Do I like to play music?' Especially after Matt quit. Clearly he didn't like to play music anymore, and I wasn't playing that much at the time either. Do I like it? Well, fuck yeah, I do. It lit the fire under me to play music and try to figure out a way to keep playing music for the rest of my life. When it stopped feeling like anything to do with a job, it freed me up, psychically."

Sub Pop released the handsomely packaged *March to Fuzz* compilation at the end of January 2000. While not actually saying the band was finished, Turner's sleeve note referred to Mudhoney in the past tense.

It ended: "So thanks to almost everyone, and I'll see you at the Grunge Reunion Tour. Coming soon to a sports bar near you."*

In November 1999, shortly before he wrote those words, Turner and Arm reconvened The Monkeywrench to make a belated followup album to 1992's *Clean as a Broke Dick Dog*. Produced by Jack Endino, *Electric Children* was released in May 2000; during the subsequent months of that year, The Monkeywrench would tour the U.S., Japan, and Europe. Prior to that, however, a very important meeting took place, prompted by the following conversation.

"Y'know?" said Dan Peters. "I wouldn't mind getting together and playing."

"Yeah," said Mark Arm. "I thought you might."

* Sleeve notes, *March to Fuzz* (Sub Pop, 2000).

9

In the Blood

Mark Arm knew that he wanted Guy Maddison to be Mudhoney's next bass player from the moment Matt Lukin announced his decision to quit. In truth, he'd known it way before then. Mark had been friends with Guy since 1989, when Lubricated Goat first toured the U.S., and it was Arm who suggested to Renestair E. J. that he invite Maddison, now resident in Seattle, to join Bloodloss in 1994. Having clattered around the U.S. on the grueling Bloodloss tours of 1996, Mark knew Guy well enough to know he would be the perfect fit for Mudhoney.

"That day, when I was going to talk to Matt, I was already thinking Guy would be an awesome person to have in the band," says Arm.

But Mark wouldn't get his man straight away. Not for the first time, it was Detroit rock that both kicked and saved Mudhoney's ass.

At the dawn of 2000, a new internet record company, Music Blitz, had offered MC5 guitarist Wayne Kramer a large chunk of dot-com bubble money to produce a compilation album called *Beyond Cyberpunk*. One of the Music Blitz founders was a Mudhoney fan and thought they would fit with Kramer's imprimatur. So the three remaining Mudhoney members, at this point unsure of whether they would even continue as a band, convened in Mark's basement to work out some songs. The thorny issue of someone stepping into Lukin's shoes—still a deal-breaker as far as Dan Peters was concerned—was alleviated by Steve playing bass.

"So we weren't actually looking for a bass player when we wrote those songs," says Peters. "That was cool; I was fine with that."

In April 2000, Kramer came to Seattle to produce the recording and asked if he might sit in on a practice in order to familiarize himself with the material. Both band and producer gravitated towards a song called "Inside Job." As he watched the trio playing, Kramer noticed a bass leaning against the wall.

"Where's the bass player?" he asked.

"We don't have one," they replied.

"Do you mind if I just thump along?"

"Oh, please do!"

"So there's a Mudhoney track with Wayne Kramer on bass," marvels Arm. "As well as being a really great guitar player, he's a really great bass player. He was into this book by Pino Palladino about how to play Motown-style bass, like James Jamerson. The original idea was for Steve to do the bass and he would have just followed the guitar line. Wayne came up with this in-the-pocket, almost bouncy bass line that really propelled the song along. That was something none of us would have thought of. We're not that smart."

Photographs from the session, which took place on April 21–22 at Private Radio, the same 16-track studio where The Monkeywrench recorded their recent album, reveal Mudhoney and engineer Jack Endino looking understandably cock-a-hoop at having a member of one of the world's greatest ever rock bands in their midst.

"Wayne was pretty cool," says Endino. "He was all business once the funny stories stopped flowing."

In terms of Mudhoney's future, aside from the new songs, the almost inestimable value of the Kramer session lay in proving to Dan Peters that there might be a life without Matt Lukin.

"That really fired us up again," he says. "Revitalized us as a band in terms of wanting to continue."

Two months later, the trio performed live together for the first time in over a year, albeit as part of a larger ensemble. The occasion was the opening of Experience Music Project—a state-of-the-art music museum at the foot of the Space Needle, funded by Microsoft's Paul Allen and designed by architect Frank Gehry. As a tribute to the legendary Tacoma garage band The Sonics, The Young Fresh Fellows' Scott McCaughey put together The New Strychnines, featuring himself on keyboards, guitarists Tom Price and Bill "Kahuna" Henderson, saxophonist Craig Flory, plus the Mudhoney trio, with Turner playing bass.

One other benefit of recording with Kramer had been to dispel the lingering notion that Mudhoney might somehow continue as a three-piece. Turner was too good a guitarist—or an insufficiently good bassist—for that to make sense. "It made me realize having a fourth person was a good thing," he says.

Mudhoney briefly considered, then rejected, the idea of a name change. "Why be willfully obscure?" says Turner. "We were already obscure enough." Their official status remained on hold. Real life, however, was about to shake things up.

On November 13, 2000, Dan Peters' wife, Donna, gave birth to their daughter, Ellie. The good news was closely accompanied by a final resolution of Mudhoney's long-stewing dispute with the IRS over alleged nonpayment of payroll taxes. Voldal Wartelle's attorney, Larry Johnson, had successfully haggled the authorities down to a payment of $56,000—a substantial sum, but way below the ruinous original figure of $250,000.

"Larry Johnson did a good negotiation," says Mark Arm. "He basically said, 'Look, this band is finished—these are their assets, there's nothing more you can get out of them.' Since we were a corporation, they couldn't go after us individually; they could just liquidate the assets of the corporation—so what, a couple of guitars and some amps? They couldn't go after our houses. But we still had to pay whatever money was left."

The easiest way to come up with the cash was to go on tour. As Matt Lukin had the same burden as the rest of them, like a good soldier he rejoined Mudhoney for a six-date run up the West Coast, finishing at Seattle's Graceland club on January 20, 2001. The shows were fun, if somewhat chaotic, though Turner detected a measure of friction between him and Lukin.

"I remember thinking that Matt doesn't like me very much, on that trip," he says. "But I don't think he really wanted to be there. It might have been a little bit of the tension between me and Bob rubbing off on him too."

Relations between Steve Turner and Bob Whittaker had turned sticky around about the time Steve began dating Bob's ex-girlfriend. The impact on Mudhoney was negligible, however, as by this point Whittaker had effectively ceased managing the band—after all, there wasn't much management to be done.

In June 1999, around the time Lukin quit, Whittaker had been pondering a move to the San Juan Islands to start a carpentry business when Peter Buck's then-wife, Stephanie Dorgan, owner of renowned Belltown club The Crocodile Cafe, told him that REM were going on tour and needed a band assistant.

"I was like, 'REM? That obnoxious bunch of new wave millionaires?!' Actually, I was never that big of a fan. I remembered Novoselic always playing me their records, and I'd met Michael Stipe over at Novoselic's house with Kurt when everyone was hanging out. So I was like, 'Nah . . . ' Then I woke up the next morning: 'What the hell am I thinking?! I should *totally* try to get that job.' So I did 1999 as assistant to the band but I basically assisted the tour manager too, and then in 2001 we went down to South America and I was functioning as tour manager, and stayed that way until they retired. Mudhoney had started to become a little less fun and a little more toxic—for me. I'm not getting quenched with the artistry of writing songs, or whatever. I basically walked away from the whole thing."

The issue of how Mudhoney should proceed, and with whom, was ultimately forced to its conclusion by an unlikely proposal. André Barcinski had first met the band in 1991. A well-respected young journalist working for a Sao Paulo newspaper and Brazilian music magazine *Bizz*, he'd embarked upon a U.S. road trip, criss-crossing the country to write a rock'n'roll travelogue: he went to New York, then San Francisco, Los Angeles, Chicago, finally pitching up in Seattle for the Nirvana/Mudhoney/Bikini Kill show on Halloween. After interviewing Mudhoney he struck up a friendship with the band. Over the years they would keep in touch via letters and faxes.

By 2001, Barcinski owned his own club in Sao Paulo and offered to bring the band to Brazil for an eight-date tour in February. "Kurt Cobain was dead seven years and nobody talked about the grunge scene anymore," he says, "but Mudhoney still had a huge following in Brazil and they had never been there. Their videos were really popular on MTV; I had a radio show at the time and we used to play all their albums. I knew they were popular. They were also famed for doing a great live show. Because they had never played in Brazil, a lot of people would want to see them."

Mudhoney were sorely tempted, but they needed a bassist. Lukin was not of a mind to postpone his retirement any longer, so Mark called Guy Maddison.

There would have been times in the not-so-distant past when Maddison would have leapt at the offer. In the late nineties, unable to make a living from playing rock'n'roll, he had taken various "jobs with dubious potential," be it as pest control technician or New Age book distributor. But now he was training to become a registered nurse and at a critical point in that lengthy process.

"I would have had to take a quarter off, then drop out of my class and join another class, which would have delayed graduation. I wasn't prepared to do that." Maddison said no.

Next, Mark asked Steve Dukich, an old friend whose band, Steel Wool, had opened for Mudhoney on more than one occasion and who had roadied for them on an early nineties U.S. tour. A skateboarding chum of Turner's, Dukich was very keen to go to Brazil. But he was also a close friend of Matt's and said he felt uncomfortable about stepping into his shoes. Lukin swiftly disabused him of any worries on that score.

"Matt had no problem with it," says Mark. "He was like, 'I quit; you can do whatever you want.' But Dukich wasn't sure he wanted to get that serious about being in a band again. Which is just as well, because Guy was my first choice."

So with Arm still holding out for Maddison in the long term, Steve Dukich got on the plane to Brazil. Even Dan was happy—or as happy as was possible, given that he was leaving behind his three-month-old baby. But in terms of playing Mudhoney shows without Matt Lukin, he was able to rationalize the Brazilian tour from a negative perspective: "When Matt was on, Matt was great. Before Matt became disenchanted and hated being in the band, there was not a funnier guy to be onstage with. One of the best things about us as a live band was Matt's incoherent rambles and people looking dumbfounded at him. Playing a song and drinking a beer at the same time. I'd look over at him, like, 'What are you doing?' 'I'm drinking a beer!' 'Well, what the fuck, we're in the middle of a song!' He's like, 'I'm hitting all the right notes, don't worry about it.' I was worried about that aspect of the band being gone. So I felt comfortable doing that tour because we had never been to Brazil—the audiences wouldn't know what they were missing."

Once there, however, Peters suffered from homesickness and the tour's punishing logistics. Amid subtropical temperatures and humidity, the band was flying from city to city, playing clubs with no air conditioning, crashing in low-cost accommodation, then rising early the next day to lug their rented backline amplification gear to the airport to catch their next plane. Until the very last show there were no days off.

"It was all fairly low budget," says Peters. "Miserably hot. We were staying in youth hostels. I wasn't enjoying playing without Matt, that was bumming me out. But the shows were good—that was the reassuring part."

With the bond never inclined to puff up their status at the best of times, Mudhoney's collective ego was at a pretty low peep by the time they went to Brazil. They didn't have a record company, their bassist was filling in as a favor because he fancied a holiday, and crowds on the last U.S. tour hadn't exactly lined around the block to see them.

So on February 21, 2001, when 3,500 screaming kids came to the Olympia club in Sao Paulo and sang along to every song, it offered a fresh perspective on their situation. "I had a great time in Brazil," says Mark. "The people were super-friendly and welcoming. That was a refreshing jolt of energy. We didn't go down there with any expectation or premeditation, only that it was a new place we hadn't been to before. Maybe it was because we hadn't been there and we'd

Everybody loves our town." Mudhoney brace themselves for the imminent release of *Piece of Cake*, the band's major-label debut, September 1992. JOE GIRON/CORBIS

Eddie Vedder and Mark Arm sing together on the first Pearl Jam/Mudhoney tour, November 1993. NEAL PRESTON/CORBIS

Mark Arm kicks out the jams with the DKT/MC5 at the Astoria, London, August 25, 2004. BRIAN RASIC/REX FEATU

Mudhoney in Seattle, 1993, circa *Five Dollar Bob's Mock Cooter Stew*: (from left) Steve Turner, Matt Lukin, Dan Peters, Mark Arm
IDOLS/PHOTOSHOT

Stick around long enough and they'll call you a legend." Lemmy offers Guy Maddison, Dan Peters, and Mark Arm the benefit of is wisdom, Portland, September 28, 2001. MARK ARM PRIVATE COLLECTION

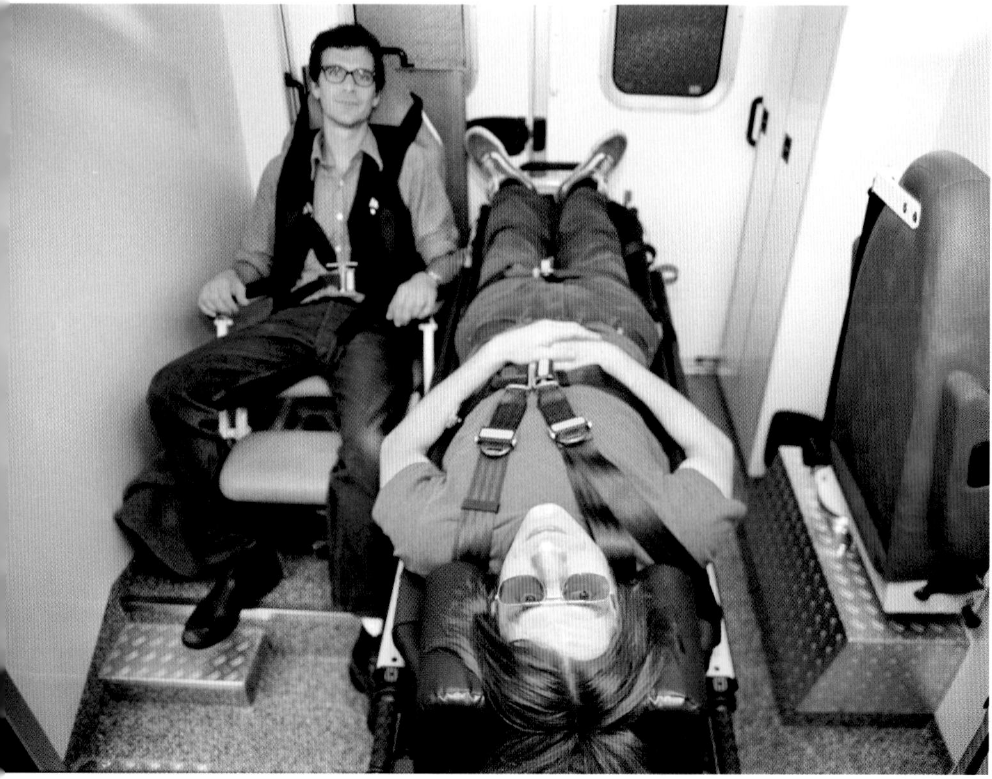

Steve Turner and Mark Arm come to terms with the budget accommodation on their first European press tour in seven years, 2002. THOMAS RABSCH/IDOLS

The new model Mudhoney, Camden Town, London, September 12, 2002: (from left) Steve Turner, Dan Peters, Guy Maddison, Mark Arm. STEVE GULLICK

nic nurse. Guy Maddison, the man who brought Mudhoney back to life, onstage with Peters, Arm, and Turner, in Portland, 2009. don't know what they would have done without him," says long-time tour manager Danny Baird. ANTHONY PIDGEON/REDFERNS

ome Together: the DKT/MC5's Wayne Kramer and Mark rm, Camden Underworld, London, December 7, 2006. ramer was instrumental in teasing Mudhoney out of their ost-Lukin limbo. JIM DYSON/GETTY IMAGES

Searching for melody. Steve Turner plays a solo acoustic performance on the LiveWire Radio Show, Portland, August 22, 2009. ANTHONY PIDGEON/REDFERNS

The Lucky Ones. Peters, Maddison, Turner, and Arm spread the love, Seattle, 2008. COURTESY EMILY RIEMAN

Recording *Vanishing Point* at Avast! Studio B, Seattle, October 26, 2012, with producer Johnny Sangster. COURTESY EMILY RIEMAN

n-set during the "I Like It Small" video shoot, Seattle, February 16, 2013. MARIANNE SPELLMAN

he short-lived quintet lineup with author Keith Cameron in Mudhoney's dressing room at the Kentish Town Forum, London, une 8, 2013. STEVE GULLICK

"My urgent urges keep urging me on." Mark Arm, back for another round at Kentish Town Forum, London, June 8, 2013.
STEVE GULLICK

been going for over 10 years, but there was a real enthusiasm from the people in Brazil."

The night before playing Sao Paulo, the band were guests of honor at a special dinner organized by André Barcinski at the behest of Ear Sick, a local teenage Mudhoney covers group. After a meal of spicy north-eastern Brazilian cuisine cooked by Barcinksi's restauranteur friend, and with the cachaça flowing in rivers, Ear Sick played a set of Mudhoney songs to Mudhoney. All aged between 14 and 16, the Brazilian band was understandably terrified. The bassist, in particular, was intent on realizing his life's ambition: to smash his guitar in front of Mark Arm.

Barcinski tried to talk him out of it. "I said, 'Don't do that, you don't have another bass.' But at the end of the show he threw his bass at the wall, and the bass broke in half. When he realized what he'd done, he knelt down close to it and started crying. It was heartbreaking."

Ear Sick's singer, meanwhile, tried to imitate the Charles Peterson photograph of an airborne stage diver as seen on the DVD of *Hype*, Doug Pray's 1996 Seattle scene documentary. That he was in a restaurant, and with no crowd to jump into, failed to deter him. The band were suitably appreciative of the kids' death-defying passion.

"We had to carry Dan to the van because he passed out," says Barcinski. "He was kissing the guys from Ear Sick and telling them they were his favorite band. At the show the next day, Mark actually dedicated a song to them: 'The best band in Brazil, Ear Sick!' The guys were crying. That's why people like Mudhoney so much in Brazil. They like to have fun, they mingle with the crowd, they're not a dressing-room band."

André Barcinski was utterly vindicated in his gamble of bringing Mudhoney to South America. He got the band's Rio De Janeiro show broadcast on Brazilian cable TV, whilst a performance on his radio show was soon widely bootlegged across the country. For the Sao Paulo gig he asked a famous Brazilian professional wrestler known as Trovão—"Thunder"—to introduce the band. "The mood was already insane," says Barcinski. "So he's about 60, dressed like a biker, and he had no idea who the band was. He wrote down their name on the palm of his hand. I told him, 'Say any stupid thing, just get the crowd going, and introduce Mudhoney.' He went onstage—'Hey motherfuckers, go fuck yourselves!' . . . and 3,500 people start throwing things at him. When he finally got to introduce the band, he looked down at the palm of his hand, but he had sweated so much he couldn't read it. So he turned to me at the side of the stage and said, 'What the fuck is the band's name?!' I said, 'It's Mudhoney! Mudhoney!' So he introduced them as 'Morones'! Mark's face when they walked on was so funny."

In Recife, Mudhoney played a free street festival as the representative of "world music." The band's schedule allowed them to stick around for the weekend's carnival festivities. "Which was pretty great," says Arm. "On day one, people were getting plastered drunk, running around in their costumes, and Steve Dukich was like: 'Brazilians are so much more laid-back—in America you couldn't have all these people getting drunk and being so happy.' By one in the morning the demeanor of the single guys roaming the streets had totally changed. They were drunk and angry because they weren't getting laid . . . It's like, 'Oh, Brazil's just like everywhere else!'"

Steve Turner was so entranced by the country that he enrolled in a Brazilian-Portuguese class upon returning to Seattle. Yet as successful as the trip had been in terms of boosting morale, the essential problem remained: Mudhoney couldn't wholeheartedly confront the future until they found a permanent bass player.

On May 11, Dukich filled in once again, at a gig to mark the 10th anniversary of The Crocodile Café, and a month later he played on his only Mudhoney recordings: cover versions of The Kinks' "Who'll Be the Next in Line" and The Circle Jerks' "Behind the Door."

Once again, Mark raised the prospect of recruiting Guy Maddison, who was by now on the point of graduating as a nurse. Dan Peters remained unsure; he didn't know Maddison very well, plus he had just been through the process of teaching the band's live set to Steve Dukich and didn't know if he had the will to do it again.

"But then I decided, 'What have I got to lose? I'll see how it goes,'" says Peters. "Guy came in to practice and we started playing—and I was like, 'Holy shit, this guy's really fucking great.' He gave the songs this weird added boost of energy and flow and groove that they never had before. I thought: 'I can get behind this. This is something.' We started writing new songs and the new songs had way more intensity and melody. Not to dismiss what we did in the past, but we became a way better band when Guy joined. I was like: 'All right, let's *do* this!'"

★ ★ ★

The best health professionals exude a calm reassurance, often in the gravest of situations. As he pads briskly through the intensive care cardiac unit of Seattle's Harborview Hospital, wearing his blue nurse's uniform and a smile, one can very easily imagine the restorative impact Guy Maddison had upon joining Mudhoney in the summer of 2001. Although not on the verge of death, the band's prospects didn't look so good. In Matt Lukin, Mudhoney had lost a founding member and a close friend. Until Maddison appeared in their midst, there wasn't a firm consensus between the remaining members that the band should even carry on. Yet within the course of a single practice session, the lights came on once more.

Maddison's public debut, on July 6, was deliberately off-piste: an extreme sports festival called the Tex Games, held at a rodeo arena in the small northcentral Washington town of Omak. The gig came through Steve Turner's skateboarding connections.

"It was a perfect place for Guy's first show, and our first show with Guy," he says, "because nobody was there. It was such a small crowd."

As they returned for an encore, Mark acknowledged the new guy: "Tonight is a special night. Not just because we're in Omak, but because it's Guy Maddison's debut with us. It might be his last show with us too. You get to decide: thumbs up or thumbs down?"*

A week later they played the Capitol Hill Block Party, a huge, open-air street festival in Seattle. Maddison was a Mudhoney fan; he didn't want to mess up a thing he loved. Given how nervous he felt in Omak, it would have been sheer cruelty to unveil him first before the 2,000-strong hometown crowd.

"The crowd's expectations of seeing Lukin was a difficult thing to deal with at first," he says. "Matt was incredibly popular, his sense of

* *Mudhoney Tourbook*, www.ocf.berkeley.edu/~ptn/mudhoney/tourbook/2001.html

humor was a big part of the live show. He's a larger-than-life figure and I don't think I would even come close to filling those shoes. At first, it was constant: 'Where's Lukin?' I don't say much, so I didn't have any witty rejoinders to those questions. That was difficult, wondering if people would even accept me. That affronts your ego, when you're the new person and people are yelling for the old guy. It's not like I deposed Lukin. But maybe it was a good thing—maybe it made me attack the strings harder and try to prove myself."

That he would ultimately succeed was never really in doubt, for beneath his easygoing charm lies a very resilient character. Born in Perth, Western Australia, on March 31, 1965, Guy Bernard Maddison is the product of classic British colonial stock. His father, Bernard Henry Maddison, was an engineer, born in India, the son of a Clarks Shoes manager who moved from Northampton to Kolkata after World War I to make cheap footwear for export back to the UK. Guy's grandfather married an Anglo-Indian woman and Bernard grew up in Darjeeling, in the foothills of the Himalayas. One of his school contemporaries was Peter Stoppard, brother of the renowned English playwright Tom. After the collapse of the Raj, Bernard was sent to boarding school in England, then studied engineering at Loughborough College before heading to central Africa, where he worked on the east-west Congo railway. Once that contract finished, he moved to South Africa and then completed his tour of the former British Empire by finally settling in Perth.

It was while working as engineer for the Roads Department that Bernard met Yvonne Janily Ward, known to all as Jan, a young draughtswoman almost half his age. Two years after Guy was born, the Maddisons added a daughter, Leila, to their perfect, middle-class sixties nuclear family.

"I grew up in the inner part of Perth," says Guy. "The suburbs, but not the far-flung suburbs. So I grew up playing a lot of sport, as Australians tend to. My mother was a sportswoman; she was a very, very good tennis player. I grew up in the tennis club essentially."

Perhaps surprisingly, given his age and background, Bernie Maddison liked jazz—especially Louis Armstrong—and Guy's first musical instrument was a trumpet, which he learned to play at the Salvation

Army. It was Bernie who also presented Guy with his first LP record: The Rolling Stones' 1964 debut on Decca. Guy's second album came from his 17-year-old Aunt Vivienne, who sought to share her love of Rod Stewart by gifting her nephew a copy of *Atlantic Crossing*. The first singles he purchased for himself were both released in 1977, the year of punk's flowering: "The Things We Do for Love" by 10cc and "Let There Be Rock" by AC/DC.

"The only record store in our area was Retravision," he says, "the place that sold refrigerators and washing machines, and it had a rack of LPs and 45s. The first album I actually paid money for might have been a Bryan Ferry solo album."

In 1978, Guy started high school, where he and his best friend Alasdair Dawson first discovered punk rock together. "Initially I liked The Damned and The Stranglers. The Stranglers had come to Australia in 1979 and had got arrested in Brisbane for drinking in the street. Back then Queensland had a very right-wing government, like the Texas of Australia. I remember being somewhat entranced by that story and then hearing The Stranglers and really liking them."

In particular, Guy loved the aggressive bass guitar of Jean-Jacques Burnel. Any ambitions he may have harbored to emulate The Stranglers' notorious, self-styled intellectual savage would not come to fruition until after he'd left school. Before then, on February 24, 1982, Guy saw The Clash at the 8,000-capacity Perth Entertainment Centre—his first proper gig, besides a couple of local tavern shows that he and Alasdair had sneaked into. The Clash concert was notable for one local oddity: all Doctor Marten boots had to be removed and checked in to the cloakroom. Perth had notorious skinhead gangs, a legacy of the city's location as the first port of call for ships from the mother country. In the seventies, a shaved head and plenty of bovver-booted attitude was a popular tribal signifier for Perth's large contingent of English immigrant youth. After skinheads had smashed up the Perth Concert Hall during a Madness gig in 1981, the PEC management was taking no chances.

"Hundreds of skinheads went up the front and berated The Clash to play 'White Riot,'" says Guy. "Joe Strummer was very pissed off, but they did eventually play it. The Clash were amazing. I'd never seen anything like that."

Perth's geographical isolation was weighing on those broad shoulders, however. During his final year at high school, Guy made plans to escape to the eastern states. His chosen vehicle was an unusual choice for a budding punk rocker: he joined the army. Both his mother's father and grandfather had served in the world wars—Guy's great-grandfather, Donald Ferguson Millar, survived Gallipoli, one of the most brutal military engagements of World War I—but, nonetheless, the reasons behind his application to the Royal Military College had more to do with a craving for independence than any deep vocation.

"I didn't put that much thought into it—I was not a very thoughtful young man!" he says. "I went through the selection process, not thinking I'd get through, but I did. And when you're 17 and impressionable you're like: 'I got selected, that's pretty good!' So I went off to Canberra, which was a real awakening to a strange version of adult life: living away from your family and earning a wage but also being in the army."

Situated in the stately colonial homestead of Duntroon, near the Molonglo River in the Australian Capital Territory, the Royal Military College is Australia's equivalent of Sandhurst or West Point, a training school for aspiring army officers. For Guy Maddison, still three months shy of his 18th birthday when he arrived, it would prove an educational experience in more ways than anticipated. As one of relatively few cadets who had not attended an elite private school, it was his first exposure to raw ambition and the manipulative psychological techniques deployed by the ruling classes.

"I'd seen bullies and high school crap," he says, "but not people actively thinking about how they were going to make their way in the world. That was eye-opening."

But subsidized alcohol proved the great leveler. With the mess bar selling beer at 50 cents and scotch and Coke at 75 cents, the whole campus could afford to get hammered. Guy had never smoked before, but with cigarettes at 50 cents a pack, it almost seemed foolish not to.

"So I got into smoking and drinking, and swearing a lot. I came home on leave at Christmas—I still feel embarrassed thinking about it—and sat with my whole family, telling a story, and letting rip with 'Fuckin' this' and 'fuckin' that'!"

With little else to spend his monthly wages on, Guy had soon purchased his first bass guitar. He was also able to take advantage of no longer living in a cultural desert. Like Seattle, Perth's remote location meant that, of the few international bands who toured Australia, even fewer would travel 2,500 miles across the island continent to play just one extra gig. So although Australia's small federal capital, Canberra, didn't have the vibrant nightlife of Melbourne or Sydney, its relative proximity to both cities meant Maddison still saw more bands than he ever did back home.

Some actually came to Canberra itself, thanks to the presence of the Australian National University. A liberal arts institution, the ANU enjoyed a rivalry with the RMC that manifested itself in typical student tomfoolery. One year, the ANU painted the RMC's artillery pieces pink, to which the RMC responded by digging a battalion position into the ANU's rugby pitch. Guy more usually entered the ANU refectory hall on civilian maneuvers: as well as seeing The Dead Kennedys and The Cure there, he would meet kindred spirits from Melbourne and Sydney, new friendships that offered the possibility of rock'n'roll furloughs during leave.

As he tasted life beyond the perimeter gates, Guy also began to bridle at the army's petty rules. He spent more and more time doing punishment drills—extra square-bashing in penance for invariably minor breaches of discipline.

"Which can result in other extra drills being added on, like if you turn up late for your extra drill you get an extra one, or if your brass isn't shiny enough, if your toecap's not polished enough, if your rifle's not clean . . . It just piled up. I think I assembled some sort of a record."

At the end of his second year, he failed his political science class, much to his chagrin. It led to him being called before the college commandant, who issued Staff Cadet Maddison with his final order: collect your pay check as you leave. He packed a bag, picked up his bass guitar, and caught the bus all the way back to Perth.

"It was a big disappointment for my mother," he says. "But I realized I didn't want to be involved in anything as organized as the military. I'm still friends with some of those guys and I once asked one of them: 'I wonder what corps I would have ended up in?' He said, 'You are not a regimented person, Guy; you would not have succeeded.' I guess even if I didn't recognize it, or wouldn't openly admit it; it must have been pretty evident if my peers thought it too. It definitely drove me in the counterculture direction."

Enrolling as an arts student in Perth, Guy moved into the same block of flats as Alasdair Dawson and was reassimilated into his old social circle as if nothing had happened. But the complexion of the punk scene had hardened during his two-year stint in the army. He discovered that the alternative lifestyle dogma espoused by UK anarcho-punk bands like Crass, Conflict, and Rudimentary Peni was taking precedence over music per se. Everyone carried political pamphlets; Buzzcocks was out, Bakunin was in.

"Anarchy was no longer a word that just got sprayed on a wall; it was something you had to think about, read about," says Maddison. "I started playing in a band—I met my buddy Ringo, who I ended up playing with in a lot of bands. He was a guitar player and he was punky, but not so much into this anarchist stuff and more into rock'n'roll. Quickly, I moved towards music like The Birthday Party, The Scientists, more garage-oriented stuff. Partly because we weren't very good and that stuff's easier to play and make it sound like something."

No band with any real ambition stuck around in Perth for long and, in 1985, Guy and Ringo moved to Sydney. Before leaving Perth, Maddison had met Stuart Gray, a.k.a. Stu Spasm, whose band Lubricated Goat were in the midst of making their first record. Soon after Maddison arrived in Sydney, he bumped into Stu.

"He asked me if I'd play in the band," says Guy. "I'm not sure what he saw, but he taught me a lot about how to play. He's a very accomplished musician whose father was a professional jazz musician. I think he just wanted someone energetic with a good haircut. I looked the part. I had black curly hair that covered my face, I had a bass guitar, and I could jump around."

In 1988, Maddison revealed these qualities, and much more besides, when Lubricated Goat performed their song "In the Raw" nude on Australian national television. A year later, the band found an appreciative U.S. patron for their lysergic leg-hump boogie in Tom Hazelmyer, who signed the Goat to Amphetamine Reptile and brought a lineup also featuring Renestair E.J. on guitar and Martin Bland on drums to the U.S. for a two-month visit. Opening up for the likes of The Butthole Surfers, Killdozer, and Sonic Youth, Maddison met the members of Mudhoney for the first time at a party thrown by a Sub Pop employee; he and Matt Lukin spent the evening in the kitchen bonding over beer.

Guy was smitten by Seattle, both its scenery and its weather—mountains and rain seemed exotic to someone brought up on the edge of a desert—as well as the locals' slightly reckless approach to life. "It's a big city with everything a city has, but it had this outpost feel to it as well," he says. "I got high on mushrooms and watched Babes in Toyland play in a primary school outside of Olympia. The roof was literally at head height, as it was a room for preschoolers. Super-surreal. Things like that didn't happen in Sydney, where there was no real alternative to the established rock industry way of pestering the living shit out of the booking agents at all the shitty clubs in town—which we had become pretty good at. You could tell there was much more going on here. There was more support for weirdness."

Several months after Lubricated Goat opened up for Mudhoney at Sydney's Kardomah Cafe in March 1990, Maddison left the band in bitter circumstances. "We were dividing up the money after a show," he says, "and Stuart felt he'd made a mistake with the division—which I guess is entirely possible as his maths skills were not strong. But he went around and started removing money from everyone's hands. At which point I snapped and punched him. Neither of us were adult enough to overcome that and I quit. The Sydney scene seemed to be disintegrating. I thought, 'I'll go abroad and see what happens.'"

In 1993, after a period in the UK—"I lived in Coventry with some relatives; it wasn't very fulfilling"—Maddison and members of his Hawkwind-inspired jam band, Monroe's Fur, moved to the U.S. They tried San Francisco first, then finally settled in the Pacific Northwest.

The peak of grunge gold-rush madness might not have seemed the most propitious time for Monroe's Fur to relocate to Seattle, but in fact they enjoyed success beyond their wildest dreams.

"We opened for Hawkwind," says Maddison. "Which for a Hawkwind-inspired jam band is a huge thing! That was the highlight of my musical career."

The band also tasted the fuzzy end of the grunge lollipop when they supported Artis the Spoonman, a Seattle street musician who found sudden and unexpected celebrity after Soundgarden named a song after him."That puts all your dreams of making it in rock'n'roll into perspective—when you're opening for a man that plays spoons."

Maddison certainly hadn't moved to Seattle in the expectation of becoming rich from playing music. But throughout Monroe's Fur and into Bloodloss, his ambition of no longer having to work day jobs to pay rent on the West Seattle house he shared with his wife, Zola, remained unfulfilled. At least his military training was of some benefit during three years as a pest control technician.

"One thing about the army is that the time spent in the field will toughen you up to a certain extent, so you can put up with things that are physically uncomfortable or unpleasant. And I kinda enjoyed the science aspect of extermination. There was a fair amount of chemistry involved."

Some of the more interesting tasks included donning breathing apparatus to fumigate the grain silos on Seattle's Harbor Island and issuing de-ratting certificates to giant container ships. "I had some entertaining days on boats. Russian vessels are very weird. Almost surreal. I remember having boiled mutton for lunch with one chief petty officer, who tagged me as someone who might be important."

But it was while crawling into a particularly nasty confined space one day that Maddison suddenly realized he couldn't kill rats for the rest of his life. In Sydney, he had applied for a job as a ward clerk at a hospital, where the director of nursing persuaded him to train as a nurse's assistant.

"You don't get to pass meds, but you do the personal care, cleaning, dressing changes. I'd done that, so I knew I wasn't particularly squeamish.

Registered nurses make a lot of money in the U.S., compared to other countries. I knew I could get a job and it's reasonably flexible, which would allow me to do other things."

Like playing in bands. So at the age of 34, Guy went back to school. For the first year, he combined pest control with studying anatomy, biology, physiology, microbiology, and chemistry, then became a full-time nursing student. Once qualified, in 2001, he got a job at Harborview and decided to undergo the three months additional training required to become a critical care nurse. By which point he had joined his favorite band.

"It seemed like there were a lot of times where stuff got put off for Mudhoney because I was not available, which they were very good about." Maddison's transformative impact upon the band meant that such restrictions were tolerated. But it was also a sign of changing times. Peters had a family and within a few years so too would Turner. Arm was a full-time warehouse manager. All were factors in the piecemeal method by which Mudhoney would put together their next album: over three two-day sessions between November 2001 and February 2002, in three different studios and with three different engineers (or four, including Jack Endino—a remixed version of "Inside Job" would make the final cut).

This unusual gestation grew from an idea Steve Turner had been toying with for years: record one song over a weekend each month until an album's worth of material was completed. That way no one would get bored and the material would stay fresh. But the writing sessions with Maddison were so productive that songs began coming together in groups of three.

"The biggest thing was having a fourth person totally engaged with the process," says Turner. "It's fun to write songs and go and record them. And we were all excited about it. As opposed to *Tomorrow Hit Today*, where Lukin was obviously losing interest, and the business around it—and us—felt . . . heavy."

The business around the new model Mudhoney was a case of "meet the new boss, same as the old boss." Shortly after January 2001's "IRS Tour," Dan Peters bumped into Jonathan Poneman at a gig. Poneman asked when Sub Pop could expect to hear the new Mudhoney album; Peters was happily surprised to learn that Poneman wanted one.

"They did great on *March to Fuzz*," says Turner, "and once we had some songs and we were really excited about it and it was going great, we certainly didn't want to get caught up in trying to figure out a record label. We were just like, 'Man—Sub Pop: let's do it!'"

The returning exile is a classic narrative, but neither party would have been well-served by an exercise in nostalgia. Sub Pop had long since pulped its original generic straitjacket. Under the calm stewardship of Megan Jasper—now the label's vice-president—who recruited a new generation of independent-minded music fans onto the staff, the label was rejuvenated as a home for idiosyncratic, somewhat self-effacing modern pop music, typified by The Shins.

Meanwhile, Mudhoney's internal dynamic had been rejuvenated by the arrival of Guy Maddison. Their first new album on Sub Pop in over 10 years was no grunge redux. The opening song, an eight-minute space-jazz psychedelic jam peppered with high-anxiety organ fills and titled "Baby, Can You Dig the Light?,' featured Craig Flory on saxophone channeling Roxy Music's Andy Mackay. It was almost four minutes into the vortex before Mark started singing.

Even by Mudhoney's standards, this was a perverse way to start a record, especially a comeback record. But as the album title itself was a tease on the band's status—*Since We've Become Translucent*—toying with their identity seemed entirely apt.

"We essentially tried to alienate people from the get-go, starting off with 'Baby, Can You Dig the Light?,'" says Arm. "Like, 'If you're still with us, either you're in it for the long haul and you enjoy all the stupid things we do . . . ' It sounds like an end of album song. Also, I think the way that *Tomorrow Hit Today* ended with 'Beneath the Valley of the Underdog,' with 'Baby, Can You Dig the Light?' opening the next record you could play those two records back to back and there would be this flow. But who's gonna pick up on that? All four of our fans?!"

As a player, Maddison clearly brought new elements to the band's creative weaponry. His aptitude for ethereal tones and improvised situations was evident in both Monroe's Fur and Bloodloss, although it couldn't be taken as given that the band would absorb his influence so readily. But the zeal with which they investigated new avenues indicated they saw their situation as an opportunity, rather than a crisis.

"It was almost like the band coming back for a second time," says Maddison. "Maybe they weren't so shackled by what had happened before, because it was a different band without Matt. It was like a new beginning and maybe they wanted to look at having some different sounds there. Why not? It's not like expectations were high." He laughs. "That's probably not the best way to put it! But no one was expecting them to rewrite 'Suck You Dry' and 'Touch Me I'm Sick' anymore. At the same time, nothing was necessarily lost: Steve's distinctive guitar sound is still present all over that record, Dan's completely unique drum stylings are still there, Mark's voice is unchanged. So in terms of composition and some of the production elements it's definitely a departure, but I think the core element of Mudhoney is still identifiable."

Two songs—"Where the Flavor Is" and "Take It Like a Man"—actually featured a three-man horn section, lending a Stax soul counterblast to material that, although inimitably grimy, had a newfound swing and swagger. With wry lyrics ruminating on the bathos of mighty egos cut down by life's vicissitudes ("Once you realize that you're not in charge/It makes your codpiece feel a little too large"), Sub Pop wanted to make the jiving "Take It Like a Man" the first single from the album. Arm thought otherwise.

"After such a long gap I don't want our first song back to be this wacky little number," he says. "Actually, it would have been a great single. But oh no, we had to go with 'Sonic Infusion.'"

It may have lacked radio-friendly crossover appeal, but "Sonic Infusion" was the record's keynote song. The closing track on the album, its smouldering introduction soon exploded into pure Hawkwind apocalyptonautics, with Mark Arm cast as a firebrand dissenting preacher ("Don't hand me that line about transubstantiation") urging his people into battle for the Truth, with a tip of the hat to The Dead Boys: "The Truth is plain to see, I'm a Sonic Transducer." The song provided the album with its title ("They think we don't exist since we've become translucent") and encapsulated the entire record's aura of sustained opposition, demarcating a standoff between "them" and "us."

"It's not for me to reveal who 'they' are," says Arm. "Either you feel it or you don't. Either you're part of 'they' or you're not. If you aren't, then you know who 'they' are."

But most importantly, "Sonic Infusion" signaled Mudhoney's spiritual rebirth. Four years after *Tomorrow Hit Today* had closed with the bleakly mordant "Beneath the Valley of the Underdog," its woebegone narrator on his knees, vanquished ("If I'm the guy you're looking for/Just look down under some rock"), the same voice was at the helm of a rock'n'roll resistance movement, beseeching his audience: "We can turn the tide with Sonic Infusion/Permeate everything/Penetrate and pull the strings/It ain't too late to make 'em sing." It felt glorious.

Released in August 2002, *Since We've Become Translucent* pulled off the considerable feat of satisfying and inspiring old followers while also enlightening a whole new generation of the grunge-curious. Mudhoney were a tangible link to an era that had already become mythologized, proving it was possible to exist in the now with dignity. With pop's endless cycle of regurgitation throwing up a new wave of garage-rock zealots—most notably The White Stripes, Detroit's latest primal scream team—the time seemed right for Mudhoney's sonic infusion.

The audiences who welcomed this new-old band back to Europe for the first time in seven years were treated to utterly carefree performances. Indeed, so obviously were the band enjoying themselves that it called into question the extent to which the buffoonery of the Lukin years had been universally endorsed.

"I think Guy made us a stronger live band," says Peters. "People might miss Matt up there pulling his pants down and yammering, but to me once we could start focusing on playing as strong as possible I started enjoying the band way more."

To suit the playfully incendiary mood, Mudhoney took to encoring with a version of "Urban Guerrilla," Hawkwind's 1973 anti-peace 'n' love anthem, and made it their own. When Mark Arm sang, "With my bullshit detector, I'm the people's debt collector" to packed houses singing along, the underdog's bite-back seemed complete.

★ ★ ★

In late 1999, Mark Arm registered with a new doctor. He spoke about his drug history, and the doctor suggested they run some tests. Mark said he didn't think that would be necessary—he'd previously tested negative for HIV/AIDS—but went along with it anyway. The results landed on his doormat with a thud: Mark had hepatitis C, a legacy of needle use, although it had been over six years since he'd stopped taking heroin. Unlike the A and B strains of the virus, most people exposed to hepatitis C experience no symptoms for many years—if not decades.

"I didn't feel ill at all," he says. "At first, I put off getting treatment, because I'd heard horror stories about it. Then I tried some herbal, naturopathic thing with my chiropractor. But that obviously didn't work—it didn't change the viral count in my bloodstream at all."

Next he decided to stop drinking, to save his liver from any more damage. Which was fine—except The Monkeywrench was about to go on tour. "Suddenly I had to play shows stone cold sober for the first time since the early days of Green River. Since The Monkeywrench is a band where I didn't play guitar, there was nothing to hide behind. I was kinda freaked out before the first show: Am I going to be able to do this? Is this gonna work? But in the middle of the show it kicked in all naturally. I realized I didn't need to be drunk to do this."

Eventually, however, in 2002 Arm decided to undergo Interferon treatment: a form of chemotherapy designed to stimulate the immune system into attacking the infection and also to halt the spread of the virus throughout the body. Because he had genotype one of the hepatitis C virus, the course of treatment would last 11 months—as opposed to six months for the other genotypes—and the side effects would be severe.

"Among the side effects of the Interferon is that it makes you emotionally raw," he says. "Some of the warnings state that you might end up having suicidal or homicidal thoughts. So I was in a mess."

Mark was in the middle of this treatment during the buildup to the 2003 Gulf War. Watching the news as the Bush administration's premeditated invasion of Iraq gathered momentum, he found himself unable to control his feelings.

"I wanted to write a song that wasn't just a didactic war-is-bad thing," he says. "But I knew I couldn't come up with anything as great as 'Masters of War,' or Flipper's 'Sacrifice.' Those are the two best antiwar songs I can think of. So there's all these people driving around after 9/11 with American flags sticking out of their cars, and it's like: Why are these people so gung-ho? I'm trying to get into the mindset of somebody who wants to send young people off to war and what their real motivations might be."

On February 15, 2003, the day of coordinated worldwide antiwar protests, Mudhoney recorded their new antiwar song. Then titled "Pushing for War," it surmised that the real motivation for middle-aged men sending younger generations to their death was sexual jealousy.

"And getting older, I can sympathize with that—not being able to get laid like you used to be able to!" laughs Mark. "Because you're no longer handsome and virile. So you rip those people out of the gene pool."

Subsequently retitled "Hard-On for War," the song brilliantly satirized the pathology of warmongering, with a leering descending guitar riff to match Arm's oily pronouncements: "See these lovely lonesome ladies/ They don't ignore me anymore . . . I'm the only game in town/And it's so easy to score . . . "

Made available initially via Thurston Moore's Protest-Records.com website, "Hard-On for War" would be rerecorded in 2005 and formed the centerpiece of *Under a Billion Suns*, the next Mudhoney album, which Sub Pop released in March 2006. The band had hoped to record in the summer of 2004, but were somewhat derailed when Mark Arm was made an offer he couldn't refuse.

In 2003, the surviving three members of The MC5—Michael Davis, Wayne Kramer, and Dennis Thompson—performed at The 100 Club in London with a variety of guest musicians and singers in place of the late Fred "Sonic" Smith and Rob Tyner. The following year, adopting the same format, they did a world tour as DKT/MC5. Kramer asked Mark to be one of the singers, initially for the two-week Far East leg. He accepted at once—though with reservations.

"These reunion things, God only knows how they can go," he reflects. "A lot of them aren't great. Especially a reunion where the original singer isn't there. It seemed like a really potentially sketchy proposition. So I was a little bit trepidatious, but also honored. And I figured, 'It'll just be in Australia, New Zealand, and Japan. There's legitimate people in all those places, but it's not like I'll be doing this in my hometown.'"

As it transpired, however, Arm ended up doing the entire U.S. and Canadian tour, plus Europe as well, after Mark Lanegan dropped out. In all, Arm was the principal singer in the DKT/MC5 for three months during 2004. Shortly prior to the first rehearsal, he watched *MC5: A True Testimonial*, the celebrated documentary about the band, which subsequently became a legal bone of contention between Kramer and the film's makers.

"And in that, Dennis Thompson is not in a good place. He appeared drunk and bitter and angry . . . I thought, 'Holy shit. What am I stepping into here?' Also, I wasn't quite sure how well can everybody play. I don't think Dennis had been playing regularly, and I'm not sure Mike had been playing regularly. But I went down to LA for a couple days of practice with them, and within a couple of songs I knew this was gonna be good—potentially great."

No one who saw Mark Arm slaying "Sister Anne," or "Black to Comm," or "Come Together," or taking his turn on the ensemble encores of "Kick out the Jams," is likely to forget the experience: the engine room of one of the great rock'n'roll bands of all time with a younger fan stepping up to earn his place on the stage as an equal. He'd now worked with the principal architects of both the sixties Detroit rock powerhouses: in 1997, through Thurston Moore, Mark wrote and sang two songs with The Stooges' Ron Asheton as part of The Wylde Rattz, an all-star band assembled to provide music for the Todd Haynes film *Velvet Goldmine*.

"Ron's a hero," says Arm. "He's one of the main touchstones for Mudhoney. I got sent music for two songs and wrote lyrics for them, and Ron was ecstatic with the lyrics. He said: 'That's exactly the kind of thing I was looking for.' It's unbelievable to me that there are two songs credited to 'Asheton/Arm.'"

During the week-long recording session in New York, Mark and Emily got to hang out with Asheton and on a bibulous night out gained first-hand experience of his gentlemanly character. "Ron Asheton held my hair back while I puked on the sidewalk," says Emily.

Stuck in proprietorial gridlock, the Wylde Rattz sessions remain unreleased, though Moore remains confident they will emerge one day: "There's original material, a bunch of Pretty Things covers, we did some psychedelic jams with Sean Lennon . . . there's three hours of music on the tapes. It was really good to see Mark sing that stuff. Plus I saw Mark play with The MC5 and he was great. What a connection to make."

Arm's contribution to The MC5 did more than just honor the memory of a great singer and offer a new audience the opportunity to witness a group of true originals. The educational process that he underwent would have benefits for Mudhoney too.

"Y'know, Rob Tyner is a *great* singer," says Mark. "I think I'm an OK singer! So I had to work really hard to be able to do some of the things that he did naturally. That also opened things up for me when we did our next two records. That stuff still sticks with me today. I think I learned quite a bit."

Some of the songs on *Under a Billion Suns*, most notably "Endless Yesterday" and "In Search of . . . ,' revealed Arm boldly taking his voice into the general vicinity of a croon. Dan Peters considers it Mudhoney's most musical album. He also finds the Guy Maddison–era albums a more rewarding listening experience than their pre-Guy counterparts. And, as Steve Turner says, Dan Peters is a very wise man.

"Particularly the first two records we made with Guy, we felt like we owe nothing to anybody," says Turner. "It's purely for us and the people that might dig it, and if they don't, well that's too bad. We certainly didn't feel any constraints. Or that we had to reinvent ourselves either. We do whatever we want—whatever we come up with, if we like it, we like it. That was a big deal to me, that was very freeing: when we realized, 'This isn't our job.' I'm not doing this for anybody but us."

It was an arrangement that suited Jonathan Poneman just fine. As he listened to the rough mixes of *Under a Billion Suns*, marveling at the eloquence and passion of the band whose first record he'd released almost 20 years previously, he was struck by how much Mudhoney had changed—and also by how much they'd stayed the same.

But one thing bothered him slightly: there was too much reverb on the vocals. When you had a singer with the arrowhead attack of Mark Arm, you didn't want mushy echo anywhere near the vocals.

Jonathan wandered out of his office and into the Sub Pop warehouse, where he said to the warehouse manager: "Mark Arm's vocals should be bone dry!"

The warehouse manager raised an eyebrow. "Interesting observation," he thought, fishing out another Shins album, slipping it into the cardboard mailer and taping it up—though not before adding a couple of stickers and a compliments slip, which, as usual, he signed, "Mark."

10

Wait, I'm Not Done

From the outside, there's nothing to tell it apart from any other house in the northern chunk of West Seattle. There's a garage at street level, plus some steps leading up to a front door. It's an unpretentious dwelling on a respectable street in a regular neighborhood. Mark Arm and his wife, Emily, live here with their two dogs, Chet and Lily, and an occasional feline friend. The couple foster rescued cats en route to new homes—although, as Emily observes, Mark often wants to keep them.

Pets play an important part in their lives. Emily is a photographer specializing in pictures of dogs and cats. For a New Year's e-card several years ago, she worked up an homage to the sleeve of the first Stooges album featuring herself, Mark, and their two old dogs, Stella and Dexter. Emily's characterful black and white portraits mock one half of that old saw about never working with animals or children. Then again, if she ever requires a real challenge Emily has been known to shoot her husband's band.

Mark explains that, soon after buying the house in October 1993, he had the walls of the basement double-thickened. "It makes the place *somewhat* soundproofed," he smiles.

Were a passing Mudhoney fan to tunnel their way into the basement, they would encounter the closest thing to a secular shrine in the band's world: amid the gig posters and set lists pinned to the walls and the tools of the rock band's trade strewn across the floor, the wall-mounted boiler and the lagged pipes on the ceiling indicate that beyond the grownup toys—the drums, the guitars, the amps, the antique synthesizer—this place is an otherwise normal domestic residence. Any fan who came here seeking the band's holy grail might just have to settle for the sports trophy plonked haphazardly on a shelf to one side: presented at a special anniversary show at The Crocodile Café on December 9, 1997, it celebrates "10 Years of Mudhoney."

At various points, the prospects of Mudhoney still being around to celebrate a 20th anniversary had looked bleak. But by the time 2008 rolled around, both the band and its members were in rude health. They had a new album recorded and ready to go—as soon as Sub Pop could find a place for it in a busy release schedule of hot and happening young talent like Fleet Foxes and Grammy-winning comedy duo Flight of the Conchords.

Just because Mark Arm worked for the label didn't mean his band got special treatment. Indeed, stalking the aisles of the warehouse and boxing up retail orders left him in no doubt as to where Mudhoney stood in the commercial pecking order. That was fine, he reflected; it wasn't as if the band was the most important thing in any of their lives. But in a funny sort of paradox, now that people's children and full-time jobs took priority, being in Mudhoney felt more valuable than ever.

So in 2007, when Steve Turner sold his Capitol Hill house for a humdinging profit and moved with his wife, Desiree, and their two sons to Portland, the 175 miles separating him from the rest of the band was just another logistical hassle to overcome—almost a test of their collective will to continue.

"We're really lucky in so many ways that we can still do this and still make it work," says Turner. "It's only because all four of us want to make it work that it works. No one's dragging their heels. We all have restrictions, and it's really hard to balance them at times, but we all want to do stuff."

Ever since becoming the band's booking agent at the end of 2000, around the time of the "Lukin/IRS comeback tour," Todd Cote has grown used to Mudhoney's unusual circumstances. Having come through the same eighties underground circles, he both understands and respects the band's nonconformist sensibilities; but still, getting Mudhoney out on the road remains a challenge.

"Guy basically gets six weeks of holiday per year," he says. "And he gives Mudhoney two two-week periods per year, and he gives his wife the other two-week period for a holiday. The nursing schedule gets posted for an entire year in November of the prior year. So Guy sends me and Mark his schedule and we look at the interest. Beyond that, we know which weekends Guy has free, so then it gets sent out: 'Who else has these weekends free?' Inevitably, Steve or Danny have some personal conflicts, but we whittle it down to the available weekends and two two-week periods, and then I go and book tours."

Ever since the band's translucent renaissance, the San Francisco–based Cote has received some very attractive proposals for gigs and festivals around the world that he doesn't even bother putting before them, simply because the offers don't fit with the Harborview nursing calendar.

"I just tell the promoter, 'That's great, and I know it's Roskilde and I know this seems crazy, but it's a pass.' And they're like, '*Whaaat*? It's eight months' notice, why can't you do this?!' It's just the way it is. If it is a weekend when Guy's available, then I send it to the band. Mark must have a cut and paste at this point that just says, 'I'm in.'"

As Maddison drily puts it: "We've been actively thwarting and stunting Mark's career since 2001."

One positive side effect of the band's restricted availability is that it makes them more attractive to promoters—and therefore increases their market value. "It creates more demand," says Cote. "Sometimes there's these crazy situations where I tell someone 'no,' and the answer's 'no' no matter what, and they think I'm playing games. They'll keep offering more money. And I'm like, 'That's great . . . you want some of my other artists?!' When they can do it, they'll do it—because they like doing it."

For 2008, the two-week tour periods were allocated to Brazil in the late autumn and, before that, in June to coincide with the release of the eighth full-length Mudhoney album, *The Lucky Ones*, a U.S. sweep from the Midwest through New England and down the eastern seaboard to Florida and New Orleans. With 16 gigs in 16 days, it was a fittingly hardcore itinerary for a record Steve Turner described as a "punk rock midlife crisis."

The Lucky Ones certainly felt like a reaction to the experiments with instrumentation and spacey textures of both *Since We've Become Translucent* and *Under a Billion Suns*. Gone was the horn section and the heavy reverb; more dramatically, so too was Mark Arm's guitar. This was part of Turner's concept for the album: punk it up, strip everything down, and record quickly. The basic backing tracks were completed in a day and a half, and the entire album took just five days to record, with Portland-based producer Tucker Martine behind the desk at Stone Gossard's Studio Litho. Interestingly, Martine had also recorded some of the . . . *Billion Suns* material; the wildly contrasting sonic textures between the two albums reflected the efficacy of form dictating function.

But jettisoning one guitar was a challenge. The band as a collective would have to ensure the material was sufficiently limber and compelling to make up for its absence. Although Arm usually performed at least one song without guitar at every gig—"Hate the Police" having been a set-list staple since 1988—his bandmates were granted a fresh perspective on his unfettered stagecraft when they watched him fronting the DKT/MC5 in Seattle.

"Mark was just phenomenal," says Maddison. "So it was suggested as nicely as possible that he try not playing the guitar. It definitely did make things go more quickly. Which had become a bit of a problem—we were taking a long time to finish songs."

Bunkered in the basement, while the other three were working out riffs, Arm would sing off-the-cuff nonsense until he found a melody. Occasionally a lyric would pop out that he liked and used as the basis for a song. The approach worked perfectly on the album's calling card, "I'm Now." With snag-toothed riffage dropping in around Peters' gobbety drums, this was a dramatically different album opener from its recent predecessors. One could almost smell Arm's prowling presence as he outlined a tragicomic tale of marital strife: a man goes to the airport to wave goodbye to his woman, not realizing "that look in her eyes" meant he was never going to see her again. Arm abridged The

Rolling Stones' "Love in Vain" (itself an adaptation of a Robert Johnson blues song)—before yammering two-fingered piano accompanied the refrain's blunt appraisal of the situation: "The past made no sense, the future looks tense—I'm Now!" In the second verse, Arm flashed back to a radio quiz he remembered from KISW, a Seattle classic rock station popular in the eighties.

"The goofy DJs would pick out a phrase and you were supposed to guess the answer," he says. "So they asked, 'What's the next thing you know?' Well, if you're a fan of *The Beverly Hillbillies*, you might go: 'The next thing you know, old Jed's a millionaire!' People kept calling in and answering whatever, and the goofy DJs would go: 'Wrong!' I just remembered that from 15 years previously. Weird."

Naturally, in Mudhoney's hands, this feverish weave of The Rolling Stones, "The Ballad of Jed Clampett," and a radio station that proclaimed itself "The Rock of Seattle" came out like premium-grade late-period Stooges. It set the tone for a writhing set of cerebral punk, with "Inside out over You" containing possibly Arm's greatest single instance of glass half-broken philosophy—"In my fucked up gestalt/ I'm a slug in salt/Losing its skin"—while the title track's incandescent soapboxer proclaimed envy for the dead, who no longer had to live in this rotten world.

The more overt political undertow to Mudhoney's twenty-first-century work reached its screaming apogee here and on "The Open Mind," an atheistic hymn to the power of negative thinking that hooked around the lyric, "The open mind is an empty mind, so I keep mine closed."

The song drew inspiration from both Jo Smitty and Emily Rieman. "That line, 'The open mind is an empty mind,' Smitty had that back in Mr. Epp days," says Mark. "I actually first used it in a Green River song, something on *Dry as a Bone*, I think.* Emily was saying she'd had it with people telling her to be open-minded and hearing people out. She said, 'Fuck that! I'm old enough and secure enough in where I'm at where I don't need to deal with bullshit.' One of her New Year's resolutions

* The song in question is "Unwind."

was to declare 2007 the 'Year of the Closed Mind'! And that of course made me think of Smitty's dictum."

Even the more pensive-sounding "We Are Rising," once again pitting "us" against "them," invoked a revolutionary spirit. "I don't feel like I have anything in common with 'normal' life," says Arm. "Even though my life has settled into a nice normal routine for me. But I don't get consumerism. I don't get religion. And I grew up with a religious background. I don't understand how people fall for it."

True to the spirit of a record that, in the brusque opinion of one reviewer, contained "nary a digression into the sort of dirge-blues nod-offs that have appeared on more recent releases,"* the *Lucky Ones* tour saw the Maddison-era lineup compacting its power and energy to an intense degree. Tour manager Danny Baird had worked with the band since 1993 and was well placed to assess the impact of the man who replaced his friend Lukin.

"Matt did what he did, but Guy's a better bass player than Matt, technically," says Baird. "So it reinvigorated them. Guy's just a wonderful person to hang out with. And he is definitely part of it in the studio and on tour. Guy's been in the band now longer than Matt was in the band. I don't know what they would have done without him."

On the summer's U.S. dates, Mark would start the set sans guitar for a blast through Fang's "The Money Will Roll Right In" and a rip through some new material, before plugging in his Gretsch Silver Jet. They typically ended with "Hate the Police," after which Mark would remain unencumbered by guitar throughout an entire encore of arched-back declamations, invariably closing with Mudhoney's idea of an early eighties medley: "Tales of Terror," *The Lucky Ones*' drawn-out, boggled-brain homage to the Californian hardcore iconoclasts, then Black Flag's "Fix Me." Acknowledging their roots seemed apt, not least because the band now attracted a pan-generational audience: fans from back in the day standing to the side and rear, while a younger demographic took care of the boisterous business at the front.

* *The Lucky Ones* review by Nate Knaebel, www.dustedmagazine.com/reviews/4301

While Mudhoney didn't publicly celebrate their twentieth anniversary, Sub Pop made amends by staging SP20, a two-day party in Redmond's Marymoor Park on July 12–13. Mudhoney played the first day, while the second featured the first official full reunion of Green River (which was technically the second, following an unannounced warm-up show three days earlier at the Sunset Tavern in Ballard). With both Bruce Fairweather and Steve Turner joining Jeff Ament, Mark Arm, Stone Gossard, and Alex Vincent, it was a six-strong, three-guitar lineup.

"Steve had to learn to play a bunch of songs he never played on," laughs Mark. "Those shows were really fun."

Although Turner was spared revisiting his nightmare trip through "Tunnel of Love," the set list did feature "Leech," which dated from the very first Green River demo tape but never survived beyond the band's earliest gigs. It had been subsequently adopted by The Melvins, whose creepy crawl style it strongly resembled in the first place. Mark enjoyed reclaiming it before an audience of 4,000 people.

"We made a demo in 1984 and passed it around to friends," he announced. "The Melvins recorded this song and pulled a Led Zeppelin by crediting it to themselves. We're the Willie Dixon of grunge. Now that we've got the combined legal forces of Sub Pop and Pearl Jam, we're taking it back."*

Momentum for the Green River reunion had been building ever since late 2005, when Mudhoney supported Pearl Jam in Chile, Argentina, Brazil, and Mexico. With the tour just over a week old and everyone getting on as famously as ever, the idea was mooted for both bands to combine for an encore of a Green River song.

"Someone suggested that we play a song from the first EP," said Mark. "We thought that 'Come on Down' might be good. Jeff found it online, listened to it, and went, 'Nah, *that sucks*!' So we ended up doing 'Kick out the Jams' and 'Rockin' in the Free World' instead." He laughed. "Which are much better songs."**

* *Green River Tourbook*, www.ocf.berkeley.edu/~ptn/mudhoney/tourbook/gr.html

** *Grunge Is Dead*, 456.

The sheer adrenalin rush from playing such combustible, anthemic material to 50,000 crowds in football stadiums was undeniable. Yet on their 2008 Brazilian tour, Mudhoney effected their own samba-grunge meltdown—albeit on a more intimate scale—performing "I'm Now" on Globo TV's *Jô Soares Programme*, a mainstream talk show similar in style and format to David Letterman's *Late Show*.

The avuncular 70-year-old Soares sported what looked like a Marylebone Cricket Club tie and seemed appropriately stumped by the performance. Indicative of Mudhoney's star status in Brazil, it was their first network television performance anywhere in the world since 1995* (or in Guy's case, since 1988—he wore clothes on this occasion). At a time when public opinion is so easily skewed by sophisticated marketing techniques, the band's popularity in Brazil—and for that matter Argentina, where audiences are equally fervent—seems a more organic expression of mass esteem. They play free festivals to crowds of 7,000 in provincial cities where international bands don't normally go, and also play smaller gigs for free, earning nothing more than two days in a hotel near great surfing beaches.

It's worth noting that this isn't some humble shtick that's been adopted in latter years. Mudhoney fans have always been able to testify to the band's disarming approachability. When 17-year-old Joel Staniec first heard "Touch Me I'm Sick" in 1990 while volunteering at WDET, his local National Public Radio station in Detroit, he felt such kinship with the band he wrote them fan letters.

"I actually got notes and postcards back from Steve Turner, which I was shocked at!" he says. Upon finally seeing the band live in 1991, his shock redoubled when they asked, "Hey, where is Joel?" from the stage. "After the show I managed to meet them, which was very cool."

"People admire their demeanor," says André Barcinski. "They're really approachable. Everyone talks about that in Brazil still. You can

* On June 19, 1995, Mudhoney performed "Judgment, Rage, Retribution, and Thyme" on NBC's *Late Night with Conan O'Brien.* Towards the end of the same year they appeared on PBS Kids' *Bill Nye the Science Guy*, miming to their version of the educational comedy show's theme song.

talk to Mark Arm and he'll just talk to you. They would watch the opening bands, they would stick around after they've played. People are impressed by that. Because the image people have of Mudhoney is of a band that was not as popular as Nirvana but was an equal to them in terms of importance in history."

Everyone knows what popularity did to Nirvana. Ultimately, Mudhoney thrived and endured by crediting the life of a rock band with no more importance than it actually deserves. Indeed, it was during the period when the band was their sole focus that things got sketchy: they toured too much, their audiences dwindled, they lost the fun factor. When circumstances removed the sense of obligation, their fortunes improved.

"It's amazing that people still ask us to go to Brazil, or Europe, or Australia," says Dan Peters. "The fact that we don't do it full time makes it easier for everybody. Certainly I think if we wanted to, we could be on tour for a year. But that's just not possible. Our limitations have kept us going. I assume that at some point in the cycle these offers will dry up again. It's something none of us have ever taken for granted. Each time we play a show I check myself and think: 'Jesus Christ, I'm in Sao Paulo, doing a rock show.' It's kinda crazy, don't you think?"

★ ★ ★

Even Todd Cote had to raise an eyebrow when he considered Mudhoney's tour itinerary for July 2012. It was a mere two shows, on consecutive days—the first in a pub, the next at a festival—but they were in Australia. The itinerary meant leaving Seattle on a Wednesday, arriving in Australia on the Friday, playing Melbourne's Corner Hotel on Friday night, traveling a thousand miles to the far northeast corner of New South Wales the next morning, playing the Splendour in the Grass festival in Byron Bay on Saturday night, then flying back to Seattle on Sunday—in order for Guy to see his baby daughter, Coco, and then go to work on Monday.

"They did the same with two Norwegian festivals a couple of years ago," says Cote. "The little time the four of them can get together they've been playing live, making a little extra income, and probably not having the time to concentrate on songwriting. I think that's partly why this new record took five years."

The five year-gap between *The Lucky Ones* and its successor, *Vanishing Point*, corresponds more or less with Steve Turner's relocation to Portland. Although just three hours by car, with family commitments already paramount, the separation between the guitarist and the rest of the band was enough to make getting together to work on new material a logistical nightmare.

"We just don't practice as much anymore, since Steve lives in Portland," says Mark. "A couple of times in 2012 he came up and stayed two days and we'd practice two days in a row, and it felt like, 'Wow, we actually got some momentum going—we actually remembered what we were working on the night before.' But if he comes up just every other week, we're back to the beginning again."

By late spring 2011, the little Portastudio in Arm's basement contained at least 30 new riffs and ideas for songs, but Mark was struggling to put words to the music. "Lyrics don't seem to come as easily anymore," he says. "I think when I was younger I used to just throw shit out there and think, 'Oh, that's good enough.' Whereas now, it's like, 'I can't do that, it's been done,' or 'That seems like a cliché.' Though sometimes I'll gladly go to a cliché!"

Perhaps more profoundly, Arm was still coming to terms with the loss of his friend and colleague Andy Kotowicz, who died in a car crash that previous October, aged 37. A native of Ann Arbor, Michigan, Kotowicz had been a Mudhoney fan since his teens and was one of the new breed of Sub Pop employees recruited at the turn of the millennium. With his ready wit, garrulous personality, and deep passion for music, Kotowicz's influence upon the record company extended way beyond his official role as VP of sales and marketing. "I know I was really affected by Andy's death," says Mark, "and I felt blank for a really long time."

Eventually, as so often with Mudhoney, it was Dan Peters who put it on the line. He declared he didn't want to come to another practice unless there was an actual song to work on. So Mark made quick mixes of all the riffs the band had recorded and put them on his iPod, to listen to them while performing other tasks. On the weekly visits to his elderly parents, for instance, he would spend the 40-minute drive listening repeatedly to a couple of riffs. Finally, he found a way through the blockage and got some lyrics down: "The way you move makes me stop/My mind is hard, my brain is soft/I try to speak, but I cannot talk/I'm frozen, and it's so hard, uh-huh . . . " Mark didn't think that much of them, but they worked well with his guitar riff. Together they would become "Slipping Away," Mudhoney's opening song for their next album.

The band's first Australian tour in over six years was the rightful occasion for the public debut of long-awaited new material. It wasn't "Slipping Away," however, but a hardcore shred called "Chardonnay" that got unveiled at Perth's Rosemount Hotel on December 3, 2011. As always, a good time was had down under, with old friends to meet and new ones to make. At the show in Sydney, Guy hooked up with John, one of his former military cadet comrades, a huge Birthday Party fan from Melbourne and now a general in the Australian Army.

"He was asking me, 'So, 'Hard-On for War' . . . are the other guys anti-militarists?'" says Guy. "It provided a very entertaining conversation."

With Mark and Steve due to meet members of feedtime for dinner in a vegan restaurant near the university, the general and another officer friend provided a route. "It was fun watching military people explaining directions to them," says Guy. "Steve said, 'I feel like I'm in the army now.' To which John played along: 'You'll proceed to your objective and destroy a Thai vegan meal . . . '"

The tour ended at the Meredith Music Festival in Victoria, where former Black Flag vocalist Keith Morris—touring Australia with his new band, OFF!—guested on the now regular set-closer "Fix Me."

Moving into 2012, Mark found that lyrics were now coming in batches of three and the creative momentum at practices intensified as the band sought to maximize their precious time together. "Slipping Away," in particular, had evolved way beyond Arm's original idea—a fairly generic heavy rock grind—into something very groovy and even soulful, an exceptionally deft accommodation of both old and new Mudhoney. Steve Turner's sinuous guitar soloing placed it very obviously in the vein of "Dead Love," yet with a jazzy undertow that simply wasn't in their 1988 vocabulary. Arm had the Maddison-Peters brains trust to thank for that.

"Dan and Guy started messing around with the rhythm and they got it to a place that I hadn't conceived of, that I think was much cooler. That's why I like working with other people." Arm laughs. "Or at least, good people who have good ideas! You'll end up with a better outcome. Because otherwise, if I was the dictator of the group, it would have been a much lesser thing."

Once they had the songs worked out, actually making the record was straightforward and quick—two weekend sessions, one in late April, the other in September, with a final session in October for overdubs: some synthesizers, a funky clavinet homage to Billy Preston, and a massed backing chorus including Dan Peters' young sons, Sam and Will. Engineering throughout was their friend Johnny Sangster, a local musician and producer, who had helmed one each of the *Since We've Become Translucent* and *Under a Billion Suns* sessions, and also produced the three solo albums of "skate folk" Steve Turner had released since 2003.

"Johnny's a great enabler," says Turner. "It can be fraught with drama in the studio, but he understands all of us and he's good at saying if he thinks we can do better."

At 10 songs and 34 minutes, *Vanishing Point* refracted its expanse and experimental yearnings through the concise prism of eighties hardcore. In places it evoked the exhilarating new world that emerged in hardcore's wake, where bands like The Meat Puppets, Squirrel Bait, and Honor Role built radical designs upon the earth scorched by Black Flag et. al. There were also traces of the murky interregnum period between psychedelia and punk, epitomized by bands like Chrome or the Dead Boys/Pere Ubu mothership Rocket from the Tombs. The album's twin midpoint bridgeheads, "The Final Course" and "In This Rubber Tomb," dug deep into this primordial soup and emerged clutching jewels.

"I really love that '74/'75/'76 period, before punk rock had happened, music made by people who are clearly not into what's happening in rock," says Arm. "Bands like Pere Ubu and The Bizarros—there's The

Stooges and King Crimson in there—because the people making this music were just listening to the stuff they could find, that they think is cool but obviously isn't anywhere near the mainstream."

Ultimately, however, *Vanishing Point* resembled Mudhoney most of all. Unlike *The Lucky Ones*, there was no guiding concept—the band were now so familiar with each other and their capabilities that they knew they could wonk the formula and still be what they are. A perfect example of the methodology was "What to Do with the Neutral."

"Dan had talked to Guy about this seventies Lee Hazlewood song," says Arm, "that has this loping bassline and a particular drumbeat. So they tried to do an approximation of that—and it doesn't really sound like it. But it reminded me of 'The Bogus Man' by Roxy Music. Then by the time I put lyrics on it, it's seventies Berlin-era Iggy!"

The eclectic jukebox's unifying factor was Arm, his ever-more expressive voice and lyrics tapping new levels of sardonic poetry. "You're the grape that launched a thousand strippers/The soccer mom's favorite sipper," he railed on "Chardonnay," the first hardcore song about white wine—prompted by too many backstage meetings with the vintner's suburban bin-filler.

"There's no depth there," chuckles Arm, "but if you're gonna rail against something you should be passionate about what you're railing against. I've had great Rieslings and shitty Rieslings, but I've never had a Chardonnay I liked."

The pounding wah-wah onslaught of "The Final Course" suggested a grotesque cannibalistic orgy—"I grabbed the throat of the nearest shrew, she was sitting to my right/Someone brained me with a skillet/Boom boom, out go the lights"—while "The Only Son of the Widow from Nain" took on the legend of an unsung New Testament hero: the first man Jesus raised from the dead, only to be subsequently eclipsed by Lazarus, whose PR guy presumably had a hotline to Saint Luke. Given the relish with which Mark voiced the indignation of the titular character, it was easy to imagine him empathizing with the figure ignored by the Gospels' rewrite of history. His spleen was vented to the illogical extreme of invoking both Foreigner's "Urgent" and Devo's "Uncontrollable Urge." This was biblical revisionism set to midperiod Black Flag gnarl.

There was yet more comedic verve on "I Don't Remember You," evocative of both Iggy Pop's "I'm Bored" and two separate Jimi Hendrix songs, where Arm is accosted in the supermarket by a scenester from hazier days, with namechecks for old school haunts The Ditto Tavern and The Lake Union Pub. "Sing This Song of Joy," meanwhile, slowed the pace without leavening the weight in its denunciation of an unnamed reaper of damage. Arm was imagining the death of Kansas petrochemical billionaires the Koch brothers, and others of their ilk:

"For years they've been funding these conservative think-tanks and climate science denial—because they just don't want to give up a fucking dime. It's kinda sick."

In keeping with the immaculate trajectory implied by its title, *Vanishing Point* felt like a culmination of the current era Mudhoney's questing impulses, but simultaneously allied to the minimalist rigor that had been the original band's founding principle. And as had also been the case since 1988, Mudhoney remained unabashed about their debt to the pioneers who had both preceded and inspired them. "We're a band that wears our influences pretty openly on our sleeves," says Mark. "It's not like we were ever trying to hide the fact that we're into The Stooges, or Blue Cheer: we basically almost ripped off a Blue Cheer song ['Magnolia Caboose Babyfinger'] and retitled it 'Magnolia Caboose Babyshit.' It wasn't like we thought we were coming up with anything new. It's more like we were trying to play music that we felt was missing: stuff that we were into and not hearing at the time. Maybe that inadvertently created something that people perceive as new . . . but to me, everything comes from somewhere."

⋆ ⋆ ⋆

Mark Arm awoke on Saturday February 2, 2013, having slept very badly. Mudhoney had a gig in Seattle that night, supporting The Sonics at the Showbox. But before then, Mark was going to his mother's 92nd birthday party. It wasn't going to be an easy visit; his father had died just over two weeks previously. Calvin was 89 and had been ill for some time.

Once the party was over and Anita's various friends from church and neighborhood had left, Mark sat with his mother and they watched a DVD slideshow of family photographs. "My mom's had a couple of strokes so she's not very communicative," says Mark. "She had no idea she was turning 92, or indeed that it was her birthday until people started telling her it was. So I think maybe she might have forgotten that Calvin was gone. I don't know. Or at least, it wasn't in the forefront of her thoughts. When the slideshow happened, she would go from being really smiley to being profoundly sad again. I . . . I just lost it."

After dealing with such deep and complex emotions, he had to suddenly jerk himself into Mudhoney mode. Back home, he tried to catch up on his lost sleep, but his nap was interrupted by the arrival of Guy and Dan with Danny Baird to start loading the equipment.

"So then I switched gears," says Mark, "and played a show. It was one of those days that felt like a year. By the end of the evening it was hard to imagine that my mom's birthday party had even been on the same day."

Opening for The Sonics was a big deal for Mudhoney, a chance to acknowledge shared geographical roots and musical sensibilities across the years. The Tacoma quintet had defined garage-rock primitivism with astoundingly visceral two-track recordings like "Strychnine" and were also unlikely Pacific Northwest pop stars. By the time Mark had discovered them in 1980—via a review in *Trouser Press* magazine of their reissued 1965 debut album, *Here Are the Sonics*, by British writer Mick Farren—the band was long since forgotten about locally.

"It was funny that I was turned on to a band from my backyard by some guy from the UK," he says. "But pretty soon, punk rock people became aware of them because of those reissues. Gerry Roslie's singing has been a huge influence on me: that screaming and singing all at the same time."

Mudhoney were offered the support slot when The Sonics reunited to play Seattle's Paramount Theatre on Halloween 2008, but had to decline as Steve wasn't available. Finally the two bands' calendars had coincided, and the long-anticipated meeting between two generations of Pacific Northwest garage rock genius took place.

"We were pretty amped up," says Steve. "We were feeling the pressure. I don't think any of us ever thought we'd play a show with The Sonics."

The show was deemed a resounding success, with The Sonics inviting the members of Mudhoney onstage to take a bow—though Dan absented himself by stepping outside for a smoke and a hot dog. Afterwards, both bands hung out and chatted. A group picture was taken with the 68-year-old Gerry Roslie proudly holding aloft two bottles of beer. Later, he would hold his head in his hands with disbelief as he and Zola Maddison discovered they both attended Tacoma's Jefferson Elementary and Mason Junior High schools—albeit some 30 years apart. Tentative plans were hatched to play together again, preferably sooner rather than later.

"I was suggesting South America, because they haven't planned to go down there yet," says Steve. "I think this is the last go-round for them. Y'know, they're healthy, but they're not that young!"

★ ★ ★

When tomorrow hits today, at such moments we find out who we really are. Mudhoney have known it all along, which is why they never pretended to be something they're not. They're four guys who got together and played music for fun, and the grand plan ended there. Their firm hold on what's important about their band also explains why they're still here: it's about integrity and civility; about growing older together; about making records with a real time/real life vitality; about knowing the identities of "them" and "us."

They say history is written by the winners: But in what way have Mudhoney really lost? By never actively playing the game, by never striving for commercial success, by never buying into the system, they eventually enabled themselves to do what they wanted the way they wanted and—give or take the odd nursing schedule or school holidays—when they wanted.

"Y'know," says Mark Arm, "despite all the shit that's gone down at times, and whatever weirdness happens, we remained friends. I think that's key. We wouldn't be able to do this if we hadn't. I guess The Ramones stuck together for 20 years while two of them didn't speak to each other, but I don't know how you'd do that! We don't have to keep doing this band 'cos it's our source of income—because it's not. I think there's a much deeper connection between us, and especially with Dan and Steve and myself, who've been doing it since 1988. Guy hopped on board when the ship had already sunk, in commercial terms! This thing was never about having a hit and getting fame and making money. The fact that any of that happened at all is just a weird luck of the draw. And the fact that we've been able to keep going for 25 years now, that's a really odd thing to me—but it makes perfect sense."

On Monday April 1, 2013, the eve of the official release of *Vanishing Point*, Mudhoney played the new album in its entirety to an uncomfortably packed crowd of 250 people at Easy Street Records in West Seattle. For an encore, they played the songs that comprised their debut single, recorded almost exactly a quarter of a century earlier. While it's arguable that the band's essence is still found wholly within the sound and fury of "Touch Me I'm Sick," it was a new song, "I Like It Small," which itemized the real reasons for the band's eternal status: "Minimal production, low yield, intimate settings, limited appeal/Dingy basements, short runs, no expectations—wait, I'm not done!"

Or, as Mark Arm put it 25 years ago: "The bigger the crowd, the lower the IQ."*

In 2001, Mudhoney opened for Motörhead in Portland and enjoyed a starry-eyed encounter to file alongside Iggy Pop. After the show, Lemmy entered their dressing room to shake hands, commend their performance, and then drink their beer.

"We had a pretty good session backstage," says Dan. "At one point, I didn't want it to seem like I was outstaying my welcome, so I moved to another corner and began chatting to some other people. Then I feel this guy tapping me on the shoulder and going, 'Yeah, that's right!' It was Lemmy, trying to join in!"

* *Swellsville* #8, Winter 1989.

The following year, Mark and Steve were at Cologne airport, waiting to check in for a flight to London, when they bumped into Lemmy doing the same. A little less perky than at their previous meeting, the great man still had one nugget of wisdom to impart: "Stick around long enough and they'll call you a legend."

Stick around longer and they'll call you Mudhoney.

Acknowledgments

Thanks to Matthew Hamilton—a rock god among literary agents—who urged me to write this book, found someone to publish it, and kept on believing in it throughout. Thanks are due to everyone at Omnibus Press for making the book a reality: in particular David Barraclough, my commissioning editor, for his reserves of patience and calm. Thanks also to Paul Woods for being such a painstaking and painless copy editor.

That this book exists at all is thanks to the members of Mudhoney: Mark Arm, Matt Lukin, Guy Maddison, Dan Peters, and Steve Turner. I will be eternally grateful to them for going out of their way to help me with contacts, and for sparing time to conduct the many hours of interviews that comprise the majority of the book's source material. The same debt of gratitude is extended to all my interviewees.

Thanks to Phil Alexander and all the staff of *MOJO* for tolerating my immersion in the book. Thanks to Chris Jacobs, Megan Jasper, Jonathan Poneman, Carly Starr, and everyone else, past and present, at Sub Pop—the greatest record label in the world.

I'd also like to thank the following people, all of whom either facilitated or encouraged me along the way: Jeff Ament, Mika Anttila, Danny Baird, André Barcinski, Francisco Bello Basilio, Nils Bernstein,

Mark Blake, Richard Boon, Anton Brookes, Stevie Chick, Todd Cote, Kurt Danielson, Steve Double, Jack Endino, Ed Fotheringham, Pat Gilbert, Steve Gullick, Barney Hoskyns, Hampton Howerton, Paul Hutton, Damian Jarpa, Sebastián Jarpa, Leila Kassir, David Katznelson, Nita Keeler, Simon Keeler, Steve Lamacq, Sarah Lazin, Bob Mehr, Mogwai, Thurston Moore, Chris Nelson, Richard Newson, Bruce Pavitt, Adam Pease, Neil Pengelly, Charles Peterson, Emily Rieman, Roger Sargent, Ann Scanlon, Garrett Shavlik, Ryan Short, Jo Smitty, Joel Staniec, Chris Stone, Kim Thayil, Peter Trahms, Cathi Unsworth, Vincent Van Nes, and Bob Whittaker.

A special word of thanks to Tim Hall, who lent me his Mudhoney press archive—an act of immense personal sacrifice for which I will be forever grateful. He's got it back now (so apologies to Tim's wife).

Finally, my love and thanks to Jenny and Hamish: for putting up with me, for looking after me, and for inspiring me.

Bibliography

Unless otherwise stated in footnotes to the main text, all the quotes in this book are taken from the author's own interviews. The following books provided source material or background context.

Azerrad, Michael. *Come as You Are: The Story of Nirvana* (Virgin, 1993).

Azerrad, Michael. *Our Band Could Be Your Life* (Little Brown, 2001).

Bangs, Lester, and Marcus, Greil, [ed.]. *Psychotic Reactions and Carburetor Dung* (Anchor, 1988).

Blecha, Peter. *Sonic Boom: The History of Northwest Rock from Louie Louie to Smells Like Teen Spirit* (Miller Freeman, 2009).

Brannigan, Paul. *This Is a Call: The Life and Times of Dave Grohl* (HarperCollins, 2011).

Browne, David. *Goodbye 20th Century: Sonic Youth and the Rise of the Alternative Nation* (Da Capo, 2008).

Chick, Stevie. *Spray Paint the Walls: The Story of Black Flag* (Omnibus Press, 2009).

Cross, Charles R. *Heavier Than Heaven: The Biography of Kurt Cobain* (Hodder & Stoughton, 2001).

DeRogatis, Jim. *Staring at Sound: The True Story of Oklahoma's Fabulous Flaming Lips* (Robson Books, 2006).

Humphrey, Clark. *Loser: The Real Seattle Music Story* (Feral House, 1995).
Kot, Greg. *Wilco: Learning How to Die* (Broadway, 2004).
McMurray, Jacob. *Taking Punk to the Masses* (Fantagraphics, 2011).
Morse, Erik. *Dreamweapon: Spacemen 3 and the Birth of Spiritualized* (Omnibus Press, 2004).
Prato, Greg. *Grunge Is Dead: The Oral History of Seattle Rock Music* (ECW, 2009).
Reynolds, Simon. *Rip It up and Start Again: Postpunk 1978–1984* (Faber & Faber, 2006).
Savage, Jon. *England's Dreaming: Sex Pistols and Punk Rock* (Faber & Faber, 1991).
Tow, Stephen. *The Strangest Tribe: How a Group of Seattle Rock Bands Invented Grunge* (Sasquatch, 2011).
True, Everett. *Nirvana: The True Story* (Omnibus Press, 2006).
Trynka, Paul. *Iggy Pop: Open Up and Bleed* (Broadway, 2007).
Waksman, Steve. *This Ain't the Summer of Love: Conflict and Crossover in Heavy Metal and Punk* (University of California Press, 2009).
Yarm, Mark. *Everybody Loves Our Town: A History of Grunge* (Faber & Faber, 2011).

MUDHONEY ON THE WEB

The following sites are run by Mudhoney fans across the world. All provided valuable information for this book and are recommended to anyone in search of more sickness . . .

www.mudhoneysite.com/
www.ocf.berkeley.edu/~ptn/mudhoney/
www.mudhoneyonline.com
www.facebook.com/pages/Mudhoney/120610017957082
www.twitter.com/_Mudhoney
www.twitter.com/Mudhoney_
www.youtube.com/user/mudhoneyofficial

Select Discography

SINGLES

August 1988
Touch Me I'm Sick/Sweet Young Thing Ain't Sweet No More
(Sub Pop SP18)

January 1989
Mudhoney/Sonic Youth:
Halloween/Touch Me I'm Sick
(Sub Pop SP26)

June 1989
You Got It (Keep It Outta My Face)/Burn It Clean
(Sub Pop SP33)
Glitterhouse 12-inch edition (GR0060) adds Need (Demo)

October 1989
This Gift/Baby Help Me Forget
(Sub Pop SP44a)
Glitterhouse 12-inch edition (GR0070) adds Revolution

June 1990
You're Gone/Thorn/You Make Me Die
(Sub Pop SP63)

November 1990
Plays Hate the Police (Au-Go-Go ANDA122)
Australian CD and 12-inch featuring: Hate the Police/Revolution/The Rose/Halloween

June 1991
Let It Slide/Ounce of Deception/Checkout Time (alt. version)
(Sub Pop SP95)
CD edition adds Paperback Life/The Money Will Roll Right In

September 1991
Mudhoney/Halo of Flies:
She's Just Fifteen/Jagged Time Lapse
(Amphetamine Reptile Scale36)

May 1992
Mudhoney/Gas Huffer:
You Stupid Asshole/Knife Manual
(Empty MT-166)
CD edition adds March to Fuzz/Firebug (by Gas Huffer)

August 1992
Suck You Dry/Deception Pass
(Reprise 5439-18687-7 WO137)
CD edition adds: Over the Top/Underide

March 1993
Blinding Sun/Deception Pass/King Sandbox/Baby O Baby
(Reprise 40741-2)

March 1994
Mudhoney/Jimmie Dale Gilmore:
Tonight I Think I'm Gonna Go Downtown/Blinding Sun
(Sub Pop SP248)
CD edition adds Buckskin Stallion Blues

May 1995
Generation Spokesmodel/Not Going Down That Road Again
(Reprise 5439-17864-7)
CD edition adds What Moves the Heart (Live)/Judgment, Rage, Retribution and Thyme (Live)

June 1995
Into Yer Shtik/You Give Me the Creeps
(Super Electro SE708)

October 1995
Mudhoney/Strapping Fieldhands:
Goat Cheese/Porn Weasel
(Amphetamine Reptile Scale76)

June 1998
Night of the Hunted/Brand New Face
(Super Electro SE716)

July 2002
Sonic Infusion/Long Way to Go
(Sub Pop SP603)

May 2006
It Is Us/Dig Those Trenches
(Sub Pop SP716)

November 2008
Mudhoney/Mugstar:
Urban Guerrilla/Born to Go
(Trensmat TR013)

April 2013
Mudhoney/Treatment:
Did He Die/Driving Me Insane
(Tym Records TYM010)

May 2013
New World Charm/Swimming in Beer/The Swimming in Beer Blues
(Sub Pop SP1025)

ALBUMS & EPs

October 1988
Superfuzz Bigmuff
Need/Chain That Door/Mudride/No One Has/If I Think/In'n'out of Grace
(Sub Pop SP21)
European release (Glitterhouse GR0034) substituted Touch Me I'm Sick for Need/Australian release (Au-Go-Go ANDA101) substituted Sweet Young Thing Ain't Sweet No More for Need

October 1989
Mudhoney
This Gift/Flat out Fucked/Get into Yours/You Got It/Magnolia Caboose Babyshit/Come to Mind/Here Comes Sickness/Running Loaded/The Farther I Go/By Her Own Hand/When Tomorrow Hits/Dead Love
(Sub Pop SP44)

July 1991
Every Good Boy Deserves Fudge
Generation Genocide/Let It Slide/Good Enough/Something So Clear/Thorn/Into the Drink/Broken Hands/Who You Drivin' Now?/Move Out/Shoot the Moon/Fuzz Gun '91/Pokin' Around/Don't Fade IV/Check-Out Time
(Sub Pop SP105)

October 1992
Piece of Cake
(Untitled)/No End in Sight/Make It Now/When in Rome/(Untitled)/Suck You Dry/Blinding Sun/Thirteenth Floor Opening/Youth Body Expression Explosion/I'm Spun/(Untitled)/Take Me There/Living Wreck/Let Me Let You Down/(Untitled)/Ritzville/Acetone
(Reprise 45090-1)
August 2003 CD reissue added Over the Top, King Sandbox, and Baby O Baby, plus the entirety of *Five Dollar Bob's Mock Cooter Stew* (see below)

October 1993
Five Dollar Bob's Mock Cooter Stew
In the Blood/No Song III/Between Me & You Kid/Six Two One/Make It Now Again/Deception Pass/Underide
(Reprise 45439-1)

March 1995
My Brother the Cow
Judgment, Rage, Retribution, and Thyme/Generation Spokesmodel/What Moves the Heart/Today Is a Good Day/Into Yer Shtik/F.D.K. (Fearless Doctor Killers)/Orange Ball-Peen Hammer/Crankcase Blues/Execution Style/Dissolve/1995
(Reprise 45840-1)
Vinyl edition included bonus seven-inch EP featuring Mudhoney Funky Butt/West Seattle Hardcore/Sissy Bar/Carjack '94/Hey Sailor/Small Animals; August 2003 CD reissue added these six tracks plus Not Going Down That Road Again

September 1998
Tomorrow Hit Today
A Thousand Forms of Mind/I Have to Laugh/Oblivion/Try to Be Kind/Poisoned Water/Real Low Vibe/This Is the Life/Night of the Hunted/Move with the Wind/Ghost/I Will Fight No More Forever/Beneath the Valley of the Underdog/Talkin' Randy Tate's Specter Blues [hidden track]
(Reprise 47054-2)
Vinyl edition released on Super Electro (SUPER10)

September 2002
Since We've Become Translucent
Baby, Can You Dig the Light/The Straight Life/Where the Flavor Is/In the Winner's Circle/Dyin' for It/Inside Job/Take It Like a Man/Crooked and Wide/Sonic Infusion
(Sub Pop SP555)

March 2006
Under a Billion Suns
Where Is the Future/It Is Us/I Saw the Light/Endless Yesterday/Empty Shells/Hard-On for War/A Brief Celebration of Indifference/Let's Drop In/On the Move/In Search of . . . /Blindspots
(Sub Pop SP700)

May 2008
The Lucky Ones
I'm Now/Inside out over You/The Lucky Ones/Next Time/And the Shimmering Light/The Open Mind/What's This Thing?/Running Out/Tales of Terror/We Are Rising/New Meaning
(Sub Pop SP765)
Vinyl edition included bonus seven-inch single: Street Waves/Gonna Make You

April 2013
Vanishing Point
Slipping Away/I Like It Small/What to Do with the Neutral/Chardonnay/The Final Course/In This Rubber Tomb/I Don't Remember You/The Only Son of the Widow from Nain/Sing This Song of Joy/Douchebags on Parade
(Sub Pop SP1080)

LIVE ALBUM

November 2007
Live Mud
Mudride/The Straight Life/I Saw the Light/No One Has/Our Time Is Now/Touch Me I'm Sick/On the Move/Suck You Dry/Hard-On for War/In'n'out of Grace/Hate the Police
(Sub Pop SP771)
Recorded in Mexico City, December 10, 2005

COMPILATIONS

1990
Superfuzz Bigmuff Plus Early Singles
Touch Me I'm Sick/Sweet Young Thing Ain't Sweet No More/Hate the Police/Burn It Clean/You Got It (Keep It Outta My Face)/Halloween/No One Has/If I Think/In'n'out of Grace/Need/Chain That Door/Mudride
(Sub Pop SPCD21a)
2008 double CD Deluxe Edition (Sub Pop SP773) restored original track sequence and added Twenty Four, The Rose, and demo versions of Need, Mudride, and In'n'out of Grace; also included entire live recording of October 10, 1988, show at Berlin Independence Days, plus six tracks recorded for KCSB in Santa Barbara, California, on November 16, 1988

January 2000
March to Fuzz
In'n'out of Grace/Suck You Dry/I Have to Laugh/Sweet Young Thing Ain't Sweet No More/Who You Drivin' Now?/You Got It (Keep It Outta My Face)/Judgment, Rage, Retribution, and Thyme/Into the Drink/A Thousand Forms of Mind/Generation Genocide/If I Think/ Here Comes Sickness/Let It Slide/Touch Me I'm Sick/This Gift/ Good Enough/Blinding Sun/Into Yer Shtik/Beneath the Valley of the Underdog/When Tomorrow Hits/Make It Now Again/Hate the Police/Hey Sailor/Twenty Four/Baby Help Me Forget/Revolution/ You Stupid Asshole/Who Is Who/Stab Yor Back/Pump It Up/The Money Will Roll Right In/Fix Me/Dehumanized/She's Just Fifteen/ Baby O Baby/Over the Top/You Give Me the Creeps/March to Fuzz/ Ounce of Deception/Paperback Life/Bushpusher Man/Fuzzbuster/ Overblown/Run Shithead Run/King Sandbox/Tonight I Think I'm Gonna Go Downtown/Holden/Not Going Down That Road Again/ Brand New Face/Drinking for Two/Butterfly Stroke/Editions of You
(Sub Pop SP500)

February 2000
Here Comes Sickness: The Best of the BBC Recordings
Here Comes Sickness/If I Think/By Her Own Hand/You Make Me Die/Judgment, Rage, Retribution, and Thyme/Dissolve/Poisoned Water Poisons the Mind/Editions of You/Suck You Dry/You Got It (Keep It Outta My Face)/What Moves the Heart/In My Finest Suit/Judgment, Rage, Retribution, and Thyme/This Gift/Into Yer Shtik/Touch Me I'm Sick/Fuzzgun '91/Poisoned Water Poisons the Mind/When Tomorrow Hits/Hate the Police
(Strange Fruit SFRSCD090)
Tracks 1–4 recorded for John Peel's BBC Radio 1 show, May 9, 1989; tracks 5–8 recorded for *The Evening Session*, May 24, 1995; tracks 9–20 recorded for Peel, live at the Reading Festival, August 27, 1995

Index